# PRAISE FOR
## *THRIVING TOGL* _

"In *Thriving Together*, David Viafora offers a pragmatic and inspiring guide for cocreating communities of depth, connection, and resilience. Drawing on a wealth of experience with mindfulness communities worldwide, Viafora shares valuable lessons for navigating the beauty and complexity of communal life. This book is a gift for anyone seeking to cultivate the transformative potential of true community."

—DAVID TRELEAVEN, PhD, author of *Trauma-Sensitive Mindfulness: Practices for Safe and Transformative Healing*

"I read *Thriving Together* while hiking the Camino de Santiago in Spain, a place where community and mindfulness merge. David's book will help us imagine another possible world, but we need to commit to peace-making and sharing love and compassion to bring it into being. When we become entangled with one another in community, we create a new fold of togetherness. *Thriving Together* is a must-read for anyone desiring a better world!"

—REV. ROBERTO CHE ESPINOZA, DMin, PhD, founder of Our Collective Becoming and author of *Activist Theology*

"What a beautiful offering in an age defined by loneliness, with nearly one in four adults worldwide reporting that they feel lonely. *Thriving Together* is a heartfelt and deeply practical guide for anyone seeking to build genuine, inclusive, and resilient communities. This book is an invaluable companion for those yearning to cocreate spaces where people of all backgrounds can truly belong and thrive together."

—KAIRA JEWEL LINGO, author of *We Were Made for These Times: Ten Lessons on Moving through Change, Loss, and Disruption*

"After several years visiting and practicing in spiritual communities around the world, David offers this book as the harvest of his quest to better understand how one might thrive in community. That hard and loving work is what makes this book special. In *Thriving Together*, through engaging interviews and deep looking into his own experiences, David lays out what it means to create Beloved

Community. This book is fresh and engaging, and anyone wanting to live in community is sure to be inspired by David's active research."

—DR. LARRY WARD AND DR. PEGGY ROWE WARD, authors of *Love's Garden: A Guide to Mindful Relationships*

"This is an adventure into our heart's calling to unite, heal, and radically transform everyday relationships in ways that welcome us home to one another, where we truly want to be. In these pages, we gain courage and know-how for applying old ways to modern dis-ease. Personal stories meld with ancient teachings to illuminate community building as a joyful way of life. Viafora writes with a perfect balance of courage and vulnerability, knowledge and mystery, practicality and inspiration as he invites readers to fully embrace what often seems impossible—a world of deep connection and belonging. Suddenly—and to all appearances magically—the radiant light and lightness of true togetherness manifests before our eyes."

—HEATHER LYN MANN, author of *Ocean of Insight: A Sailor's Voyage from Despair to Hope*

"The liberating power of Buddhism rests on the teachings of The Three Jewels: The Buddha, the Dharma, and the Sangha. Zen Master Thich Nhat Hanh has said that the next Buddha will be the sangha or community, not an individual. The energy of the sangha, a committed group of people dedicated to living in harmony and understanding, is a powerful force for good in a troubled, polarized world, sending ripples of peace outward. *Thriving Together* is an important guidebook for creating, maintaining, and visioning sangha. David Viafora shares his passion for community and brings extensive lived experience both as a former monastic in the Plum Village tradition and world traveler living and researching the art of building community. Filled with lively stories of visiting and living in spiritual communities around the globe, Viafora has written an important guide for those seeking to understand community, spiritual friendships, and relationships, and move closer to realizing Beloved Community."

—VALERIE BROWN, coauthor of *Healing Our Way Home, Black Buddhists Teachings on Ancestors, Joy, and Liberation*

"David Viafora's book *Thriving Together* offers a powerful and personal glimpse into the experiences of people who have spent years dearly and dutifully creating long-standing and supportive communities. I learned about the struggles that arise when people dedicate their lives to growing together, and the patience required to keep learning so that friendship becomes the foundation of our growth."

—CHARLES H. VOGL, M.Div., author of *The Art of Community: Seven Principles for Belonging*

"There's an adage that the best way to learn something is to teach it. Such teaching is best done after directly experiencing this something, and David Viafora does precisely this in his book of lessons about community. Sharing stories of his visiting, joining, and forming intentional communities and reflecting on them through the lens of his Buddhist practice, David invites us to join him on his own voyage of discovery. In the process we will all find there is more to discover than we supposed."

> —RICHARD BRADY, author of *Short Journey Home: Awakening to Freedom with Thich Nhat Hanh*

"There has always been a deep need for conscious community to move our species towards surviving and thriving. Tragically, we have lost this solid ground in the ever expanding technological age of "connection." *Thriving Together* is based on extensive experiential research of both flourishing and struggling mindfulness-based communities around the world. This book and his life's work are fundamentally vital for the future of children and families on our planet."

> —DR. VIKTOR PAUL GIANGRASSO, author of *2: Awakening The Mystery of You and I*

"An essential road map for creating Beloved Community. Powerful, honest, and vulnerable, David Viafora boldly shines a spotlight on what breaks communities and fearlessly confronts patriarchy and internalized racism. This book provides real-life advice for anyone longing for an inclusive and stable community."

> —CELIA LANDMAN, author of *When the Whole World Tips: Parenting through Crisis with Mindfulness and Balance*

"For those of us who are interested in nurturing and sustaining intentional and lasting communities, *Thriving Together* is an indispensable book. Having lived in, developed, researched, and written about communities, communes, collectives, fellowships, and Beloved Community Circles over decades of my life, I can truly say that this is the best, most complete guide I've ever read. Why? David Viafora artfully uses intimate stories from his own life, including many mistakes and false starts, to illustrate nine core principles of building strong communities, which include how and why to foster harmonious relationships, set appropriate boundaries, resolve interpersonal conflicts, unearth and heal internalized oppression, and navigate the tensions between individual freedom and collective well-being. David Viafora's writing is fluid, lush with poetic flourishes, and intimately personal yet grounded in a wise and wide view of both the literature about and the lived experience of community. *Thriving Together* book is immensely readable, accessible, and informative. I keep going back to it for nourishment. I wish I had had this guide decades ago."

> —JOHN BELL, author of *Unbroken Wholeness: Six Pathways to the Beloved Community*

# THRIVING TOGETHER

## Nine Principles for Cocreating True Community

## DAVID VIAFORA

FOREWORD BY SISTER TRUE DEDICATION

PARALLAX PRESS
BERKELEY, CALIFORNIA

Parallax Press
2236B Sixth Street
Berkeley, CA 94710
parallax.org

Parallax Press is the publishing division of Plum Village Community of
Engaged Buddhism, Inc.

Cover Design by Katie Eberle
Text design by Maureen Forys, Happenstance Type-O-Rama

Printed in Canada by Marquis on FSC-certified paper

Parallax Press's authorized representative in the EU and the EEA is SARL
Boutique La Bambouseraie Point UH, Le Pey, 24240 Thénac, France.
Email: *europe@parallax.org*

"Creating an Inclusive Welcome" is reprinted courtesy of its author,
Valerie Brown.

ISBN 978-1-946764-96-6
Ebook ISBN 978-1-946764-97-3

Library of Congress Control Number: 2024950273

1 2 3 4 5 MARQUIS 29 28 27 26 25

MIX
Paper | Supporting
responsible forestry
FSC® C103567

The mindful community-building practices offered in this book
have been resourced from the wisdom, knowledge, and inspiration
of many sources, including social justice movements challenging
systemic conditions that create and perpetuate trauma, the stories
of struggle and resilience of political and economic refugees, and the
timeless spiritual traditions of Vietnamese Buddhism. In light of
this, 50 percent of the author's proceeds from this book will be shared
equally between the following three organizations:

**ARISE** (*Awakening through Race, Intersectionality, and
Social Equity*) *is a community of mindfulness practitioners
and monastics who come together to heal the wounds of racial
injustice and social inequity, beginning with looking deeply within
ourselves and using the energy of compassion, understanding, and
love in action.* arisesangha.org

**Karam** *offers community, mentorship, and innovative education
to Syrian youth and families, helping them harness their power
and shape their own future, so they can define themselves not by
what they've survived, but where they're going. Karam encourages
radical generosity and holistic support to change the lives of Syrian
refugees, with the goal of self-sufficiency.* karamfoundation.org

**The Thich Nhat Hanh Foundation** *works to continue the
mindful teachings and practice of Zen Master Thich Nhat Hanh,
support Plum Village mindfulness practice centers around the
world, and engage in Sangha (community) building in order to
foster peace and transform suffering in all people, animals, plants,
and our planet.* thichnhathanhfoundation.org

## Communities featured in *Thriving Together*

* **Athens Refugee Project**
  Athens, Greece
* **Avalokita,** Castelli, Italy
* **Blue Cliff Monastery**
  Pine Bush, New York, USA
* **Deer Park Monastery**
  Escondido, California, USA
* **Dharma Gaia,** Coromandel, New Zealand
* **Greatwoods Zen** Charlotte, North Carolina, USA
* **Honor Oak Community,** London, United Kingdom
* **Intersein,** Hohenau, Germany
* **Meppel Mindfulness Community,**
  Meppel, Netherlands
* **Morning Sun Mindfulness Community**
  New Hampshire, USA
* **Mountain Lamp Community,** Washington, USA
* **Plum Village France**
  Dieulivol, Loubès-Bernac & Thénac, France
* **Riverside Smiling Sangha,** Riverside, California, USA
* **Sugarplum Sangha,** Ukiah, California, USA
* **Wake Up London Houses,** London, United Kingdom
* **World Beat Sangha,** San Diego, California, USA

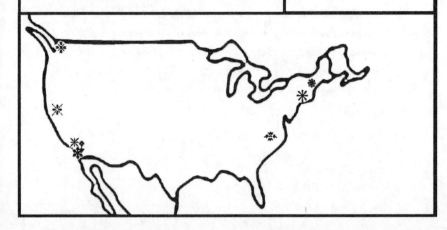

# CONTENTS

# FOREWORD

*by Sister True Dedication*

In an age of increasing isolation and polarization, we are called to examine new ways to live closely in community again. How can we create tolerant and inclusive communities of resistance? Communities that nourish us and offer connection, healing, resilience, joy, and fearless courage to imagine a different future—a future that honors not only our collective well-being but the well-being of the Earth? This book, *Thriving Together*, is both a beacon of hope and a practical roadmap for answering these questions.

David Viafora's quest to explore the essential elements of healthy communities of mindfulness has taken him on a multi-year journey across continents, visiting and living with dozens of communities in the Plum Village tradition. David has dug deep into the reality of community life, discovering what determines whether a community will "sink or swim in the deep pond of relational dynamics." This book, the fruit of his exploration, draws on the collective wisdom of over 100 community-builders who have shared their lives and insights with courage and vulnerability.

What shines through in *Thriving Together* is the need to be bold, loving, and authentic. David does not shy away from the challenges that arise when humans live and serve side by side: the conflicts and reconciliations, the attractions and aversions, which are there alongside the shared joys and quiet transformations. David invites us into frank conversations about boundaries, power, friendship, silence, and shared spiritual practice. He inspires us to ask not just how communities survive, but how they thrive in ways that honor everyone's deepest aspirations, and how they can help us heal our relationship with Mother Earth. Living simply in community is not only a path to deeper connection but also a vital way to lighten our collective footprint on the Earth.

Building true community is both an art and a practice. David's research is a precious resource to encourage us to step into this practice ourselves—whether we are founding a community, joining one, or simply seeking to bring a more meaningful communal spirit to our neighborhood, workplace, or network of friends and family.

This book reminds us that while living in community is messy, it is also profound. David shows us that when we live together with intention, compassion, and the insight of interbeing, we can touch something much larger than ourselves. In these pages, you will not only find practical guidance but also the possibility of transformation—for yourself, your community, and the world. In these times of ecological crisis, living together is not just a necessity but a path to collective awakening—which can nurture both our human resilience and the resilience and healing of the Earth.

**SISTER TRUE DEDICATION**
Plum Village, France

# INTRODUCTION

*Rarely, if ever, are any of us healed in isolation.*
*Healing is an act of communion.*
—BELL HOOKS

*Happiness is not an individual matter.*
—THICH NHAT HANH

*There is hardly anything more appealing,*
*yet apparently more elusive, for humans at the end*
*of the twentieth century than the prospect of living*
*in harmony with nature and with each other.*
—ROBERT AND DIANE GILMAN

Nestled between lakes abundant with star lilies and within a rich forest of pine, beech, maple, poplar, oak, and birch trees, Morning Sun Mindfulness Community was built on the land of an abandoned quarry mine. In more recent decades, this land had been a hangout spot for target practice and beer drinking. Scars of the past remain: dilapidated machinery, a hollowed-out silo of crumbling concrete walls, rusty metal cables weaving in and out of the earth's surface like a Chinese dragon statue, swaths of previously cleared forest steadily reclaiming their home, and the colored glass shards of thousands of broken bottles. Yet the mining also left something that the current inhabitants of this land enjoy. Huge sand deposits formed lakeside beaches and dune hilltops overlooking Blueberry Pond, where kids and families play, adults gather for retreats and days of mindfulness, and the entire community barbecues over campfires throughout the summer.

Morning Sun has also become a refuge for humans to enjoy natural beauty as a nurturing background for mindfulness and meditation retreats. Every year, several hundred visitors from across the United States come to unwind, rest their eyes on the infinite shades of green, blue, and brown in the lakes and forests, and discover new ways of connecting to themselves and the world around them.

Over the last several years, the land has been steadily transitioning back to its essence—a quiet forest refuge where deer and moose roam. Beavers thrive in this habitat, and wild blueberry bushes encircling the lakes offer dessert to shy black bears on quiet summer afternoons.

For over five years, Morning Sun Mindfulness Community was my home, wilderness refuge, a source of inspiration and support in my mindfulness practice and life learning, and an avenue of service. Together, the resident members guide programs and retreats year-round with the aim of creating a more mindful and compassionate society for ourselves and future generations. I've learned that building a residential retreat center in a pristine forest that both protects and is nourished by the wilderness cannot be accomplished by one person or even a few individuals. Ecological sustainability needs a healthy and thriving community of people who work harmoniously together so that the land and her guests can flourish as one.

## Building the Dream

Morning Sun began in 2009, when Fern Dorresteyn and Michael Ciborski, both meditation teachers who had lived and studied extensively as monastics with Zen Master Thich Nhat Hanh, planted the seeds of mindfulness and community living on the rolling forest hills of the Catawba or People of the Dawn Land, commonly known as New Hampshire. Over time, as Morning Sun residents, we dedicated ourselves to realizing this shared vision of building a retreat center where hundreds and eventually thousands of people would come each year to train in the art of mindful living and receive the blessings of its gorgeous forest and wetland habitats. Through a hodgepodge of fundraising, one resident with construction genius, an enthusiastic crowdfunding video, a small village of wholehearted volunteers, and boundless inspiration, we scraped together enough funds to buy most of our materials. And then, with limitless gratitude for our mindfulness practice, we subsidized construction labor with our own hands.

Aside from building sheet and pillow forts in my childhood living room or working on sketchy tree houses as a kid, I had never done any construction. What made it possible for a scholarly social worker and meditator (that's me) to get out on the construction site every day? We've heard the old adage, "Where there's a will, there's a way." Where there's a collective will, the way is even stronger! Each day, a community force energized me through the challenges of construction like a river carrying me through a canyon. I found myself climbing up ladders (big ones!) with a nail gun in one hand and plywood in the other, hauling forty-pound bundles of tile to the roof, cutting out sheetrock, screwing in ceilings, nailing in bamboo flooring—basically becoming a full-on construction worker. We tiled the roof from dawn to dusk under blazing summer rays and nailed in wooden siding around the building amidst the snow and frosty winds of late winter and early spring. No matter the season, the work was dirty, sweaty, and exhausting. Just as importantly, it was invigorating, challenging, and fun to be out there working together as a tribe. We were building the temple of our beloved community with our own hands and it bore our signatures.

At times, our physical and emotional energy felt sapped by the intensity of doing construction in between offering multiple five-day summer retreats. The more challenging it was, the more we leaned into our community practice. We encouraged each other to attend morning meditation sessions before construction, often took moments to pause, breathe, smile, or laugh between tasks, and rested while eating lunch in mindful silence together every day. We encouraged anyone who was feeling overly tired to care for their body and mind by lying down for a nap outside or taking five for a tea and dark chocolate break.

When our spirits were low, even when things seemed beyond busy, we still made time to gather in a circle and share appreciations for one another's brightest gifts of time, presence, and generosity. This simple act repowered our spirits almost beyond belief. On days off, we practiced being as lazy as possible. We frequented a hidden river spot to lounge on sun-heated rocks, swam with our kids in the small rapids, picnicked from noon to sunset, and completely forgot about lifting anything.

Building our retreat center taught me a lot about construction, but most of all I learned about building community. There's an often-quoted African proverb that says, "If you want to go fast, go alone. If you want to go far, go together." I would like to add to that wisdom: "If you want to go joyfully, go in friendship." There are some things, and some distances, that we can't or wouldn't want to cover alone. We need the power and momentum of trustworthy friends and a loving community to accomplish our most important, far-reaching dreams.

## The Great Need for Community

When practiced in community, mindfulness strengthens bonds of acceptance, appreciation, empathy, and joy between close friends and loved ones. Mindfulness is the living awareness of what is happening within and around us at each moment, in a spirit of curiosity and compassion. Everyone has this innate capacity, and we can strengthen it both within ourselves and within relationships through sustained practice. Mindfulness helps us access the living intelligence of our own body and mind, grow our capacity to face suffering with both gentleness and fierce compassion, understand and transform the roots of our difficulties, open our eyes to the many wonders of life, and dwell more happily in each moment. Voyaging even farther on the path of mindfulness, we discover a profound interdependence with other people, all life on earth, and even the outermost reaches of the universe—and we realize we are less separate and more connected than we ever imagined.

Practicing mindfulness depends on the guidance, motivation, and relational support that arise in a community like Morning Sun. Daily practice thrives in environments where slowing down and cultivating moment-to-moment awareness is collectively encouraged, compared to the extreme busyness of mainstream society. Trying to practice mindfulness without collective support we are like birds separated from the flock, struggling alone against the wind. In community life, we naturally learn from others how to uniquely adapt mindfulness to our lives where we need it the most.

In the Buddhist world, we call a community that practices mindfulness in a spirit of harmony and compassion a Sangha. A Sangha, though, does not need to be Buddhist—it can be our family, congregation, workplace, or any community where people try to listen with an open heart and support each other's deepest aspirations. Time and time again, my teacher, Zen Master Thich Nhat Hanh, spoke about the necessity of building Sangha wherever we are. Thich Nhat Hanh, more affectionately known as Thay, which means "teacher" in Vietnamese, famously said, "It is possible the next Buddha will not take the form of an individual. The next Buddha may take the form of a community, a community practicing understanding and loving kindness, a community practicing mindful living."

A Buddha is someone who embodies unconditional love and compassion for oneself and all beings and manifests liberating insights into the nature of suffering and happiness. Perhaps our future hinges not just on one individual person or Buddha attaining these peaks of spiritual awakening, but rather, on a community whose collective compassion and wisdom can support and guide our individual paths. Thay often told us, "My friends, you are my Sangha body. I take refuge in you. I also need you." If having a Sangha is this important even for such an accomplished Zen teacher, then how much more so for the rest of us? No matter what tradition, belief system, or congregation we adhere to, our spiritual and emotional wellness depends on the nourishment and love of a true practice community.

Many people wish to live in or be surrounded by supportive, wholesome, communal environments where mindfulness is the norm and compassionate ideals are shared by everyone. Yet where can we find these places, or how can we create them? Typically, only Buddhist monasteries offer an all-inclusive environment of mindfulness practice where people can visit or live. For those of us not destined for monastic living, lay mindfulness residential communities and practice centers are sprinkled around the world. There are few guides for helping people create flourishing Sanghas, residential or not, that can support our practice and help transform our ailing society.

The need for oases of mindful living and compassionate human connection is as great as at any time in history. Our society has reached a critical juncture, as people are more disconnected from each other than ever before. Research over the last few decades, both in the US and abroad, shows us that the fabric of community life is unraveling as our social resources deteriorate. Even before the global COVID-19 pandemic, more than one in five Americans reported feeling lonely,[1] having not a single close connection with others,[2] and the average person's social network had shrunk in size by over one-third.[3] A 2018 study discovered that at least a quarter of our population feels we don't have anyone in our lives who understands us.[4] Nearly three-quarters of our nation, 74 percent of us, don't know most of our neighbors,[5] and a full one-third of us have never had an interaction with a neighbor.[6] It turns out that we are not alone in feeling lonely at all.

The longest research project on happiness is an eighty-year study by Harvard University, which highlights two critical findings. The first is that strong social connections support and enhance people's well-being. The second finding is that loneliness kills. Hundreds of studies similarly reveal that when people experience significant loneliness, live alone, or are more socially isolated than they wish to be, they are less happy, likely to die much earlier, their health deteriorates faster, they sleep worse, and their brain function heads downhill more quickly.[7] A 2015 review of over seventy international studies and more than three million global participants concluded that social isolation, loneliness, and living alone were all associated with increased risk of death in that year. Interestingly, it wasn't just older adults who were most at risk; middle-aged folk living alone suffered more of these consequences than older adults. It turns out that poor relationships have a greater influence on health than even physical inactivity and obesity.[8] Vivek Murthy, former surgeon general of the United States, wrote about "the loneliness epidemic" in the *Harvard Business Review*: "Loneliness and weak social connections are associated with a reduction in lifespan similar to that caused by smoking fifteen cigarettes a day."[9] Loneliness, it turns out, is killing people. Perhaps one of the few things worse for one's health than loneliness is being a lonely smoker.

It seems our society has largely forgotten about the ancient, innate power of community. In her book on building flourishing relationships and true community, *All About Love*, bell hooks writes, "I think that part of what a culture of domination has done is raise that romantic relationship up as the single most important bond, when of course the single most important bond is that of community."[10] Research shows those with stronger and more intimate relationships with family, friends, and community are happier and healthier, and they live longer. The happiest and most resilient people are not without conflict, but they lean into their closest relationships, especially when facing tough life challenges. Once we wake up to community's pivotal influence on the health of our bodies, minds, and world, we can begin to build more trustworthy, supportive connections and meaningful lives.

Even in the shadow of our societal loneliness and separation, the wisdom of community lies dormant within us like ancient seed buried deep in the earth, waiting for a strong rain to burst them open again. Community is in our bones and our blood; it is our survival and our birthright as a species. Every one of our cells contains the wisdom, whether known or forgotten, of the strength, love, challenge, and happiness of living harmoniously and interdependently as one communal organism. Community-building skills are not merely for us to learn anew; they are a forgotten art for us to rediscover, renew, and strengthen. In her masterful portrayal of African American community culture, *How We Show Up: Reclaiming Family, Friendship, and Community*, Mia Birdsong writes with unshakable trust and confidence in the communal strength of countless generations before us: "All of us have ancestral memories of what it's like to live connected, interdependent lives. We may be cut off or too far away from those traditions to claim them, but we can listen to our needs and our longings, and, through ritual, rite, and practice, build a way of being in the world that honors and makes tangible our connections to one another, to nature, and to spirit."[11] What are your ancestral sources of communal wisdom, joy, and tradition, and how will you manifest them in our world today?

## Researching Communities from the Inside Out

This dilemma of loneliness, individualism, and separation in the world and my personal quest to find a community home restlessly churned within my heart and mind for years when I was young. In my early twenties, I had fallen in love with the practice of mindfulness and Sangha building, and I dreamed of living in a community where mindfulness, harmony, and service were at the core of our lives. I explored Buddhist monastic life for several years, lived in a lay urban Zen center in Southern California, and worked as the temple keeper for a meditation center in rural Washington for eighteen months. I grew and learned tremendously from each of these communities, yet I didn't find an enduring fit for my life. Finally, at the age of thirty-four, I resolved to visit and research lay residential mindfulness communities and retreat centers around the world to thoroughly study their shared practice and then pass their inspiration, knowledge, and lessons on to others. I knew mindful communities offered a rare medicine to help heal our society's estranged hearts, and I was ready for the adventure.

I felt inspired to study communities that practiced mindfulness as taught in the Plum Village tradition founded by the Zen monk Thich Nhat Hanh and nun Sister Chan Khong. This tradition had been my path for over a dozen years by then, and I was passionately driven to learn how to build community according to its teachings. Visiting communities that shared a common culture of practice together would also streamline my research, learning, and insights. I was primarily interested in exploring *lay* practice communities, which are inspired by and rooted in Buddhist monastic communities but not immersed in them. These lay communities are founded and led by practitioners who often have loving partnerships, families with children, and diverse jobs in the world alongside a sincere dedication to deepening mindfulness practice and sharing it with others.

In the spring of 2017, my then-partner and fellow Sangha enthusiast, Vanessa Ixil Chavez, and I set out on our global quest. We journeyed across the English-speaking world and several countries in Europe, staying for weeks and even months at various residential communities and young adult mindfulness houses, as well as briefly visiting dozens of local weekly mindfulness groups in thirteen countries. We focused primarily on residential communities, but also visited and learned from many non-residential Sanghas. Knowing that 50 percent of communities fail within the first two years, we asked questions about what made each community sink or swim in the deep pond of relational dynamics.[12] Our understanding of creating community grew rapidly with every encounter.

In North America, we visited two residential retreat centers; one urban mindfulness house for young adults in the Wake Up youth mindfulness movement, known as a "Wake Up house"; and dozens of local Sanghas in various cities across the US, Canada, and Mexico. Then we traveled to ten communities in Europe, including three residential retreat centers and seven mindful living houses, along with several dozen non-residential weekly Sanghas. We spent one month at a residential community and retreat center in New Zealand, and hopped over to Australia to visit a few local Sanghas before heading back to the States. We finished our year-long expedition by visiting residential centers in Washington state and Northern California in the spring of 2018.

In most residential centers, we stayed for about one month to really taste the life of their community as well as steadily build trust before discussing personal and often vulnerable topics with the community members. With every community, we practiced meditation, ate, slept, followed their schedule, hung out, and played music and games with the residents to understand how mindfulness was woven into the fabric of their everyday lives. We were hungry to learn how residents first envisioned their centers, how they handled hardships along the way, how conflicts brewed internally, whether they found ways to reconcile hurts, and how they managed money, shared meals, hosted retreats, and shared good times.

We interviewed more than a hundred people and found ourselves enthralled by their founding stories, hard-won lessons, and ongoing challenges as well as their genuine happiness in dedicating their lives to Sangha building and supporting each other's practice and growth. In surveying the many communities, our goal was not to compare. Rather, our underlying aspiration was to understand: *What can we learn from one another, and how can we support our learning and development as fellow communities?* We hoped to better understand each community's strongest gifts, genuine difficulties, and overall trajectory in light of its similarities and differences with others without getting caught in better-than or less-than evaluations. Our interviews often evoked vulnerable accounts of the interpersonal challenges, organizational frustrations, and spiritual crises that inevitably arise. Our conversations also brought to life the most meaningful moments and heartfelt successes of people's lives. Notwithstanding inevitable rough patches in relationships, we heard across the board how much people loved living, practicing, and growing together as a family of sincere practitioners. The full power of collectively cultivated compassion, communal joy, accelerated learning, and purposeful impact on society and the Earth cannot be experienced alone.

During our voyage, we were able to put many of the lessons we were learning from others into practice in our own lives and communities: how to nurture communal harmony, strengthen joyful relationships, and boldly put a communal vision into action. We spent four months building a service-based residential mindfulness community in Greece during the ongoing refugee crisis. Over a dozen young adult practitioners from around Europe came to live and practice with us as we dedicated ourselves to befriending and supporting Middle Eastern refugees. Even though we were in touch with much suffering, our community provided a stable foundation of compassion and joy for us to sustainably offer our support as well as receive priceless gifts of friendship and resiliency from our migrant friends and each other. Because of the profound friendships we built, it became one of the happiest experiences of my life, and I learned more about community building and service in those four months than ever before.

Throughout our tour, people's stories and answers to our questions ranged widely. Still, we noticed that there are conditions and practices which support communal harmony and growth. Conversely, others clearly do not—not all community-building strategies and cultures are created equal. At Dharma Gaia Community in New Zealand, near the end of our world tour, I was offering a presentation with photos and stories of the many centers we had visited along our journey. A wise ten-year-old girl boldly asked the last question of the night: "Which place were you happiest at? And why?" The question still rings in my heart. It is a question for each of us to intimately ponder and courageously answer with our own lives as we find our way back home to community.

This book is my attempt to answer this young girl's powerful question—to illuminate the core practices of community building that beautifully foster individual and collective well-being and to respectfully challenge those that do not. These communities and their stories offer tangible and loving proof that another way of living, beyond isolation, individualism, and separation is not only possible—it is emerging and thriving all around us.

## The Essence of Community

In a project similar to our journey around the globe, environmental studies professor Karen Liftin visited and researched fourteen of the most renowned ecovillages across five continents. Responding to our planet's growing ecological disaster, the rural and urban intentional communities she visited aim to restore and regenerate social and natural environments through locally owned, participatory processes, much like mindfulness communities. Liftin found that as a result of their belief in the sacred web of life, ecovillages are unusually open to sharing. She surmised that if there were one word to express the "taproot" or essence of ecovillage life, it would be "sharing."[13]

This synopsis of community life may appear overly simple, like a kindergarten lesson, but the depth and significance of sharing is multifold. The word "community" is derived from the Latin root, *communs*, which means "shared in common." On a material and resource level, community life, or sharing, is more efficient than living more individually. Community living also encourages generosity and collaborative friendships through communal use of land, tools, and living space, while enabling learning from shared knowledge and skills in areas ranging from conflict resolution to child-rearing.

On a deeper level, true community is the expression, discussion, and embodiment of whatever shared ideals and virtues its members hold to be true. Sharing an ethical understanding is the soul of any community. Without such a foundation, community life ultimately fails. In *The Buddha's Teachings on Social and Communal Harmony*, teacher and translator Bhikkhu Bodhi illuminates this truth simply and boldly: "Harmony in any community, whether a small group or a whole society, depends on a shared commitment to ethical conduct."[14]

Bhikkhu Bodhi's book highlights some of the most salient virtues of mindful community living that are similarly expounded in this book's nine elements of flourishing communities.

On yet a more profound level, sharing life through community is an attempt to express the deepest truth of our existence; namely, that despite our socially conditioned inclinations toward individuality, our lives and destinies are intimately and beautifully interwoven together. The Buddhist insight of interbeing demonstrates that every phenomenon in the universe is interconnected with everything else. Therefore, in community, we share food because we are one living and breathing communal body; we share resources and ideas because we have a common purpose and destiny; we share joys and sorrows because our hearts and nervous systems are inexpressibly intertwined. Every shared smile, word, and interaction impacts us and changes us forever. Community teaches us the gifts and truths of our shared existence.

Thriving together in these ways is no easy feat. Sharing a living space, work, and internal struggles with others will certainly be messy at times, both literally and figuratively. In the world of intentional communities, people often refer to living together as the longest, most expensive personal growth workshop we will ever take. But practicing and living in community will inevitably change how we relate to others, our environment, and ourselves in ways we can hardly imagine. This personal development and group transformation is essential for us to contribute to the greater healing that our planet is asking of us. Community practice is a shared practice and community life is a shared life. In this light, sharing is the common thread running through each chapter and principle in this book.

## Nine Elements for Building the House of Community

The ensuing chapters lay out nine foundations of building a thriving mindful community based on my own experiences as well as my global explorations. Each chapter offers concrete practices and community exercises based on these nine elements to experiment with at home in your own family, group, or community where it counts the most.

## NINE ESSENTIAL ELEMENTS FOR BUILDING COMMUNITY

1. Sharing a Vision
2. Sharing Friendship
3. Sharing Service
4. Sharing Joy
5. Sharing Silence
6. Sharing Appreciations
7. Sharing Conflict and Reconciliation
8. Sharing Racial Healing
9. Sharing Boundaries, Addressing Power

While building our retreat facility at Morning Sun, I realized the powerful parallels between constructing a house and creating a flourishing community. For example, the first step in building is sketching the blueprint. The intentions of the design, whose ideas influence the blueprint, what's included, and what's left out all have a crucial impact. Changes to the blueprint are always easier than remodeling. Similarly, the process of envisioning a community, determining who is invited to shape it and how the founders' vision is consciously, semi-consciously, or haphazardly strewn together will impact the entire lifespan of the community. In chapters one and two, the communities at Avalokita in Castelli, Italy; Morning Sun in rural New Hampshire; and the East Bay Meditation Center in Oakland, California, teach us how collective visioning lays the most solid foundation for a flourishing community of sustainably engaged, harmonious, and resourceful members.

The next step in building is laying the cornerstone and setting the foundation. The cornerstone of any community, especially a Sangha, is the integrity and trust of its closest relationships; everything grows from solid friendships. If the cornerstone is squarely set, then the foundation and walls of our house will rise solidly, able to withstand pressures from any direction. Just so, if the core friendships are resilient, then community will thrive from the ground up, unshakable under the inevitable tensions that arise. Chapter three illustrates the creative and resilient power of spiritual friendships in every community.

The electricity running throughout our house is the shared spirit of service, both to one another and to the world around us. Service brings a spark of light to the community mission, filling the house with energy and brightness. Without the spirit of service, our lives lack the vitality and inspiration that are crucial for living together with purpose. Chapter four details our adventure of creating a mindfulness community of volunteers in Greece as we partnered in solidarity with many friends from migrant backgrounds.

Many welcoming buildings have a big fireplace, the source of warmth and joy in a home. A fireplace creates warm connections between people and a reason to huddle together during spring nights or cold wintry days. Just like a fireplace, joy is an inexhaustibly reliable source of warmth and bonding in community that helps people feel energized, relaxed, and comfortable. Without joy, cold feelings between members can become almost unbearable. Joy helps us get through darker times and offers endless motivation to continue connecting and growing together. In chapter five, we learn from communities young and old that inspire play and joy as a way to nurture bonds of strength, trust, and happiness.

Positioned squarely upon the foundation and directly connected to the chimney are a house's structural beams. These hidden supports, quietly upholding everything, are the pillars of silence. Even if we don't always recognize its power, silence is an essential component of mindful attention and provides nourishment, sensitivity, and strength to everyone. Without the strength of rejuvenating silence, the walls of our practice can feel overwhelmed, weak, and shaky. Chapter six takes us into the quiet gardens and silent retreats of Intersein, Mountain Lamp, and other communities where the mysterious power of silence transforms those who enter.

Within the walls of any house, we need to carve out windows of light and inspiration to see each other and our world more clearly and refresh our attitude. This is cultivating a culture of appreciation where the gifts and beauty of our friends truly shine. Without the light of appreciation, our house will feel dark and almost unlivable. Opening these big bright windows brings joy, gratitude, and freshness to us and others every single day. In chapters seven and eight, we see how the art of appreciation invigorates community happiness and how it fueled people's spirits while building Morning Sun community.

Any house also needs plumbing and a septic system to circulate fresh water for nourishment and cleaning as well as to flush out waste. This is akin to a regular reconciliation and forgiveness practice in community, which not only resolves old resentments and hurts that build up naturally over time but also provides new sources of healing connection. When the plumbing of our relationships is not working well, things smell bad real quick! On the other hand, proper plumbing leaves our community fresh and perky. Chapter nine reveals the messy, painful, yet very valuable heartaches and lessons of conflict that manifest in any community, family, or group of humans working closely together. Through patience, persistence, and wise action, we can climb out of difficult scenarios while building even stronger community and more resilient friendships through it all. Chapters ten and eleven offer nuts and bolts guidance and stories of genuine transformation around a particular Plum Village practice of reconciliation called Beginning Anew.

The natural landscape, native plants, and surrounding gardens are potentially the most beautiful and dynamic features of any residence. In order to grow a flourishing garden, we need to carefully assess whether the soil is healthy, deficient, or poisoned, and whether weeds are dominating the landscape, preventing other plants from growing

and thriving together. This mirrors nurturing a community's awareness of racial dynamics and oppression in which the cultural tendencies of white supremacy and isolation choke off the community's
garden of joyful diversity and inclusivity. Chapter twelve offers stories
and insights in healing longstanding patterns of racial suffering within
a mindfulness community context. Chapter thirteen offers thorough
guidance and discussion around the path of racial affinity groups,
which can transform the very soil of racial distress and strengthen
multicultural harmony and true allyship, the most fragrant flowers in
a community garden.

While we would never forget to put a roof on our house, we often
don't realize that the roof of healthy boundaries protects the entire
community from forces of nature that can quickly damage or destroy it.
Without a roof impervious both to torrential rains and the subtle effects
of water leakage, our house is in peril. Similarly, every community is
susceptible to inappropriate romantic and sexual relationships when we
lack well-crafted, wise, and clearly communicated boundaries. Chapters
fourteen and fifteen explore power and vulnerability dynamics, lessons
of misconduct, and the path of creating healthy boundaries to protect
our communities from both the top down and bottom up.

With these basic elements, our house or community will be up
and running strongly and beautifully! We may want to prioritize additional principles and values, but if we have established these pillars, we
are well on our way to creating a safe, happy, and thriving community
or family wherever we are.

These ideas are ready to be adapted to the unique community and
relationships we are each creatively growing—the best lessons are
the ones we discover ourselves. The aim of each chapter is to always
lead you back home to your own community, to embrace your real
difficulties and potential, where you will realize your own insights,
breakthrough practices, and joys. While these nine principles are the
fruits of community building that I have found and seen to be most
essential, please, don't take my word for it—what is most important is
to experiment with them yourself.

## Going Forward

We can't all go out and build new residential mindfulness communities. But if we cultivate these nine principles wherever we are, our
homes will already look more like intentional mindfulness communities already. We can apply these lessons to our families, neighborhoods, local Sanghas, work settings, and cities. The basic intention is
simple: sharing—sharing ideas, joys, sorrows, conflicts, reconciliation, silence, service, activism, and more. Sharing across these realms
will help transform the loneliness and isolation inside of us, and even
heal the world around us.

I don't believe mindfulness communities are the only answer to
humanity's problems. But it's clear from my life experiences and travels that they offer a profound opportunity and viable path forward
through the many challenges facing us as a human family. Karen Liftin
sees ecovillages as "seeds of hope sparsely sown across the global landscape."[15] I see mindfulness communities as seeds of healing and transformation spread across the landscape of humanity.

The mission of my research was to document these mindfulness
communities not only for those who wished to build new ones, but
for those who could take inspiration and lessons back to already-
established communities. Even if you live in an apartment block in a
city, a suburban subdivision, or a rural village, you and your neighbors
can benefit from the greater friendship and mutual aid that mindfulness inspires. This book is a curated collection of the insights that I
gleaned throughout my travels and lived experiences; it also show-
cases my own humbling mistakes and rewarding lessons learned in
community building and relational growth. Since it's impossible to
share the totality of amazing stories and wisdom we gathered from
every community, I've attempted to share the lessons, stories, challenging scenarios, and unique voices I found most relevant and to
blend them with my own personal stories of failure, heartache, great
learning, and adventure. To say I wrote this book solely to share
insights for others' communities would be untrue. At the deepest

level, I wrote this book because it is what I need most: a guidebook packed with inspiring insights, concrete practices, and humble lessons to further support the growth and flourishing of beloved community in my own life.

May the treasures of creativity and compassion from the communities we visited and the people who intimately shared themselves and their stories shine a bright light on your path forward in community.

# CHAPTER 1

# VISIONING A COMMUNITY

*When we understand each other's deepest aspirations, we become soulmates.*

—THICH NHAT HANH

*When I dare to be powerful, to use my strength in the service of my vision, then it becomes less and less important whether I am afraid.*

—AUDRE LORDE

During the first few months of our global tour in 2017, we visited Avalokita, a residential community and retreat center nestled in an Italian mountain range two hours east of Rome. The locals call this region the "Italian Tibet." The range is geologically young, so time hasn't eroded sharp peaks into gently sloping ridges; jagged crests and austere cliff walls, potent with inspiration, greeted us as new visitors.

Avalokita is built at the foot of a massive peak that towers majestically over her guests. The morning after our arrival, I sauntered up the long grassy hill that rises and rolls steadily toward the mountain behind the center. After about twenty minutes, I stopped at the hilltop edge of Avalokita's hundred-acre property and sat in the shade of an oak next to a wild cherry tree bursting decadently with burgundy-colored treats. Indulging in the sweet abundance, I soaked in the sights below: golden flowing hills, bucolic Italian countryside, and farms sprinkled between dark green forests on both sides of the valley.

At Avalokita, each day offered myriad splendid encounters with the mountain. Walking out to the meditation hall just before sunrise, bright pink beams bounced off glowing east-facing walls. On late evening summer strolls, we were treated to golden peach and fuchsia light dressing the west-facing slopes like an elegant gown. Stepping out for some refreshing air before bed, we witnessed moonbeams lighting up blanched cliffs as if a vast Buddha were meditating under a lunar halo. No matter the hour, the mountain's stable stature was omnipresent, a continual reminder of the glorious solidity always residing within each of us.

While sitting quietly on the hilltop that first day, I wondered to myself, "How did they manage to build this center in such a gorgeous place?" With the mountains behind me and sprawling fields and forests ahead, I felt deeply grateful that mindfulness oases like Avalokita exist in such naturally beautiful locations. "Well, they must have had some big donors," I surmised, knowing they were a fairly small community. Over the next few days and weeks, my curiosity guided me into many stories and conversations with founders and residents. I soon discovered Avalokita to be much more than a visual and sensory paradise; it had even sweeter offerings than its many wild and cultivated fruit trees.

In 2003, fifteen Italian practitioners and friends were inspired to create a community and retreat center together. They had no idea how to do this, so they sought counsel from two deeply experienced Dharma teachers from the original Plum Village community in France, Karl and Helga Riedl, who lived at Intersein, a residential mindfulness center in Germany. A Dharma teacher is someone in the Plum Village Buddhist tradition who embodies the qualities of wisdom and compassion and has formally received encouragement and the authority to guide and teach others from their own teacher. Under Helga and Karl's guidance, these Italian friends began meeting together one weekend per month to enjoy a meditation retreat and spend time visioning. From Friday evening through most of Saturday, they attended to their mindfulness practice only: sitting meditation, silent meals, walking reverently in nature,

listening to talks, and taking time to unwind from the city—whatever
nourished their togetherness. By Saturday afternoon or Sunday morning, they were refreshed and ready to begin visioning. They called
themselves the Explorative Core, and month after month they invested
themselves in weekend visioning retreats at different locations around
Italy. They took time to vision both individually and collectively, sharing
views, discussing, and refining their ideas over and over again. If even
one person did not agree on a decision, they did not move forward;
they patiently listened, discussed, and waited until everyone was in
accord—a much more time consuming and emotionally intensive process than they had anticipated. Yet the bonding, co-creative inspiration,
and consistent time for shared practice were more enjoyable and fulfilling than any of them had imagined.

They met every month for two full years before finally crafting
a vision they all could stand behind wholeheartedly. Everyone in
their core community was invested in its creation and success, laying
Avalokita's foundation on solid bedrock. Consequently, their collective enthusiasm and trust became like pillars planted deep in the earth.

Success came, but not overnight. They spent two more years
fundraising before they had enough money to look for a community
home. It was another two years before they found the piece of land
that Avalokita now rests on. Finally, they spent three more years dia-
loguing with the local community, purchasing the land, rebuilding
the dilapidated structures, and building a new meditation hall before
opening the retreat center's doors. Silvia, a founding member and
Dharma teacher, shared with me, "Avalokita has been our baby; we
gave birth together. But instead of nine months, her gestation period
was nine years!"

Stefano, another Avalokita founder, teacher, and resident,
responded to my inquiries as we sat across from each other at the
dining table one evening. We silently savored our last spoonfuls of
leek and potato soup and sopped up locally harvested olive oil with
country-style bread made fresh that morning by Marco, another resident. Following their custom to eat in silence, I waited until we had

both finished our last bites in mindfulness. Then I asked, "Stefano, what is the most important thing about the founding of this beautiful community?" Without hesitation, he responded, "The vision is so important. The center is what it is now because we started with a vision. We are still growing with that vision." Stefano explained how their Explorative Core evolved into a Founders Council of about twenty members in charge of all major decisions. The Council is divided into several committees that continue to steer the community forward in different domains, such as finances, education, residential life, and groundskeeping.

Our conversation meandered to ownership and financing. I thought rather skeptically to myself, *Sure, they all visioned it, but who actually owns the place?* I asked Stefano how they paid for it. He explained, "Italy does not have a strong fundraising culture like the United States. But still, we were able to fundraise enough money to buy this land, renovate this main building, and build the other two smaller residences nearby." I was amazed that they could do this with a fairly small group during the first years of development. Stefano went on, "When we attended larger Italian retreats with several hundred people, we shared with such enthusiasm and conviction about our project that people really believed in us. That's because we believed in our vision and our togetherness first. The most important lesson is that we took time to vision together and to *live* our practice center, even before it was built." Stefano recounted their story with delight, confidence, and a dash of pride in his beloved community.

In further conversations, he and other founding members clued me in: the majority of the seed money had come from the founders themselves. Their emotional investment in the community's vision was strong enough to catapult them into financial resource investment. By the time they finished, their Sangha had fundraised over one million euros. They placed Avalokita into a trust owned by everyone with the community founders as its stewards.

Even though their visioning process was slow and required tremendous commitment, the founders developed an inclusive decision-making process inseparable from the heart of their community. This gave them extraordinary power to build upon a stable and resilient foundation of communal cohesion. Among the two dozen core members, I never heard anyone refer to Avalokita as "their community." Instead, they always lovingly called it "our community." The retreat center is still guided by the same principles of sharing views and decision making used in those first years. Major decisions require consensus, and almost all of the founding members are strongly involved in committees and programming that support the center's ongoing functioning. With so many pillars holding up its walls, Avalokita has the conditions for a long-lasting and thriving future.

Across our tour, it became clear which communities had a collectively empowered vision and which ones didn't. The level of members' engagement, the number of people serving as pillars, and how resources were collectively accessed were key indicators. Avalokita's story taught us that the first and most important step of community building is taking time to vision together, including everyone's ideas and aspirations as much as possible. This is akin to consciously and collectively designing the blueprint of the house we feel called to build or sketching out the map of the wilderness we are bravely bushwhacking through—essential and worth every second.

# CHAPTER 2

# SHARING A VISION

*Do not be afraid to build castles in the sky.*
*That is where they belong.*
*But once the dreams are in place,*
*Your job is to build the foundation under them.*
—THOREAU

*If you don't know where you are going, you might end up*
*someplace else.*
—YOGI BERRA

As Stefano shared and the Avalokita community has experienced, every group begins with a vision, a dream that either one or more people hold sacredly. In building the house of community, a shared vision is the blueprint of your collective dream that may manifest into reality. The process of visioning unfurls not just before one's community is built, but throughout its lifespan. Hearing the potential unleashed when others give voice to their tucked away aspirations ignites mysterious forces of creativity and communal bonding. This is what community building is all about—collaboratively growing something that is both a part of and greater than any one person could ever achieve alone. Community life is the quintessential expression of interbeing—we depend on each other's partnership to fulfill our deepest dreams.

During our global tour of communities, we always asked the founders, "How did you start all this? How did you begin visioning your community? Who was a part of those first conversations? What were the biggest challenges early on?" Many amazing and diverse stories came forth from these questions, too many to tell in just one chapter or one book. Sometimes the vision began with a couple huddled in a cabin for weeks, drawing on whiteboards and drinking up inspiration. Other times it was a group of committed young adults, fastidiously brainstorming plans on laptops to change the world through their plans for their community residence.

Teacher and writer Diane Leaf Christian has spent a lifetime studying and supporting ecovillages and other intentional communities to form, function effectively, and thrive around the world. In *Creating Community*, she explores the conundrum of why 90 percent of intentional communities either don't get off the ground or fall apart in just a few years. Through research and her own experiences, she espouses the qualities and practices that help the 10 percent to wildly succeed. What was at the *top* of her short list? Yes, a clear, strong, and collaboratively forged vision.[16]

There are countless ways to vision as individuals or as a community, and each may lead to different fruits and failures. An inclusive visioning process can help lead a community down the road of further harmony, diverse voices, empowered participants, unfolding resources, and—most importantly—emotionally invested members. And yet, the visioning process or lack thereof is so often at the root of communities' biggest challenges, breeding exclusion, stifled power, lack of clear purpose, miscommunication, emotional withdrawal, and missed access to resources. How the vision is grown and who is included will affect a community's entire lifespan.

Who's drawing the map, directions, and destination where your community is going? If you want people to come along for the journey, hearing where others want to go and including their ideas might be important. Think about how far you wish to go, and then see if it's worth spending the extra time to travel together.

Through stories and examples from teachers, members, and communities around the world, this chapter illustrates the values of collective visioning, ways to include others, concrete steps toward engaged collaboration, and how to articulate your vision to others. Although many of the stories speak about residential mindfulness communities, the principles apply to virtually any group, whether residential or not, mindfulness-based or not.

The visioning process goes well beyond those first years of starting a new community; it can and needs to be applied throughout the community's lifespan to renew focus, reinvigorate ideals and participation, and respond to ever-changing circumstances. Just as maps need to be updated and routes amended based on changing environmental conditions, we need to continually reassess our collective navigation to flexibly meet our aspirations in the evolving world. Visioning as a community can be meaningful, fun, and even very simple. It's not rocket science to steer the process forward. But it does take humility, honesty, willingness to listen, trust in vulnerability, and, usually, a small mountain of patience. By having fun and building friendship along the way, we are already living into the community we have dreamed of creating.

## What Is a Vision and Why Is It Important?

Is a vision a fancy sentence to impress people in your fundraising brochure? Or perhaps it's a dream your leader mystically receives on a full moon night and then proclaims to her followers? Is it something one person declares or that many voices contribute to? Is it written down or just tacitly understood?

The *Oxford English Dictionary* states that a vision is "the ability to think about or plan the future with imagination or wisdom." Diane Leaf Christian captures it more poetically: "Although written down, it's much more than a collection of words. It begins as a quality of energy that grabs you and doesn't let go. It's like a beam of energy leading your group from where you are to where you want to go." A true vision is all at once the stable taproot, the nutrient-rich sap that feed's your communi-ty's growth upward, and the flowers inspiring your future.

However, most communities I have visited have neither a clearly articulated vision for others to see nor an understanding of its far reaching influence in daily community life and gatherings. In both residential centers and local mindfulness groups, I saw striking con-nections between their visioning and decision-making process and the cohesiveness of their community. A friend of mine in the United Kingdom confided to me that she and a handful of other young adults weren't feeling inspired to participate in their local Sangha's leader-ship. She explained, "We often hear them saying things like, 'We want more young adults to be involved with us. But we don't under-stand why they don't want to help work on our projects.'" My friend laughed as she reemphasized the words, "Our projects!" In another community, a teacher once shared with me privately, "People don't understand this is their community. They always refer to it as 'your community,' but it's 'our community,' I keep telling them."

I have often heard community leaders struggle to find support for the many roles needed to run a community. Their sense of overwhelm tends to sound like this: "We need more people to be involved." On several occasions, teachers shared concerns that they feared their com-munity wouldn't continue after they were gone. The problem we heard the most often from teachers and leaders in both residential communi-ties and weekly groups was that not enough people were taking respon-sibility for leading or doing things.

Many of these challenges are universally shared in organizations around the world and don't have simple answers. Yet they all lead back to the same issues of collaborative engagement, inclusive partnership, and collective visioning. Over time, I started responding to these con-versations with a question, "Who is visioning these ideas of things for people to do?" When people come up with ideas themselves, usually an overflowing wellspring of energy, creativity, and joy bubbles up. Con-versely, when people don't have a strong voice in what the community is doing, they often choose to do something else, somewhere else.

A friend of mine, Susan, told me a story of her friend inviting her to start a weekly mindfulness group together in the town where they both lived. Susan had more experience practicing and facilitating meditation, so she facilitated the programs each week. The first few months went well—they enjoyed a weekly meditation practice with a growing group of people. After a few months, Susan's friend and cofounder said she really wanted to share readings from different teachers. Susan's vision for their group was to only read books from one teacher, Thich Nhat Hanh, whom they had both been studying; she vetoed her friend's idea completely. Soon after, the woman's participation in the group stopped abruptly, as did her friendship. This cofounder, of course, most likely felt her ideas were not valued and included, or that didn't even matter if she was present. Perhaps she felt hurt, surprised, resentful, or even betrayed.

Our need to feel heard, included, and to matter in community go very deep. Many of us carry old wounds of not feeling seen or included in decisions when we were children. I still remember how frustrating and wrong it felt as a child when my opinions and feelings were not taken seriously just because I was small. Yet now, as an adult in community leadership positions, I have surprisingly found myself repeating these old intergenerational patterns, trying to push certain ideas forward during meetings while dismissing or downplaying others' views. Fortunately, our core team at Greatwoods Zen is founded on ideals of consensus, respect, and inclusion, and the members also hold me lovingly accountable. Such old habits don't change quickly—they need patience, personal investigation, and group maturity to transform. A spiritually mature community harnesses the creativity and power of each community member's unique voice, experiences, and aspirations.

I recently asked Sister Flower, the eldest monastic sister at Blue Cliff Monastery, for advice on building a thriving Sangha. She impressed upon me the importance of inviting other community members to share their ideas in order to grow true harmony. She explained, "In our meetings, I always ask others to share their ideas first. I know that as the elder sister, if I share first, they would never contradict me. But if they can't share what they really think, it leads to more problems later for us. Any time the seniors impose their ideas, the younger ones don't like it, even if they don't say so." Sister Flower invited me to always listen to others' ideas, to be flexible, and to go with the group ideas rather than imposing my own will as a senior community member and cofounder.

## Searching for Community

Ultimately, each member may ask themselves, "Whose community is this?" It's a very interesting experiment to ask people in your community this question and to see whether they feel content with their answer. Our responses can be very telling.

I found myself asking this question often while exploring different communities in my young adulthood. A few years after disrobing from monastic life in my late twenties, I lived as a layperson for a number of years at Deer Park Monastery, a Plum Village center in California. I loved the serene meditative environment, the community of deeply engaged practitioners, and the abundance of pristine nature. Yet as a layperson living in the monastery, I wasn't invited to community decision and direction meetings. The traditional Buddhist monastic code, thousands of years old, skillfully and inclusively provides decision-making guidelines for monastics. Historically, laypeople were never intended to take part in community decisions. Over time, I realized I was a guest in someone else's house; I longed for inclusive partnership in my home and aspired to live in a long-term spiritual community where I could fully contribute.

A few years later, I moved to Mountain Lamp, a small residential meditation community where I worked as the retreat center caretaker. Before coming onboard, the founding teachers promised to support my aspirations to organize and facilitate retreats for young adults and families, which I was passionate about leading. I was thrilled to finally move to this lay practice center where my voice and ideas could be shared wholeheartedly alongside others, combining our insights and aspirations to grow our community. But I slowly learned that aside from my personal pet projects, this was not their way of doing things either. The nonprofit board met once per month to discuss affairs and make decisions about the practice center. I enthusiastically asked to participate in the meetings, and sometimes they included me, but more often they did not. Although I lived and worked there full-time as one of only a few resident staff, the board was the primary visioning and decision-making body.

After about a year there, I remember half-sitting, half-lying on the sofa in my quarters one evening while the board met in the meditation hall during their yearly visioning retreat to discuss the center's future trajectory. I felt a sinking sensation in my chest, and my whole body felt lethargic and depleted; I was feeling left out again. I didn't have a voice or a seat at the visioning table in the community I was trying so wholeheartedly to build alongside others. Even if I wasn't a decision maker, I wanted to take part in discussions and be part of the yearly brainstorming process. I longed to be included at the heart of the community. But I had misunderstood the organization's culture and vision: here, the role of residents was to dedicate time to work and meditation practice without being caught up in the center's "business" affairs. I could not see this community for what it really was and for the gift it offered to residents; I could only see what I yearned for, and what I lacked. This was not their mistake or responsibility—it was mine.

I still genuinely loved many other aspects of community life there—growing our own food, rehabilitating clearcut forests, powerful retreats, and consistent access to meditation teachers—but living and working without a feeling of inclusive partnership steadily winnowed my enthusiasm until I finally departed.

Not every community or organization intends or needs to offer a seat to every staff member and volunteer at the collective visioning table. But in my experience, the most sustainable path of community building entails wholeheartedly engaging its members' ideas, inspiration, and dreams so that everyone feels included in the collective vision forward. Each gathering, meeting, and decision-making moment is an opportunity to empower each member and the whole community at once. Then, people are less likely to feel that leaders are steering the ship by themselves, telling everyone else what to do. When this feeling arises, a community's foundation can become wobbly. Whether due to this feeling or other reasons, the retreat center where I had been a caretaker shut down just a few years later.

## SEVEN STEPS TO CREATING A VISION

So, how do you ensure that you include members of a community in a visioning process? There are seven basic steps to guide communal visioning. They are simple enough and may appear to be common sense; but our enduring lesson in studying communities is that "common knowledge" isn't always common practice. These seven steps are a basic outline for visioning, whether you are starting a new community, engaging in an annual members' meeting, or beginning a new project as an already-established community. My experience is that when a community skips a step, they likely return to it later or even start the process completely over. Please reflect on what aspects your community already applies and which ones you can still learn from.

1. **Decide who** is part of the community and invited to take part in the particular community visioning or decision-making process.

2. **Contemplate questions** individually and collectively, such as "What is our aspiration this year as a community? What do I want or need the most in my spiritual community? What are our goals this year?"

3. **Listen** to everyone share their dreams, needs, fears, and ideas without interruption. Elicit participation, feedback, and guidance from everyone present.

4. **Discuss**, appreciate, and reconcile views as needed.

5. **Agree** upon your vision together, both short- or long-term goals. Collaboration will be the axle carrying your vision forward into the future; it needs all wheels turning.

6. **Come together** as many times as needed to fulfill the purpose of the visioning process.

7. **Write down** a clearly articulated vision and share it with others.

Let's bring these steps of the visioning process to life in the following section about the community in which I lived for several years, Morning Sun.

## Visioning Morning Sun

Morning Sun is an example of a community that was initially visioned by its two founders but is continually re-envisioned every year by its residential members, staff, and board members. When the original founders Michael Ciborski and Fern Dorresteyn first conceived of Morning Sun, they huddled together for weeks in their tiny flat behind Michael's sister's house to dream and scheme their ideal community. They jotted down ideas on whiteboards and notebooks, meditated on their deepest aspirations, visualized their ideal community, and embraced their fears and resource limitations. Fern and Michael had lived as monastics in the Plum Village tradition and studied closely with Thich Nhat Hanh for about ten years before returning to lay life.

Fresh out of the monastery and with very little money in their pockets, they began as a two-person community. Soon after, Fern's mom, Candace, joined their visioning team. Over the course of fifteen years, the three of them steadily helped grow Morning Sun to where it is today: a vibrant residential community of over twenty people, a burgeoning retreat center, a pristine nature preserve of 240 acres, and a spiritual home for hundreds of people. But it was not easy by any means. As Fern recollects:

> In the beginning, we could see and imagine the end result: a beautiful farm with people, children, animals, and all that. A community space where people could come together and cultivate programs around many different ideas and creative expressions of the practice. We could see all this in our minds, like a beautiful picture. But how would we get from here to there? How do you talk about that and then work it back to where we were, two people with absolutely no material resources in the world? And what is the glue that will hold it all together?

While they had no material resources, they had a wealth of spiritual and social support. Fern and Michael were both established Dharma teachers, personally mentored by Thich Nhat Hanh, and strongly connected to a worldwide Buddhist tradition. Fern and Michael shared a powerful vision and a stable mindfulness practice to uphold and empower that dream.

Long before Morning Sun was realized, Fern and Michael reached out to hundreds of practitioners throughout North America with questions about living in a mindfulness community. They sent out surveys inviting people to describe what facets of community life and residential structure might work best for them. They sorted through dozens of survey results, analyzed people's preferences, and explored options of community living that seemed to best fit people's needs. Most respondents expressed a deep wish to live in a residential community, have abundant access to nature, and share communal spaces such as the meditation hall or retreat facilities while having their own private dwelling space as a couple or family. This process greatly informed Morning Sun's pioneering vision. After reaching out to Sangha friends and family for low-interest loans, Michael and Fern reached received enough to buy a significant piece of raw land in rural New Hampshire.

At this point, Michael, Fern, and Candace asked not only friends and family about their vision, but just as importantly, they asked the Earth herself. Upon first visiting the land where Morning Sun now rests, Michael recounted, "We were walking here, thinking about it, getting to know the land, and we asked the land, 'Do you really want us here?' The response was a clear and resounding 'Yes.'" The trees, rocks, ferns, and even the dragonflies seemed to echo their deep wish to build a community home where they could live harmoniously with the entire land.

Soon after purchasing, Michael, Fern, Candace, and a group of friends in their budding community did a celebration and dance, connecting with the forest. Since then, they've tried to steward that relationship, staying in touch with the forest, talking to her and listening to her often. Fern reflected, "And we feel very supported by the land, it's been very clear in that way."

## From Teachers to a Team

While Fern and Michael established the initial vision, Morning Sun has grown because of the robust dedication and involvement of many residents and local members. I understood this was intentional from when I first met Fern in 2014 during a twenty-one-day retreat in Plum Village, France. Fern and I stood next to each other at the edge of the basketball court in Upper Hamlet, where the monks live. There was a pick-up game between the brown-robed, shaven-headed monks and the long-haired lay ballers, and Michael had just subbed in for me. Fern and I watched the entertainment for a few minutes before stepping away to talk. I asked Fern, "What is your and Michael's vision for the community?" Fern paused, looking toward the forest in quiet contemplation. Her eyes looked both serene and concentrated as she spoke. "Michael and I really hope to not just have our own vision but to have a community vision grow organically. The ideas, talents, and inspiration of the whole community will guide the ways we create and grow together." My ears perked up as she spoke. *That's what I'm looking for!* I thought to myself, and I promised Fern that I would soon come visit.

After touring communities around the world, deciding to plant my roots into Morning Sun's soil was an easy choice, and I spent the next five years living there and helping grow their burgeoning retreat center. Each month the Morning Sun residents come together to discuss programs and other issues that affect the community. Every fall, residents and staff reflect together on what retreats they would like to offer together the following year, since the residents are the main volunteer organizers and facilitators. Everyone discusses what they're inspired to offer, what worked beautifully last year, what was difficult or exhausting, and the realistic capacity for the year ahead. Everyone's thoughts are welcome, and consensus is the goal. At the same time, if someone really wants to lead something and has the energy for it, the community generally tries to support them. This allows residents to feel empowered with creativity and agency in the programs for which they are taking responsibility. At Morning Sun, it's not someone else's community they're serving—it's their own!

Not all the work of visioning and decision-making at Morning Sun is done absolutely equally and inclusively. As a growing retreat center and residential complex, Morning Sun has a multilayered decision-making framework with different tiers of responsibility. The residential community meets monthly to make autonomous decisions about residential life and significantly weighs in on programming decisions, whereas the retreat center is ultimately governed by the nonprofit board. The resident community makes decisions about prospective residents. A homeowner council stewards the permanent resident community. At the same time, any resident or non-resident member can volunteer or serve on committees overseeing different programs or projects. There is a wide spectrum of decisions that impact the community's short and long term well-being, so each domain requires different levels of commitment, experience, inclusion of voices, and membership.

## The Wisdom of Discernment

As a balance to inclusivity, my conversations with founders at both Morning Sun and Avalokita also strongly emphasized thoughtfulness about who they included in visioning and decision-making circles, especially during their nascent stages. When you're deciding *who* is involved in creating a community from the ground up, healthy discernment is key. A strong sense of friendship is important, as we'll see in the next chapter. Don't invite a black hole inside your inner circle if you want your Sangha solar system to shine bright and long. If you believe you are not able to build community harmoniously with someone, taking them on board for inclusivity's sake might derail the whole project. At the same time, visioning is an opportunity to open to others' ideas and learn from those we don't always get along with—it's a careful balancing act. Wisely choosing founding members or other leaders who shape the community's culture and path forward is arguably the most important decision a community will ever make.

## Visioning with the Larger Community

A visioning process that carefully includes as many voices as possible, from prospective members to interested neighbors and varied stakeholders, can unleash previously unknown sources of creativity, insights, and empowerment that send the community's sails flying into the future. People's ideas and collaboration can be included in many ways: surveys, focus groups, open house events, and cofounder relationships, for example.

In Oakland, California, the East Bay Meditation Center (EBMC) offers an inspiring story of engaging the local community to build its vision from the ground up. Its founders and leadership council focused first and foremost on relationships with their local community before building anything. Founding teacher Larry Yang writes in his book, *Awakening Together,*

> As practitioners, we had all been involved with mainstream meditation centers built on the power of the charismatic leadership of a specific Dharma teacher. These centers often assume that they know what is best for the community at large. The attitude might be described as 'build it and they will come.' Such centers have a certain quality of imposition: they were conceived without discerning what the needs of the potential participating community actually were.[17]

Rather than presume that they knew what their community needed most, the EBMC founders sought to involve the community from its very inception, having several meetings with local community groups and individuals to better understand both general interest and, more specifically, needs. They analyzed the demographics and asked how to represent the diverse communities who lived in the area. Their research revealed very practical points about planning the center. First, public transportation to a downtown location was indispensable in order to reach a diverse population, especially those in lower income communities. The community meetings also clearly conveyed the need for culturally specific programs that fostered community cohesiveness, trust, and safety, especially for people from marginalized groups consistently facing systemic oppression.

Out of these community engagement efforts, EBMC began offering classes, workshops, and informal gatherings for communities of color and LGBTQIA+ communities even before the center physically manifested. When they were finally ready to open their new center, as a gesture of solidarity, they hung a rainbow flag in the meditation hall instead of a Buddhist statue. Yang writes, "It was critically important to give diverse communities the experiential sense that they were not only included from the inception of EMBC but also cocreators in developing the center."[18] Like those at Avalokita, the EBMC founders didn't wait for their center to be physically built before experiencing the heart of their community vision. For there is no way to inclusiveness—inclusiveness is the way.

Larry Yang reminds us that it is much easier to establish a cocreated vision of inclusiveness, diversity, and equity during the embryonic stages of community development. Rather than tear down the walls and reconstruct a house that has already been built upon historical models of classism and White supremacy, integrate these ideals into the very blueprint and foundation of your community house from the beginning.

## Annual Meetings

Visioning can be done before a center or group is created but also any time throughout the life of the community. Whether your community has just opened its doors, been on the block for a dozen years, or is dreaming up new plans, it is always possible to reassess how its ideals are actually serving the target population and to renew the vision. Annual meetings are a wonderful opportunity for harnessing and guiding the wider community's aspirations for the upcoming year.

Shortly after leaving monastic life, I started practicing in a small weekly group called the World Beat Sangha, which met and took its name from the beautiful World Beat Center in San Diego, California. Our group size rapidly increased and we outgrew the original leadership model in which the two founders carried all the responsibility for decision making. We started a small "Caretaking Council" (CTC) of several volunteer members to steer the group's direction and organization. One of the CTC's first responsibilities was to host an annual meeting for all members. We started by meditating together for half an hour before inviting everyone to reflect and remember the past year—the mindfulness practices, our schedule, events, and days of mindfulness. "Please share, what you would like us to keep doing well? What areas would you like the Sangha to do differently? This is your spiritual community—what do you wish for the most?"

Based on the responses, the CTC did its best to organize and prioritize the group's activities for the coming year. However, the CTC's responsibility was not to execute all of the Sangha's ideas itself. For example, someone wanted the group to host a fundraising event for a member who was applying for American citizenship. So, the CTC invited those who suggested the idea to organize the event themselves and let the CTC know what material, logistical, or emotional support they needed. In this regard, the CTC helped the Sangha to brainstorm and fulfill visions that could not be implemented within its own framework—a win-win situation for everyone. The more that the CTC enthusiastically supported members' ideas and gave them the opportunity to realize their dreams in community, the more the members realized they were, in fact, the Sangha! The Sangha did not belong to the steering group of the CTC or anyone else; the Sangha belonged to everyone and everyone belonged to the Sangha. This realization is one of the greatest achievements in the life of any community.

## Listening to the Community

Building trustworthy relationships and including the voices of people you aspire to serve is at the heart of successful visioning. If you don't invest in listening to those who are crucial to your definition of success, your vision won't amount to much, no matter how eloquently crafted it is. A friend of mine asked me to provide a consultation for a retreat center project being designed in Europe. She was the project manager for a six-person steering committee who had been dreaming of this center for years and had enthusiastically crafted a vision together. Nonetheless, they had gained only minimal traction within the larger community and through fundraising efforts.

The committee wished to build a physical center that local groups from around the country could call home, a center where people could live and serve as caretakers. They envisioned young adult retreats, family retreats, and BIPOC* events each year, which local mindfulness groups could support. I happened to be in frequent contact with the facilitators of the local young adult, family, and BIPOC groups in the region at that time; naturally, I asked them how they felt about the project. "Retreat center? We haven't heard anything about that." I was shocked—most of them barely knew what was happening. The committee wanted to build a home for these groups, yet they hadn't built relationships with individuals in those groups. I encouraged the steering committee to completely let go of their vision and to start over with step one of the visioning process: "Decide who is part of the community and/or visioning process." Including these communities' voices, aspirations, needs, and insights could then grow towards a larger shared vision and reality.

The committee felt renewed enthusiasm to engage in larger visioning sessions with a broader coalition of community leaders from around the country, especially with groups not previously represented. I cautioned them that they still ran the risk of inviting these other groups to "*their* project," a trap in which the committee listens but ultimately feels singularly responsible. But if they listened deeply, remained open to how others wished to be involved, and sought genuine collaboration, opportunities for partnership and greater community might naturally unfold.

## When Visions Are Not Written Down

After forming your team, contemplating your ideals, and arriving at a shared vision together, the next step is putting it on paper. A concretely articulated vision is the blueprint of the house you are

---

* BIPOC stands for "Black, Indigenous, and People of Color." The term acknowledges that people of color have faced different levels of discrimination and oppression, both currently and throughout history; Black and Indigenous people have been and continue to be severely impacted by systemic racial injustices.

building. Without posting it clearly for everyone to see and follow, people will be confused about what they and everyone else are constructing! A well-crafted vision will harness the community's focus, agency, and resources and will draw more of the people you want toward you.

Even in the best of circumstances, without a clearly articulated and communicated vision, each community member's unique vision and values will be slightly different, if not grossly divergent! I have heard story after story of people who joined a community because they liked the vibe and the people and fell in love with the unspoken purpose, without reading the vision. After months or years of investing time and resources, they felt estranged and deeply bothered by the community's direction. Then one day, they realized that the community's vision was fundamentally different from their own! A clearly articulated vision attracts those who align with our deepest aspirations and sends a clear message to those who don't.

Clarifying community agreements early on and writing them down can save some huge headaches. Ten years after Morning Sun was founded, the community struggled with whether members would need to be vegetarian or not. Initially, the first few families were vegetarian, and most believed that they were creating a vegetarian community. But over time, one family transitioned to an omnivorous diet, and new people moved in who also preferred a mixed diet that included meat. Meanwhile, some residents had assumptions that everyone needed to be vegetarian. However, these assumptions and values were never articulated in the original vision statements or resident bylaws.

Many residents believed with all their heart that a plant-based diet was crucial for mitigating the impacts of climate change and land degradation, as well as being a compassionate response to the horrors of animal factory farming. Others felt that a balanced omnivore diet was a more practical and healthy diet for themselves and their growing children. The tension over this issue became a prolonged source of discomfort, confusion, and resentment in the community for years. Ultimately, the community settled on the understanding that, while everyone absolutely wanted all the current residents to stay, no matter their diet, any prospective residents would need to have strong vegetarian aspirations in order to be accepted into the residential community. We also decided that all community events would be plant-based or vegetarian.

A community that is all things to all people runs the risk of disappointing, frustrating, and confusing its own members. Concretely articulating a vision enables your community to stand behind the values you have clearly chosen together. Whenever the community's direction feels shaky or if opinions start straying in myriad directions, you can look back to the clearly drawn circle of your community vision and core values. They become an enduring force of integrity, purpose, and the heart of who you are. As your collective visioning process ripens, I encourage you to write down your vision so that both current and prospective members can easily see it and be inspired! You can freely share it on your website, in brochures, your community hall, or on social media. Don't be too vague. Share what the vision is and what it is not. Let your vision shine openly and widely. May it illuminate your community path during dark nights and be a lighthouse for others to seek refuge.

## Trusting the Wind at Your Back

Even after mapping out a clearly articulated vision, sometimes the community will still sail in a different direction than you anticipated. I spent a year meeting monthly with three other Morning Sun residents to envision a young adult community center, the Wake Up Center, where young people could flourish in residential community. We shared our ideals and goals, crafted an inspiring vision, and created a breathtaking building design. But after a year of meeting together, the visioning wind that had been briskly filling our sails suddenly stopped. Each time I tried to reinvigorate our meetings, something else got in the way; people were busy, email threads grew more distant, and enthusiasm waned. I felt disappointed and tried to keep rallying the troops. But after pushing for several months, I got tired and frustrated, so I decided to stop chasing the dream and just listen. Several months later, our community decided to start building a main retreat center facility at Morning Sun. All of our enthusiasm, time, and resources for the Wake Up Center were reborn in this new endeavor. The wind was at our back again, and stronger than ever; but it was blowing in a slightly different direction. We just had to let go, listen to the breeze, and be ready to hoist our sails again. Soon, our new facility became the main hub of retreats and community life year-round at Morning Sun.

Not all visioning processes eventually manifest according to our desires. Your community dream may launch majestically, or it may tank. The best we can do is nurture the soil. Even then, each community sprouts a life of its own. But if we wholeheartedly share our deepest aspirations with others, listen deeply to many voices, befriend others as partners, and ask for support, then we give the precious seed of community its best chance to bloom bright, strong, and happy.

## Getting Back in Alignment

Visioning can be helpful throughout the lifetime of a community, especially when the community vision goes awry. This past year, two friends and I launched a new meditation center and mindfulness intentional community in the land of the Catawba people, in Charlotte, North Carolina. While living at Morning Sun community, a man named Roger Grosswald called me one day out of the blue to share that he wanted to build a meditation community in Charlotte, a relatively large city. Initially, I was not interested in moving, and my energy was totally focused on Morning Sun. But the prospect of building a mindfulness residential community and retreat center close to an urban area was too compelling. The land included twenty-eight acres of diverse mid-growth woods, a creek, and large ponds with bobbing turtle heads and seasonal geese. Herds of deer roam through the woods, infant speckled fawns silently taking refuge in the leaves during spring, and flocks of geese spend the fall and spring seasons there, too. It was much more beautiful than I had imagined, and Roger and I soon began working on our dream—building a meditation community where city dwellers could access the healing forces of a gorgeous natural landscape through the wisdom of mindfulness practice.

We spent almost two years visioning together before I finally moved across the country for this new venture, and my longtime friend and Sangha-building partner, Nick Neild, followed me there shortly after. Several months into living there, we uncovered a huge misunderstanding between us. We had spent most of our time visioning the intentional community before finally realizing that we weren't on the same page at all regarding the retreat center. Roger, the property owner, had envisioned only daylong retreats and did not want people staying overnight on the property, whereas Nick and I had clearly planned for multi-day overnight retreats, which require a different level of infrastructure and investment. It was a scary moment; we seriously questioned our viability moving forward together. I was honestly shocked how easily we had misunderstood such a key component of our mission and questioned our visioning process together. I requested that we immediately schedule a visioning session among the three of us to clarify our collective aim, identify other potential elements that needed to be reconciled, and determine whether we could proceed in our mission together.

First, we set aside half an hour to simply meditate together at our beautiful pond, effortlessly enjoying the turtles inquisitively poking their heads up at us and feeling the cool breeze blow off the rippled shore and onto our faces. Even if we couldn't resolve this today, we could at least enjoy the present moment together. These peaceful moments together also gave us the best chance of succeeding. We spent the next twenty minutes clearly writing out our individual visions independently. When we were finished, we shared our visions, what each of us wished for the most in our budding community dream, out loud. After each person's sharing, we asked questions, celebrated ideas, and clarified points.

During Roger's turn, he spoke honestly. "Well, I originally didn't foresee an overnight retreat center because I don't want to run a damn hotel business! That's a lot of work, cleaning up after people. But, after reflection, I am willing to go along with it, since it is clear how much you both want this. But I have some ideas about it...." Together, we brainstormed ways to make the housing infrastructure and accommodation responsibilities easier for us as administrators.

After we reconciled this topic, I probed Nick and Roger's visions in detail to see if there were any other hidden elements that could throw us off the rails again. But there were no visible traces of misalignment between us in building our beloved community. After reaching harmony of our views, I felt so elated—a combination of relief, confidence, clarity, and deep trust in collective purpose. The process of collective visioning had not only rectified the concern, but had brought out the deep, hidden power of harmony and solidarity of purpose. This power continues with us even today.

## Weaving a Vision

Time and patience are necessary for the most beautiful collective visions to grow to fruition. Different individual visions organically bloom into a greater shared vision that both includes and surpasses individual ideas. The culminating tapestry is not merely a sum of multicolored threads; individual visions are woven into a creation that is more colorful, dynamic, and complex than any single thread could ever be alone. Van Gogh didn't paint sunflowers with only yellow. He needed to blend shades of gold, orange, green, brown, and white for his masterpiece to be possible. Just the same, we need a diverse palette of colors and shades from every member's unique voice to meld into the most beautiful community creation.

# CHAPTER 3

# SHARING FRIENDSHIP

*Your friend is your needs answered.*
*He is your field which you sow with love and reap with*
*thanksgiving.*
*And he is your board and your fireside.*
*For you come to him with your hunger, and you seek him*
*for peace.*
—KAHLIL GIBRAN

*A measure of liberation will be found in our capacity for*
*intimacy.*
—PRENTIS HEMPHILL

*Friendship is the medicine for the isolation we often feel*
*within supremacy societies.*
—KATE JOHNSON

One day, the story goes, the Buddha and his friend Ananda were sitting alone on a hill together, overlooking the plains of the Ganges. Having served as the Buddha's attendant for many years, Ananda often shared his reflections and insights with him. "Dear respected teacher," Ananda said, "it seems to me that half of the spiritual life is good friendship, good companionship, good comradeship." I imagine that Ananda said this with some level of confidence in praising the merits of spiritual friendship. But the Buddha quickly corrected him: "Not so,

Ananda! Not so, Ananda!" Ouch—probably Ananda wasn't expecting such a stern rebuke. But the Buddha offered a powerful teaching. He continued, "This is the *entire* spiritual life, Ananda: good friendship, good companionship, good comradeship. When a monk has a good friend, a good companion, a good comrade, it is to be expected that he will develop and cultivate the Noble Eightfold Path," referring to the eight branches of the path of happiness.

Some of early Buddhism's most powerful teachings resulted from someone, often Ananda, sticking out their neck only to be corrected by the Buddha. In this case, the Buddha skillfully removed Ananda's idea that the Sangha and the Dharma are separate. One is not half of the other; the Sangha is not merely helpful in realizing the path. The Sangha is the path. Spiritual friendship is the path.

The practice of Sangha building may be considered one long story of sharing spiritual friendship. Strong communities depend on the personal relationships between their members, like a quilt woven together of various threads and seams. By strengthening each individual friendship, we strengthen the entire fabric.

## Kalyana Mitra

In Sanskrit, *kalyana mitra* means "spiritual friend." *Kalyana* may be translated as "good, true, virtuous, upright, or beneficial," and *mitra* is the root word for *maitri*, which means kindness. A kalyana mitra is not just any pal you hang out with to hit the clubs or go barhopping. A kalyana mitra is someone who helps you realize your deeper aspirations, someone who uplifts your path to a higher level of ethical and spiritual well-being. In comparison, the word "friendship" stems from the Old English *freon*, meaning "to love," and *freo*, meaning "free." So, at its root, friendship means to "love freely." Thus, both translations point to a selfless kindness toward others.

Many people, presented with a body of teachings that praise the practice of meditation and solitude, think Buddhism is a practice for loners. But the Buddha's encouragements to practice in solitude were balanced with an ardent emphasis on cultivating worthy friendships. Throughout his teaching career, the Buddha spoke about the pivotal importance of kalyana mitra to succeed in one's practice, stating that no other factor is so conducive to the arising of the noble eightfold path as good friendship. "Just as the dawn is the forerunner of the sunrise, so good friendship is the forerunner for the arising of the Noble Eightfold Path," the Buddha says.[19] The Discourse on Happiness Sutra, which extols thirty-two blessings of a happy life, begins: "To avoid foolish persons and to live in the company of wise people, this is the greatest happiness."[20]

Not just the Buddha, but spiritual teachers of various backgrounds throughout millennia have praised the merits of friendship as integral to self-realization and a cornerstone of spiritual community. A few years ago, under the shade of green olive trees at Deer Park Monastery, I was sharing a cup of tea with Jack Lawlor, a senior Dharma teacher and close student of Thich Nhat Hanh. Jack edited *Friends on the Path*, the first book in the Plum Village tradition that specifically offered guidance for building Sangha. When I asked Jack for words of wisdom, he replied without hesitation: "After all these years of practicing, it's clear to me that it all really comes down to one thing. The key is friendship." Perhaps it really is that simple.

There is no factor in our environment so influential to our lives as our closest friends. I once heard a quote, "If you want to know what you will be like in five years, take a look at your five closest friends now." The Buddha's emphasis on the profound impact of friendship is similarly captured by Joseph Rubano's poem, "Friend by Friend":

> Who is my mother,
> Who my father,
> When I am being created friend by friend?
> I don't remember who I was without you.[21]

Whether during times of crisis or peace, whether on momentous occasions or very subtly, wherever we live, those around us impact our life and consciousness at every moment.

## FIVE CLOSE FRIENDS, FIVE QUALITIES

I consistently find that my own Sangha's discussions on the theme of kalyana mitra offer the richest insights; I encourage your community to learn from each other.

1. Ask people to write down their five closest friends and what quality they appreciate the most in each of them.

2. Then write down five qualities of friendship you personally offer to others.

3. Lastly, name five qualities you want, need, or value the most in a friend at this time in your life. Invite people to share their insights with the whole group.

If we wish for our community to deepen its friendships, we can invite people to offer suggestions and guidance. We may ask, "How do you think we can grow friendships and stronger connections within our community? Does anyone have ideas?" Someone may like to offer tea and snacks after meditation is over. Another may invite the community to embark on a camping or skiing trip together. One of my closest friends invites community members to attend rock concerts with him as a Sangha! A new magic of friendship can take place in these different environments. Listen to the group's wisdom; their ideas will likely be the best and make all the difference.

## Friendship, the Cornerstone of Community

As I reflect on all the Sanghas and meditation centers I have observed, read about, and built alongside others, an enduring feature shines forth like a faithful star: they were all built with *at least one* powerful friendship at the very core. The Buddha had powerful disciples such as Shariputra, Maudgalyayana, Mahakassapa, Ananda, and others to help build his most precious and enduring legacy—the monastic Sangha. Thay had Sister Chan Khong to build the Plum Village international community, one of the largest and most diverse international Buddhist Sanghas today. Upon leaving monastic life in Plum Village, Michael and Fern teamed up to build the Morning Sun community. During our research tour, Vanessa and I met with the advisors for Avalokita, Karl and Helga Riedl, the two German Dharma teachers who lived in Plum Village France for many years before founding Intersein retreat center in their home country. Sister Shalom and Anton founded Dharma Gaia in New Zealand. The list goes on.

My journey of community building is no different. The yearlong research tour of global communities that forms the very heart of this book would never been possible without my then-partner Vanessa's boundless encouragement, support, and effervescent enthusiasm for Sangha building. While Vanessa and I eventually parted ways as a couple and she now lives many states away from me in the Pacific Northwest, our Sangha service project in Greece, numerous mindfulness retreats we led along the way, and the hundreds of interviews and discussions we had with community founders and members would never have come to fruition without her immense capacity for friendship, compassionate service, and communal joy. My gratitude for Vanessa's companionship and contribution to this book reaches across the world.

When I first moved to the land of the Catawba that would become the new mindfulness center, Greatwoods Zen, I began leading days of mindfulness and other programs. While I felt dedicated, inspired, and full of energy, I also felt quite alone, overwhelmed, and burdened with tasks. When my longtime Sangha friend Nick Neild moved all the way from the Czech Republic to partner with me in building this center, everything changed: our Sangha tripled in size in just several months and our momentum seemed to roll effortlessly downhill. Not only was the work half as much when divided between us, it was also twice as fun! As a duo team, we inspired our community with overnight backpacking trips, spontaneous community game nights, and new retreats.

Nick and I became an invincible team, the solar nucleus of our Sangha planetary system.

My experience is that to build a thriving community, whether brand new or renewed in spirit, we must find at least one person whom we can trust and partner with, to travel the distance of our dreams. It makes all the difference.

## The Sangha Solar System

While living at Deer Park Monastery in California, I once overheard a retreatant asking Brother Phap Dung, one of Thich Nhat Hanh's most senior Dharma teachers, how to build a Sangha in his hometown. Brother Phap Dung replied, "The most important thing is the core friendships you create together. That's everything. You practice every day by yourself, and you share the fruits of your daily practice with the closest members, those who are the core of your group—you know who they are. You offer your freshness, joy, and deep listening to them, and help those friendships to bloom. You can't fake that kind of thing. Build that core community, and when people come to your Sangha, those friendships will radiate out. People will see it, and they'll gravitate to that energy."

Brother Phap Dung likened the Sangha to a solar system in which the core friendships are the bright sun at the center. These core friendships radiate out warmth, light, and gravitational pull for everyone else to orbit around. Some people will be drawn right into the sun's center, beaming bright with kindness and affection. Some will orbit very closely, like Mercury and Venus, while others will come less regularly, like Saturn or Neptune. Still others, like Pluto or Halley's Comet, may visit your Sangha only once in a long while. But they all will feel the magnetic draw and nourishment of the sun's strength, warmth, and light.

When I visit Sanghas, I pay close attention to the quality of their friendships. Do people look at each other with eyes of affection and ease? Do they look at each other at all? Do they spend time hanging out after gathering times or at other times of the week? How do they speak about others when they are together or, more importantly, when they are not together? What do you observe in your own community?

Many Sanghas strive to serve as many people as possible. Our society consistently promotes the message that bigger is better, more is superior, and that size validates our self-worth. This habit energy of supersizing can dilute and distract from the Sangha's deeper purpose and power. A Sangha's true power lies in its depth of spiritual friendship and harmony, not its number of followers. Friendships that embody safety, intimacy, and compassion are what people everywhere in our ailing world are so hungry for—in fact, friendships are what we need to heal. There is nothing wrong with growing one's community and sharing the blessings of meditation practice more widely. But are the roots of connection dug deep into your Sangha's soil? Is the trunk of your togetherness strong enough to withstand the storms? Deep roots of friendship will nourish the Sangha no matter how tall and wide your community grows.

My friend Joseph started a young adult Sangha called Wake Up Happy Valley in Massachusetts a few years ago. He told me that the week before COVID-19 erupted, his burgeoning Sangha was about to transition their meeting space from his bedroom to a large and beautiful indoor yoga hall that would quadruple the space available. But due to the pandemic, they changed their plans and held small online gatherings with their current community instead. This was a blessing in disguise—they focused more on the quality of their close friendships and how to support each other through the pandemic rather than trying to expand. Every week after their evening practice, most members would stay online talking, hanging out, and having fun together. Joseph noted that although the Sangha stayed small, their friendships grew closer and more intimate during this period. They organized a buddy system "second body" practice for Sangha members to pair up for walks, weekly talks, or hang out sessions after Sangha to strengthen the existing friendships and offer support through the pandemic.

## The Art of Friendship

Young people display some of the most creative and sophisticated means of friendship building. I have spent time, for example, with Wake Up London, a young adult Sangha that masterfully combines practice with the art of play, joy, and service. After their Saturday meditation practice downtown, they often go out for pizza or hang out together in St. James Park with tea and snacks among the trees. My friends Karen and Dave began offering Sangha hikes outside the city with time for both walking meditation and enjoying each other in conversation. Once or twice a year, they organize concerts where all are invited, as well as encouraged, to offer music, poems, skits, or anything else creative. During the pandemic, a large group of friends went camping on the coast for several days, keeping the flames of joy and companionship burning bright even during those dark times. Many of them have chosen to share apartments together, living in mini-Sangha houses to share their daily lives. They spend time together not merely for practical reasons or to get ahead in their practice but because they like it!

Kareem and Jasmine, a former couple who have been practicing in the UK Plum Village community for many years, said to me, smiling, "Our Sangha friends have become our best friends now!" They frequently hosted weekend gatherings for other Sangha facilitators at their house outside the city, offering time for meditation practice as well as hiking in the beautiful countryside around their home in the town of Stroud. These intimate gatherings strengthened the very core of their community through the years, deepening both their practice and their connections.

The tight-knit circles of companionship in Wake Up London have brought Thich Nhat Hanh's legacy of socially engaged practice into the streets. One of Wake Up London's founders, Joe Holtaway, shared, "I believe our Plum Village–inspired activism has bonded us in action." The Sangha has organized numerous sitting and walking meditation events in public spaces and offered their compassionate and collective presence to peaceful protests for environmental and humanitarian causes like Extinction Rebellion.

Having profound exchanges through meditation and Dharma sharing circles is important, yet that's only one dimension of building friendship. To see the full sphere of someone's world requires different types of conversations, socially engaged projects, and good old hang out time. Especially after steeping in meditation together, the atmosphere is ripe for meaningful connection and joyful service.

One of my first Sangha friends ever, Alicia Rowe, and I started the Riverside Smiling Sangha over twenty years ago in Southern California, in the town where I had grown up as a child. When I visited her last year, she said practically the same thing as Jasmine and Kareem. "When we first started, none of us knew how the Sangha would affect our lives. Now, even after all this time, we are best friends with each other!" The average age in Alicia's Sangha is over seventy, and Alicia herself is ninety-two years old! Yet they have built their friendships with as much vitality and joy as my young friends in London. They love being with each other, and it feeds their love for the Sangha.

When Alicia and I first started hosting the Sangha each week at her house, Alicia always offered cups of Japanese herbal tea and a tray of cubed honeydew melon and cantaloupe that we slowly ate with toothpicks while we hung out after meditation. Even now, twenty years later, the Smiling Sangha still stays after meditation every Monday evening for a potluck dinner and conversation. Having profound exchanges through structured sharing circles is precious, yet it's only one dimension of getting to know someone. If I want to know the full sphere of someone's world, then it requires different types of relating, including some good old hang out time. After steeping in meditation together, the atmosphere is so ripe for joyful vibes, meaningful connection, and a sense of belonging—what people often crave the most in community.

## Second Body Practice

A few decades ago, Thich Nhat Hanh invented a Sangha-building practice at Plum Village called the "second body" system. A second body is a companion in the community who shows up for you, and who might be someone you don't know well yet but with whom you will develop a closer relationship. Whether you live in a monastery, reside in a lay community, or practice regularly in a local Sangha, the second body practice is one of the easiest and most powerful ways to strengthen relationships in your community and help everyone to feel more connected to the Sangha itself.

Many years ago, when I was a novice monk at Plum Village France, I became ill and needed to stay in my room for several days, apart from the rest of the Sangha. I was feeling lonely and cut off from the community, so it was a total surprise and joy for me when my second body delivered hot oatmeal and fruit to my room. I slept right through breakfast and woke up to find the caring gift on my nightstand. Every meal thereafter, three times a day like clockwork, my second body came with a bowl of hot soup or steamed vegetables and rice and, most importantly, his caring presence! He often stayed to eat with me, enjoying the simple meal in silence as if we were sitting together with the whole Sangha. We gazed at the lush forest outside, content with each other's presence without words. Even though he was my only visitor, he was like an ambassador of the Sangha, helping me feel seen, cared about, and a sense of belonging. Throughout the pandemic, when so many people felt isolated and starved for human connection, the second body practice helped connect every member of the community in which I was living to the whole.

In this practice, everyone looks after themselves first; we care for and attend to ourselves as our own first body. Then, those who wish to participate are assigned someone else as their second body—an intentional, caring friendship for a period of time. Each participant has both someone who they are caring for and someone who is caring for them. Thus, the entire Sangha is tied together in a circular chain of intentional friendships.

We approach this practice with lightness. We're not trying to be someone's therapist or guru. We are simply keeping friendships alive and growing the circle of our community. One of the intentions of this practice is to pull us out of our habitual forces of self-interest, busy-ness, and isolation from others and gently pull us into a spirit of more openness and connection. Focusing on one's second body each week extends people's attention outward; it encourages everyone to expand beyond their typical and most frequent connections. This practice is powerful for the whole community—you don't need to improve your relationships with everyone in order for friendships to bloom across the Sangha. When you care for one person, you care for the whole group.

At Morning Sun Community in New Hampshire, we started our second body practice during the pandemic. It was amazing to see what happened when people were given permission and encourage-ment to have fun with people they normally didn't spend one-on-one time with. Joaquin accompanied Mary Beth on a ten-mile bike adven-ture around Lake Warren during her typical weekday ride; Candace, who was a second body to me, invited me to plant tomato and sweet potato seedlings on Saturday afternoons; I treated Fern, my second body, to some dark chocolate and tea during my lunch break, which stimulated some great conversations—Fern shared her family's new-found interest in playing Dungeons and Dragons together. Without our second body practice, I would have never learned that Fern, our senior Dharma teacher and a former nun, enjoys Dungeons and Drag-ons with her family so much!

Several months later, we were all assigned a different second body. I asked Aurora, my new second body, to go for a walk and have some tea together. She wrote back, "No thanks, but how about you go for a run with me?!" I groaned, realizing I was paired up with an ultra-marathon runner! It had been a while since I ran regularly, but that all changed with my new second body. As it turned out, Aurora was doing a multi-marathon training that month, so I started running alongside her for as long as I could a few times per week. But instead of being a chore, running with Aurora for even a fraction of her epic adventures became quite fun for us both. After several weeks, I was able to run with her for two-and-a-half hours one day—I would have never gotten that strong so quickly without my second body. But more importantly, our friendship became stronger than ever.

Our Morning Sun community found it helpful to have a minimum amount of time each week or month that everyone agreed to spend with their second body. We decided that spending about thirty minutes each week, or one hour every two weeks, was reasonable. Sometimes the second body relationships connected very easily, and other times they didn't really click. Relationships are always shifting and changing, and one never knows how spending time with a random person in the Sangha will be—that's part of the fun and growth! We also discovered that a clear end date was helpful so that people don't let the limited time go by without crafting meaningful experiences together and so that they can find closure.

I encourage you and your community to explore the second body practice together for three months. It's a bold experiment in building friendships in the heart of your community. Even if not everyone wants to participate, it is still fun and worth exploring for those who are game. Once a month, remind people of the time frame and offer suggestions on ways for people to connect so they can benefit from each other's companionship. Aside from the half-hour weekly commitment, people may like to offer other gifts of friendship, such as bringing fresh flowers to brighten someone's day, a card full of genuine appreciations, or simply getting together to meditate. It is up to each second body pairing how they wish to connect. Most important is to be creative and make this practice your own. No one will do it perfectly, and people will make mistakes.

In her book, *Radical Friendship*, Kate Johnson reminds us, "We don't have to get ourselves 100 percent together to be available for radical friendship. Rather, it is through the practice of friendship that we get ourselves together."[22] In this light, true friendship is both our highest ideal and our daily practice. Through sincerely striving to serve others, we end up realizing our own heart of happiness. With your second body, see what you may learn, offer the fruits of your daily practice to each other, and then watch your Sangha bloom with cross-pollination in front of your eyes.

\* \* \*

If it was easy to succeed on the path without the guidance, compassion, and joy of good friends, then kalyana mitras wouldn't be so precious. Walking the path alone can be a confusing, lonely, and difficult journey. Voyaging with poor friends is like sailing across the ocean with your anchor dragging on the floor—no matter which direction you try to go, you are always pulled downward.

Good friendships are like rays of a spring dawn pouring beams of warmth and light onto the frozen forest floor. Every part of the forest is brought to life by such brightness and vitality. The practice of kalyana mitra is learning to breathe new life into every relationship, beginning with ourselves and then expanding to our closest relationships and beyond. Each one of us has a kalyana mitra inside, ready to step forward. We can start by cultivating just one quality of good friendship, with one person in front of us, in one moment. We can even start right now.

# CHAPTER 4

# SHARING SERVICE

*Even a wounded world is feeding us. Even a wounded
world holds us, giving us moments of wonder and joy. I
choose joy over despair. Not because I have my head in the
sand, but because joy is what the earth gives me daily and
I must return the gift.*

—ROBIN WALL KIMMERER

*"To act with the eyes and heart of compassion, to bring joy
to one person in the morning and to ease the pain of one
person in the afternoon. We know that the happiness of
others is our own happiness, and we aspire to practice joy
on the path of service."*

—THICH NHAT HANH

Since 2012, Greece has been a doorway to the European Union for
millions of migrants seeking refuge from war, persecution, and economic distress. They have left their homeland, livelihoods, and family
members, and risked even their lives in search of a new home and
hopeful way of life. For years, I felt called to volunteer with migrants
in Greece, especially while traveling in relatively affluent communities
throughout North America and Europe. I witnessed a stark contrast
between the relative luxury of middle- and upper-class communities and tourists and the abject poverty of migrants fleeing from violent oppression and social devastation. Unsettled by the pain of this

injustice, I felt compelled to find ways to help. But I feared that if I headed there alone, my motivation and capacity to serve others would dry up like a lone tree without water and forest.

I had worked for some years as an environmental and social activist and a social worker in high-crisis situations. Even with a stable meditation practice, I was no stranger to vicarious trauma, empathy fatigue, and the burnout that often comes with these fields. The last time I joined a nonviolent civil disobedience action, about seventy of us slept on railroad tracks for a few days to temporarily shut down an oil refinery polluting the coastline of federally protected Indigenous lands and fishing waters. To help ground our collective efforts in peace and stability, I offered morning and evening meditations for myself and the other activists. These circles helped, but engaging in a political action without a community of safe and dependable friends left me emotionally exposed and vulnerable. Having confrontations with armed state troopers, hearing verbal assaults from those who disagreed with or hated us, risking arrest, and feeling the despair and rage of fellow activists depleted my energy. I felt wrecked and told myself I would never engage in activism without trustworthy friends and community again.

These experiences encouraged me to think differently about Greece. Going as a solo volunteer could lead to another emotional burnout—then how helpful would I be to others? Buddhist teacher Muslim Ikeda from the East Bay Meditation Center offers a more inspiring and sustainable approach in her yearlong mindful activism program for students. Before participating, she requests they undertake this sacred vow:

> Aware of suffering and injustice, I [name], am working to create a more just, peaceful, and sustainable world. I promise, for the benefit of all, to practice self-care, mindfulness, healing, and joy. I vow not to burn out.

This was the nature of the aspiration with which I and my partner Vanessa set out for Greece. I felt overjoyed to hear that my partner

Vanessa shared my enthusiasm but I knew we could do better than just the two of us. This time, we were determined to go as a Sangha. This story is about the power of service, not merely as individuals, but as a community.

## The Wake Up Retreat in Plum Village

Midway through our global tour of mindfulness communities in 2017, Vanessa and I helped to facilitate a retreat in Plum Village, the monastery and retreat center in the southwest of France I had lived in as a monk. It was a retreat for young adults—over six hundred of them between the ages of eighteen and thirty-five—all opening their hearts to cultivate peace in themselves and compassionate action in the world. I thought to myself, "One couldn't ask for more perfect conditions to start a mindful volunteer project!"

Midway through the retreat, I asked a senior Dharma teacher to speak about our project after a morning talk while everyone was gathered in Still Water Meditation Hall in Upper Hamlet. Hundreds of young people would be there to hear about our vision, and the proposal was well received.

Vanessa and I then offered information sessions every day at lunch, encouraging people to consider this profound opportunity for service: "Let's fuse our strengths of mindful living and compassionate action with our aspiration to support the refugees landing in Greece. We can live together, support each other, and show up for those in need! We will begin this fall, when volunteers are especially needed due to colder conditions and lack of volunteer support in the camps. Who's interested?" I shared as confidently as possible that this would be a fulfilling project to embark on together—one not to be missed!

Although I had been studying the migrant crisis for years, at that point I still had no idea where we would live or what organizations we could partner with. Instead, I focused on the power of Sangha responding communally and compassionately to the world's problems. Others added their own experiences, inspiration, and healthy skepticism to the discussions, and slowly, a core team of inspired young adults began to form.

To our delight, about half a dozen people committed to the project right there during the retreat! Over time, fifteen young adults from eight countries decided to join this rare adventure. Vanessa and I were thrilled by the enthusiastic response, knowing they felt inspired by our vision, trusted our leadership, and felt similarly called to serve in this dire situation. As this group of dedicated young adults began scheduling their flights, I realized I felt responsible for the whole thing—travel plans, lodging arrangements, coordination of volunteers, not to mention my friends' well-being—all in an unfamiliar country steeped in crisis. "Oh no!" I thought, "What am I doing? Where will we stay? What exactly will we do there?" In a matter of hours, my feelings flipped upside down from elation to serious concern. Walking slowly around the monastery lotus ponds, I pondered this dilemma and then quickly sought guidance from a few senior monastic brothers I trusted.

## Advice before Greece

On the last day of the retreat, I sat beneath the large linden tree in the middle of Upper Hamlet, where the monks reside. Across from me sat Brother Phap Dung, also known as Brother Embrace. As a Dharma teacher for almost twenty years, he'd been one of my strongest mentors ever since I had arrived at Deer Park Monastery in California, where he was formerly the abbot. His insights could be fierce, but I always trusted his genuinely compassionate heart and intentions. Besides, I desperately needed his advice before setting sail for Greece in six weeks.

I shared with Brother Phap Dung my inspiration for initiating and leading this project. As part of our service in Greece and given my experience teaching social workers, educators, activists, and youth, among others back home, I was excited to teach mindfulness to volunteers and staff at NGOs and refugee camps. Brother Phap Dung soon had something else to say about these grand ideas: "What you need to do is to go there and just listen—don't go trying to teach anything, mindfulness or whatever. Yes, you want to offer something and you want to help, but what you need to do is listen because you don't know anything, David." He paused to make sure I received those last words before continuing. I swallowed a gulp of humility during the silence. "You're going to a whole new country, and you're meeting a whole new culture. You don't know them; you don't know anything about them. You can't teach mindfulness because you don't know what they need. So, you just listen, that's your practice. You're not teachers, David, you're listeners."

I listened for about twenty minutes to everything he had to say. It felt as if he emptied out the contents of my brain, spun my head around 360 degrees, and then set it back on straight. I walked away feeling slightly disappointed and at the same time relieved, clear-headed, and more confident. What a fortune to have mentors who are not afraid to offer a Zen punch when necessary to help my intentions stay rooted in the ground of reality instead of floating in the clouds.

The following day, under the shade of the same supportive linden tree, I sat across from Brother Phap Linh, a long-time friend and monk from the UK. On the other side of the tree's fifty-foot branch span, a young woman playfully pushed a giggling friend on a wooden rope swing hanging from a thick branch above. As if taking cues from these childlike sisters, Brother Phap Linh said, "Don't forget to nourish your joy together, David. That's essential because when you nourish your joy, that's what you'll share with others. You don't keep it for yourselves—offer that beautiful energy to those you'll be with. Especially with this kind of work, if you feel down and drained of energy, you won't have anything to offer to others. They need for you to be nourished and replenished deeply so you can offer your reserves; it's a constant cycle of nourishment and offering."

I'd been considering ways for our Athens community to enjoy the beach or nearby islands, but in the back of my mind I judged these fantasies as self-indulgent. We would be working with people experiencing dire poverty and recovering from war zone traumas and displacement, so even small vacation outings felt absurd. As if

Brother Phap Linh were reading my mind, he added, "And don't feel guilty about it either. If you're just serving all the time without any joy and you exhaust yourselves, then it's over, you're done; you'll have nothing to offer. You need downtime to be happy, to be joyful, in order to be there for others and to really be effective. You aren't keeping it for yourselves, you are nourishing yourselves for everyone. So yes, no guilt!" I laughed with surprise and relief at his strict encouragement to have fun.

A giddy excitement started lightening up my mood, balancing out my seriousness toward the project. That afternoon, eight members of our newly formed cohort sat together on the grass in the shade of several towering pines. We passed around a small bucket of coconut-based ice cream and shared our visions and inspiration together. Feeling excited about all the new advice, we immediately started brainstorming ways to both listen to each other and sustain our spirits. "There are tons of beautiful islands there—we can visit them and meditate there!" one person shared. "I'd love to take a day off each week to visit the Parthenon, the Acropolis, and all the museums of this ancient city," sparked another. "I hear there are incredible hikes over hills and mountains rising over the Mediterranean Coast!" burst another. After half an hour of excitement, we laughed while reminding each other that our primary purpose was to support refugees in Athens and not to plan a vacation.

## Landing in Athens

To our good fortune, a young Dutch woman at the retreat had been living in Athens for a year and was thrilled to partner with us. She invited us to use her apartment as a Sangha home base and we rented another one down the street. By the beginning of October, a dozen of us young idealists crammed into these two small apartments, some of us sleeping three or four to a room. We knew we needed to meditate as often as possible and have lots of playful fun together or else we'd kill each other before helping anyone else!

Some of us worked in refugee camps, others in community centers and NGOs. We provided art therapy, physiotherapy, soup kitchen staffing, refugee camp staffing, mental health support, legal support, construction for NGO buildings, hot meals for those living on the streets, animal shelter care, community gardening, language instruction in English, French, and German—and more!

We chose Sunday as our weekly "Funday," purely dedicated to enjoying our new friendships and the paradisiacal elements of Athenian landscapes, museums, and culture. We decided to gather in a sharing circle every Wednesday evening to listen to each other and hold space for whatever we were going through. We knew that to be a stable source of compassionate listening for others, we had to begin with ourselves. We also formed a cooking rotation so that a hot meal would be ready for us every morning before work and in the evenings when we came home exhausted.

We started every day with the spark of mindfulness: sitting and walking meditation, a short inspirational reading, and a silent breakfast to nourish our wellsprings of inner peace and joy. We never knew what challenges and opportunities the day would bring, so we dedicated ourselves to diligently coming home to our bodies, centering our hearts, and finding a calm refuge in the rhythms of our breathing. Not everyone could participate in the morning sessions, but our collective intention to start the day with serenity and caring attention cultivated a settled and energized presence to channel into our volunteer jobs.

We started a weekly meditation group in town with the intention of benefiting ourselves first. We enthusiastically invited other international volunteers, migrant friends, and Greek residents who wished to come. We tried to be very aware and talk openly about unconscious motivations that we as all-White volunteers from affluent and "developed" countries may be bringing in as mindfulness "teachers," especially toward our friends coming from Muslim, Arabic-speaking countries. At the same time, we wanted all of our friends to feel welcome to participate if they were genuinely interested.

Establishing this refuge of mindfulness practice throughout the week was crucial to keep our presence fresh for ourselves and others over the long haul. Our Sangha home was filling with peace and joy, steadily becoming the foundation for our service for others.

## A Day under Apollo

Our apartments were located in a lower-income and migrant-rich neighborhood in Athens. This was a tremendous blessing for us—we were able to live, walk around, and hang out on the same streets as those we wished to befriend and serve.

While finding our way home from the metro during our first week in Athens, Vanessa and I got lost and asked a young man for directions. He had a finely trimmed beard, a clean-shaven head, and a black leather jacket offset by his beaming, innocent smile. His warm brown eyes, humble yet sincere efforts to speak English, and gentle insistence on walking us home that night made us fall in love with him immediately.

Omar was a twenty-seven-year-old father from the war-ravaged city of Aleppo in Syria. Two-and-a-half years earlier, he had left his wife and baby in Syria and fled for his life to Istanbul, then Athens. He arrived just a month before we did, and he was volunteering every weekday as the main chef of a soup kitchen down the street from where we lived. Omar enthusiastically welcomed us to have lunch there as his guests the following week. "How charming and generous!" we thought. We accepted and countered Omar's proposal by inviting him to hang out with us at the beach that weekend. We were thrilled that our new friend could spend our first "Sunday Funday" with us under the warm blessings of Apollo, the sun.

Even in October, the midday sun hovering over the Mediterranean coastline poured warmth and freedom over our bare skin. As others played in the water, Omar and I relaxed quietly on the beach together. I watched him stare dreamily into the aqua blue horizon, his hands planted firmly behind him in the warm sand as if he had just come home from a long journey. We were looking in the direction of his former home, several hundred miles across the treacherous sea that had delivered him here.

Finishing a slice of melon, I pointed to our Sangha friends who were goofing off in the water. "They're having so much fun out there. Let's go join them!" After slowly standing up and regaining his twenty-seven-year-old athleticism, he smiled at me and said, "I'll beat you to the water." I laughed out loud at his playful taunt. Even though I was a good ten years older, my competitive nature was excited by his boyish challenge. Within moments we were both sprinting as fast as we could down the beach, laughing all the while, water soon flying out behind our heels as we plunged into the refreshing waves.

An hour later we were back on the sand, lazily soaking in the warmth. "This watermelon is so sweet, Omar. Thank you for bringing it to share with us." Despite the inexpensive cost of produce in Greece, I assumed he didn't have much money and I was touched by his generosity. Omar put his hand on his heart and gently bowed with an abundantly warm smile. "We're so thrilled that you could join us today!" I added. Omar responded, "Thank you very much, David and all my friends here, for inviting me. I forget how I love the ocean." Omar was still learning English, but he always managed to communicate his sentiments very well. "In Syria, the sea is very close. It's our home. But now it's already some years since I visit like today." Like other refugees we met, Omar was consumed with survival needs and the hope of gaining asylum in northern Europe; he rarely took time to enjoy the playful side of Athens.

But on this day, Omar connected with everyone in our group while playing Frisbee, teaching us his kickboxing skills, snacking on chocolate tahini sticks, having one-on-one conversations, and just roasting lazily under the sunshine. We effortlessly spent the entire day between the warm sand and cool waters, nearly forgetting where we were and the cold shadows and crowded problems of the city behind us.

As Apollo's chariot finally descended over the island-speckled sea, we gathered everyone together to sit in silent appreciation for the day's ending. Seated upon sand-made meditation cushions, we returned to the foundations of our mindfulness practice—bringing awareness to our whole body, relaxing in an upright and stable posture, and resting our attention on the waves of our breathing. We sat with open-eyed awareness, allowing the ocean-mirrored sunset to fill us with light. A wavy golden pathway stretched endlessly along the water from shore to horizon.

## Making Friends

Omar is one of nearly 12 million forcibly displaced Syrians who have fled from violence, persecution, and economic despair in Syria after the civil war began in March 2011.[23] His migration west took him to the crowded cities of Istanbul and Athens, where he hadn't visited the beach in over two years. Athens' narrow streets and multistoried walls span for miles in every direction. For tens of thousands of migrants, the daily quest for food, safety, or shelter blocked out much of the day's sunshine as well as the coastline that lay just a bus ride away.

Omar cooked at HopeCafe, a soup kitchen and distribution center for clothing and infant supplies, which primarily served the Syrian community. We loved visiting Omar at this vibrant, boisterous social scene and meeting the friendly regulars. Some of our Sangha members started volunteering there, but a few of us just went there to hang out with Omar and meet new friends. If we had been too proud or caught in our self-ascribed roles as "volunteers," "international helpers," or "benefactors," we might have missed this profound opportunity to receive their gifts, allow them the joy of serving us, hear their incredible stories, and make meaningful connections.

Hanging out and getting to know people became one of my most important tasks as a volunteer. Sometimes I felt quite uncomfortable and out of place, standing around as the only White person and non-Arabic speaker in the room. But I patiently hung out while slowly sipping my drink until the right conversation opened up, and many did. Many wonderful friendships started this way. One day at HopeCafe, I met an Iraqi teenage girl who told me that her family was moving to France as part of the European refugee resettlement program. A few years prior, she, her three siblings, and their parents had abandoned their home when conflict entered their village, only to risk their lives by crossing the perilous Mediterranean Sea. Along the journey, they watched another small boat of refugees sink a half mile away from them, not knowing whether the floating survivors would be rescued and praying their own crowded vessel would safely deliver them across. They finally arrived upon the sandy shores of Lesvos island and were soon placed in an apartment in Athens. The family waited in limbo for two full years before hearing the news—rare among refugees—that their family was chosen for relocation to France. They were beyond excited; yet they were also anxious, as none of the family members spoke a word of French or had any French friends. Having lived in France for a few years, I offered to give them French lessons twice a week for the next few months before they departed, and they gladly welcomed me to their humble apartment.

A French-Irish brother from our Sangha also joined me each week. After the hour-long French lessons, we played games, took silly photos, and did Acroyoga with the younger kids. The mom always insisted that we stay for dinner, so we sat on the floor with them and ate traditional Syrian food as the teenagers translated into English and Kurdish. While I can't say they mastered French in those few months, we always had a fun time together! Most importantly, our friendship helped them feel more at ease with preparing for yet another move to a new country, knowing that they would meet kind people on their path—even if they didn't yet speak the same language. If I hadn't hung out drinking free cappuccinos that day at HopeCafe, we all would have missed this opportunity for greater connection.

## Listening

Whenever Omar was cooking at HopeCafe, he came out to greet us with a genuine smile and warmly asked how we were doing—"Hello, it's my brother and my sister!" he always called while putting his right hand over his heart. "Come, come, let me get you a drink—cappuccino, tea, hot cocoa?" Omar loved playing host, and we felt like distinguished restaurant guests, sometimes forgetting we were at a refugee soup kitchen. Vanessa and I both loved visiting him, being around his cheerful spirit, and hearing his incredible life stories. Indeed, it felt like we were siblings. But like most or all of our Syrian friends, Omar fought hard every day to keep his spirits afloat. He had survived countless traumatic experiences during the devastation of Aleppo, where streets, blocks, and entire communities had become a near-endless maze of white rubble.

One day, Omar and I were sitting over the signature HopeCafe cappuccinos, and his mood was more inward than usual. He shared stories of survival and loss with me as I bore witness to his depths of resilience and strength in overcoming despair. While they were standing in line for bread in the streets of Aleppo, Omar's younger brother had been shot in the neck by a sniper and died in Omar's arms. Less than a year later, Omar was thrown into a correctional prison after refusing to give his family's newly bought tank of propane to bullying government soldiers. After surviving a week in torturous conditions, Omar was released from jail, apparently by mistake. When ordered to return, he fled after saying a final goodbye to his wife and baby son that same day. It's against the law to leave Syria, punishable by prison or death. Yet Omar felt no choice but to flee and seek asylum in Europe, praying he would reunite with his family one day. He crossed the Syrian border overnight and eventually reached Istanbul, where he worked and saved money for almost two years before crossing the Mediterranean Sea separating Turkey from nearby Greek islands. He bought a spot in a small boat filled to the brim with other Syrians risking their lives to cross cold, dark waters at night in hopes of reaching a new home.

Whenever we listened to Omar's stories, we were deeply inspired by his courage and uplifting spirit in the face of trauma and pain he endured over several years. Omar was one of the most admirable young men I have ever met. He exuded an indomitable force of goodness and positivity toward others, fierce faith in life, and gentle humility. These qualities continued to rise to the surface amidst turbulent waves of suffering and despair around him. I heard countless stories of Omar helping others during dire situations. While living in Aleppo, Omar had a female acquaintance who began prostituting herself with soldiers in exchange for food to feed herself and her young children. She offered herself similarly to Omar, who refused and implored her not to hurt herself in this way. Instead, he offered to bring her bread twice a week so she wouldn't need to endanger her body and family anymore. Omar later shared that along his perilous migration north, he could often feel the prayers of friends he had helped, like this woman, supporting and blessing him to safety.

Listening to Omar's struggles and overpowering resilience was like receiving a handful of gems mined from the Earth's innermost core. Omar didn't need us to be volunteers or to teach him English. He simply needed a friend to bear witness to and receive his stories of loss, love, and strength. Omar was our teacher, revealing to us that "service" was much more about receiving others' gifts than offering our own.

## Syrian Stew

One evening Vanessa, Omar, and I were walking home from Hope-Cafe, and I asked Omar where he lived exactly. He confided in us that when he first arrived in Athens, he was denied entry to any of the refugee camps—they were all at maximum capacity. He spent the next few weeks homeless, which took a serious toll on his health and spirits. He eventually scrounged up enough money to share a crowded room with several other Syrian friends. This was officially illegal, so he rarely told people where he lived. "I can't be on the streets again. That's no good for me," he shared while looking down and shaking his head in determination and painful remembrance. "A warm and safe place at night is all I need." He sighed with relief, his gratitude for his tiny refuge and restful sleep unmistakable.

About a month later, Omar nervously shared with me and Vanessa that he was afraid of not being able to pay the next month's rent of one hundred euros, and it was really stressing him. He asked for our help, followed by several apologies and visible feelings of shame. Vanessa and I reassured him that it was more than okay to ask us, that we wanted to support him. We could have easily given him the money right then and there, but I knew that it was difficult for Omar, like many Syrian migrants, to receive handouts. Syrians have deeply rooted values of self-sufficiency, education, hospitality, and generosity. Yet migrants rarely receive work visas in Greece. We knew that being unable to contribute to society through gainful livelihood steadily eats away at one's self-worth. Omar needed the cash, but he also needed a way to contribute his value, to be seen as a hardworking earner and not only as a beggar. Vanessa and I thought about it for a few minutes and then decided to offer Omar a chance to share his culinary and baking skills, as he was a master pastry chef back home. In return for compensation, we asked Omar if he would teach us how to cook traditional Syrian cuisine and make a surprise birthday cake for our Irish Sangha brother. Without hesitation he accepted!

The rest of our Sangha was thrilled at the opportunity to learn Syrian-style cooking, and everyone threw down some cash for the dinner. We provided all the ingredients Omar requested and asked him to guide us as the head chef. Some of us chopped and washed under his direction while others patiently watched him prepare the feast. The aroma of tomatoes, rosemary, garlic, eggplant, and squash stewing for hours under his adept hands permeated our house and spirits. After the meal, when our chef needed to leave, we all got up from the table and surrounded him with a thirteen-person cinnamon-swirl hug. From inside our snug embrace, a few tears managed to slip down his stoic face.

## The Seed of Joy

A month later, we hadn't seen or heard from Omar for several weeks, and we began to worry about our friend. Then one day, we unexpectedly encountered Omar at HopeCafe, looking safe, healthy, and bright as usual. As he prepared his signature cappuccinos, consisting of instant coffee mix, condensed milk, quite a dose of sugar, and a big heartfelt smile, he recounted his latest struggles to find employment and entry into northern Europe. A Spanish physician had befriended him in Athens and offered to host and provide him with employment on the coast of Spain. Omar had tried several times to enter the country by boat and plane using fake identifications, a common strategy for migrants trying to seek asylum in the north, but despite his best efforts and resources, he was turned away at the border each time.

Feeling locked out of his dreams and seeing no hope for the future, Omar sank into the dark waters of depression that lapped at the shores of his and other refugees' lives. His aims to reunite with his family in a safe and prosperous land seemed like an arrow shot blindly into the night. Where could even his best efforts take him? The smothering shadow of despair overwhelmed all but a few traces of light left within him.

Standing near the bar with his mug still in hand, Omar shared, "Whenever I was feeling down, very sad, and had no more energy, I lay down and thought about that day at the sea with you and all my friends. It was like the sunshine came down into my heart and brought me much happiness." He paused for a moment before sincerely adding, "You don't know how much that day with you all brings me, David." The rest of us had been simply having a fun time, totally delighted that Omar could join us. But for Omar, our collective energy caused the seed of joy to flourish within him, a seed he needed for the trials that lay ahead.

After not seeing Omar again for several weeks, we finally received word in early 2018 that he had reached the Netherlands, his long hoped-for destination. We knew he was safe and we were thrilled for him, but that was all the communication he could share at the time. It was not until the following year when Francie, one of our Athens volunteers, and I were able to visit Omar in a city near Amsterdam that we could finally hear about his perilous journey. We were overjoyed to see Omar's smile, bursting like sunshine, just like when we had last seen him. The three of us took an entire day strolling through cobblestone streets and city parks as Omar recounted his long and harrowing journey there. Omar had traveled with two Syrian friends, trekking by foot across mountain passes in southern Austria and narrowly escaping guards who patrolled the alpine borders. He sometimes went days without eating and slept under the trees with just the clothes on his back. They encountered wolves and robbers along the way, yet also friendly police officers and generous strangers, and they never turned back. Over the course of several weeks, Omar took a combination of buses, trains, and car rides as well as lots and lots of walking to finally arrive at his golden destination.

At the end of our day, Omar brought us to his house, where he introduced us to his wife and toddler son, with whom he was able to reunite after finally attaining asylum in the Netherlands. Francie and I were filled with boundless joy to finally meet them and witness their happiness together. In the beginning of our relationship, Omar was our kind friend who played with us and asked us for help. In the end, he had clearly become our hero. I am forever grateful to him for sharing his bravery, inspiration, and companionship. Not all stories, especially concerning war refugees, end with happiness, but ours with Omar did.

## Blooming Community

Our Athens community aspired to practice joy as an expression of our compassion, like bringing a bouquet of winter flowers during the colder, darker time of year to a friend. Pansies, snowdrops, winter jasmine, holly bushes, and camellias bloom brightly in the winter. Their array of colors, freshness, and enduring vitality encourages us, if only temporarily, to let our sorrows and struggles fall to the earth.

Throughout the months in Greece, we found limitless ways to celebrate life, sustain our work in the refugee camps, and, most importantly, include our migrant friends in our communal gatherings. Our work with NGOs and soup kitchens was important, but we soon realized it was the quality of our relationships within the Sangha and among new friends that made the difference. We forged meaningful friendships (many of which continue to this day) with Syrian, Iraqi, Afghani, Senegalese, and Pakistani migrants who lived in our neighborhood and had fled from armed conflict, religious persecution, or economic despair.

With these new friends, we journeyed throughout the city and its environs, finding ways to enjoy our lives together despite the depressing conditions. We watched a free concert in the ancient Odeon theater, perused massive columns of the Olympian Zeus's second-century temple, hiked up to the landmark Acropolis and Parthenon, enjoyed weekly Pakistani and Indian curry dinners, walked up various hills to watch sunsets, and savored loads of tea and chocolate in parks overlooking the city. These unforgettable moments with friends were the highlight of our lives in Greece.

The three Americans among us hosted a traditional Thanksgiving dinner in November and invited our Syrian and Senegalese friends to join our celebration of family and gratitude. The next month, we collaborated with an NGO led by Kenyan Christian women in our neighborhood to organize and host an alcohol-free Christmas dinner for migrant families and anyone who wished to come. Almost twenty nationalities were represented! We handed out small toys for the kids, and everyone enjoyed music and dancing. It was the most diverse and memorable Christmas celebration I've ever been a part of, and the food was excellent—mostly because Omar cooked the main dishes!

If strangers had walked into our celebration that night, they never would have dreamed that a very depressed city waited just outside our walls. That night together, there were no economic woes, war, refugees, unemployment, or trauma; there was only our celebration of life and each other. This is the magic of community.

## Nourishing Sangha Harmony, 1-2-3-4

It also took time, through trial and error, to learn how to best support our group's harmony. During our weekly sharing circles, many of us admitted at one point or another that when we didn't pay enough attention to each other's words, spend quality time with one another, or attend to our communal harmony, we felt empty and listless in our path of service. We were often exposed to dire social conditions, and were still adjusting to a new culture as well as living very closely together. Community living, especially in small quarters, naturally breeds interpersonal conflicts and triggers a range of unresolved internal difficulties. Sometimes the combination of these challenges spontaneously erupted in a deluge of tears or fiery emotional outbursts. Where does one turn in those moments of overwhelm and confusion, especially when one's original intentions are to help others?

The flip side of service is being vulnerable and open enough to receive the support we need from others. For some of us, asking for help can be a much more daunting task than helping others. But to offer our genuine presence outside, we had to be there for ourselves first, both receiving and offering the compassion we needed from friends and community during difficult moments.

During these upsets, we patiently listened to one another and waded through the rocky shores of interpersonal struggles. We renewed our efforts over and over to empathize with one another's difficulties and needs, never giving up on anyone. Most importantly, we gave everyone the space to just be themselves as a whole person, in all their bright gifts and unique internal blemishes.

To ramp up our harmony, on special occasions—like a birthday or a friend's departure from our Athens Sangha—we celebrated them with rounds of tea and sumptuous Greek pastries. We all took turns voicing heartfelt appreciations for their personal gifts and contributions to our community. These circles of celebration and verbal acknowledgments were incredibly redeeming, and they greatly enhanced our feelings of joy and positive regard for one another.

Meditating every morning, listening deeply to each other's difficulties, appreciating one another's gifts, and enjoying Sunday Fundays together became our 1-2-3-4 combo for renewing our relationships and reinvigorating our spirit of service. Our Sangha's harmony was the foundation for genuinely reaching out to others. Most importantly, we learned to build an extended family of friendships—the deepest teaching we received through our quest to serve. Through our aspiration to support others, we touched real community and friendship, and received encouragement and insights from our teachers. We need a true family for ourselves in order to truly serve others.

Many of us stayed weeks or months longer than anticipated, and several people continued living, community building, and creatively serving in Athens. After almost four months in Greece, Vanessa and I knew that it was time to continue onward with our community research tour. Many of our friends, including Greeks, international volunteers, Syrians, and others with migrant backgrounds strongly encouraged us to stay and continue building a mindfulness community center there in Athens. Yet Vanessa and I knew that the healing power of mindful community building was also desperately needed back in our home country, where there is also much suffering, and we felt committed to returning and serving.

## Community Practice for Sharing Service

You don't need to travel halfway around the world with a dozen enthusiastic young people to contribute something valuable or relieve suffering in the world. The best place to serve is usually right where you are, in your home or neighborhood, with a community of spiritual friends. About ten years ago, I founded a young adult meditation group in Bellingham, Washington, and every Friday evening we gathered to meditate, read some teachings, listen deeply to each other, and then enjoy a potluck dinner and games together. It was such a fun way to let go of work and kick off the weekend. After about a year, several of us expressed that something felt lacking in our community. People wished to extend our happiness beyond our typical gatherings through a service project for the wider community. After tossing around various ideas, we planned to meet the following week at a local park with a sizable number of unhoused neighbors to offer them a meal. We first gathered at a quiet spot on the lawn and meditated together for thirty minutes before sharing our intentions for this experience and any other feelings that were alive in us. Then we moved to a more central location in the park and brought over several containers of food and outdoor games from our cars, forming a wide circle on the grass that looked open and inviting to others.

Several of us walked around the park to greet those who appeared to be park residents. We said, "Hi there! We have a bunch of extra food at our picnic. We would love to have you join us for some croissants, watermelon, chocolate, or Frisbee." It is amazing how friendly strangers can be if you just ask. In almost no time, a dozen new friends were checking out our picnic scene! While eating some cantaloupe, a young man mentioned that he used to play football in high school. I had my football and tossed it over to him. "Go long!" he yelled. We instantly started running wide receiver routes for one another. Our Sangha members Shannon and Jaren started tossing Frisbees around with others.

To call this a service project felt wrong—we were just having fun, laughing, and playing with new friends at the park. It was nothing special, yet it was more special than we could have imagined. We enjoyed pastries, cherries, veggie wraps, kombucha, and ice cream sandwiches. But more than that, we shared the most satisfying nourishment of all—human bonds. We shared stories, and we came out with the intention to offer food, love, and connection to our larger community. We left having received more joy, hope, and gratitude than we could have asked for.

# CHAPTER 5

# SHARING JOY

*If you never did, you should. These things are fun and
fun is good.*
—DR. SEUSS

*Joy is a net of love by which you can catch loves.*
—MOTHER TERESA

*It ain't no sin to be glad you're alive.*
—BRUCE SPRINGSTEEN

Through our community-building experiences in Athens described
in the previous chapter, I came to understand the importance of joy
and making time to play, and how such moments increase our resiliency when times get tough. When it comes to building a community,
play is just as important as spiritual practice.

During my first year living in Plum Village France, my cohort
of aspirant siblings and I, all hoping to become monastics, enjoyed
a rare lunch together with Thich Nhat Hanh and a small group of
senior monks and nuns after a day of mindfulness. We walked down
the grassy hill to Son Ha, "The Foot of the Hill Hamlet," where we
gathered at Thay's hut, a small, cozy building with a large fireplace
at the back wall. On an adjacent wall was Thay's calligraphy, *Smile to
the Cloud in Your Tea*. After gathering our food, we waited for Thay to
arrive; he was taking some time to rest after having just officiated a

ceremony and given a talk. I would never have guessed, but one of Thay's attendants told us that Thay had not slept well the night before due to some chronic health issues. When he finally entered the room, I noticed his eyes looked red, but they still glowed with great warmth and vitality. His eighty-year-old cheeks radiated joy, and his entire demeanor looked relaxed. Since it was a rare occasion for us to be so close to Thay, my aspirant friends and I were feeling shy. As usual, we ate in silence for the first several minutes. As each of us focused on our bowl of food, Thay's bright eyes and smile hovered confidently over us like a double rainbow, lightening the mood and easing our nerves.

Among us at lunch was a guest monk from China. He had come to practice with the Sangha for a few weeks and was hoping to have an audience with Thay. After the silence, Thay began talking playfully with the monks and nuns in the circle. Thay asked the guest monk where he was from and the monk shared which monastery and teacher had trained him. Then, Thay spontaneously asked the monk a bold question in front of everyone. "Your teacher, is he the kind of monk who likes to *play*?" Thay paused briefly after emphasizing the word "play" in a higher tone of voice and raising his eyebrows. In a more serious voice, he continued, "Or does he like to practice?"

The monk seemed totally caught off guard. He paused nervously, feeling on the spot in front of everyone. The air was slightly suspenseful as we all watched eagerly to see how he would respond. Mustering some confidence, the monk answered, "He likes to practice," ending with a serious nod.

Thay wore a slightly mischievous smile, knowing he held the crowd's enthralled curiosity in the palm of his hand. The monk was caught, as I think we all were. Thay quietly chuckled, as if pausing to let the question ripen within each of us for just a moment longer. Then finally, he revealed, "to play or to practice? When you know how to really practice, then you are just playing. And when you know how play, then you're really practicing." I felt the room breathe out a collective exhale and smile at the humorous yet profound exchange across the circle. This monk would likely remember this question for the rest of his life.

Thay's teachings are often something between a riddle, a personal question, and a magic trick that leaves his listeners in deep inquiry. The point of Zen practice generally, as far as can be articulated, is to dispel one's notions, especially opposing ideas, to arrive at a greater truth that slices through the limited perceptions that create suffering. In this case, Thay's question about play and practice was not simply for monastics, but for anyone with mindfulness, psychological, or spiritual aspirations.

Play and practice, practice and play: Which do you and your community lean into? When do you feel these two worlds merging?

## The Meaning of Joy

Thay shared that in order to be a spiritually mature person, we need to know how to cultivate joy. It's the same for the developing life of a community. A Sangha or family whose members do not know how to water seeds of joy in one another cannot be said to have wisdom. Like the hearth or fireplace of a home, sharing joy is at the heart of any blooming community.

But what does joy mean to you? To your family and community members? And how do you cultivate it, individually and communally? In the West, there is a deep belief that joy comes from obtaining what we want. Consider the Merriam-Webster dictionary's definition of joy: "The emotion evoked by well-being, success, or good fortune or by the prospect of possessing what one desires." Joy is often pursued in regard to objects of sensual pleasure. In this regard, conventional wisdom might suggest that buying a new car, eating chocolate fudge sundaes, drinking IPAs on a tropical beach, or having as much sex as possible will bring you unlimited joy, as much as you could want.

Perhaps having these things will help you feel good for a while, but will they really offer lasting joy to yourself and your loved ones? Many sages from the East have revealed a different relationship to joy, one that is less temporary and more dependent on service and cultivating one's mind-heart. For example, the Dalai Lama explains, "Compassion is one of the principal things that make our lives meaningful.

It is the source of all lasting happiness and joy." A Tibetan lama and friend of mine in California once shared with me, "Happiness comes from strengthening your capacity for virtuous action." In the Buddha's teachings, joy arises naturally from four different practices: loving kindness toward oneself and others, releasing tension in one's body and feelings, maintaining concentration on wholesome states of mind, and letting go. Whereas a shadowed valley tends to follow the peaks of sensual pleasure, these inner states of joy are longer lasting and without such drawbacks. Joy is a practice, a state of mind you can grow within yourself and your community.

In the communities I visited, I found that a community's joy was strongly reflected by the degree to which they prioritized being in harmony with each other and having fun together. M. Scott Peck similarly writes that true community is a body of individuals "who have developed some significant commitment to rejoice together, mourn together, delight in each other, and make others' conditions their own."[24] Joy is the lifeblood of a ripened community. Dharma teacher and writer Larry Ward once told an inspiring story about valuing joy when he lived in an intentional spiritual community years ago—if someone wanted to hold a business meeting, the community had to do something fun first! You can imagine the harmony, joy, and work-life balance that prevailed in this community.

Walking into a community for the first time, Vanessa and I could instantly feel whether joy permeated the atmosphere. Ease of laughter, looking at others with warmth and affection, smiles without hesitation, and tones of enthusiasm about the community's life and programs all subtly yet powerfully convey the life-force of communal harmony. Whenever Vanessa and I entered such environments, especially after many hours or days of traveling, our muscles softened, our nerves steadily quieted, and we felt both humbled and touched by the gentle outpour of kindness.

## Community Models of Joy

When Vanessa and I visited Wake Up houses in London, San Diego, and the Netherlands, we were inspired by the amount of fun they had.

Having fun together isn't the only major factor of well-being, yet it's paramount for an assembly of thriving relationships. The Honor Oak Community of young adults in London wore contagious smiles as they shared how play helps them make decisions that are mutually satisfactory to all. One of their founders, Ramanprit Sandhu, shared with me, "We couldn't decide whether to choose smooth or crunchy peanut butter for our bulk order, and we were split fifty-fifty. So, Karim suggested we have a spontaneous rap battle between the two parties to decide." I laughed and asked, "Okay, but who won?" Ramanprit explained, "Well, crunchy crushed the competition. We didn't know that Brendan actually had rapping talent! But because of smooth's heartfelt efforts in the contest, we decided to get both in the end."

The Meppel Mindfulness Community in the Netherlands, though small, is one of the most powerful examples of a community taking responsibility for their joy and happiness together. Upon retiring, the two founders, Vimh and Greetje, had a deep wish to live in community. When the house behind theirs went up for sale, they seized the opportunity by co-purchasing it with their friend Joan, removing the fencing between the two properties to create one seamless sprawling garden, and renting out the free bedroom to their friend Rudi, to create a four-person residential mindfulness community. This remarkable landscape included flowing hedges of raspberries, blueberries, white and yellow gooseberries, a small stream, a thriving vegetable garden, benches to enjoy tea with a view, bursting wildflowers, and walking paths that meandered under trees, over bridges, between bushy hedges, and under flowering vine canopies. The crown jewel of their property was a hexagonal meditation hall with large glass windows that looked out over blooming yellow daisies during our visit. Even though none of them knew much about construction at the beginning, they had devoted themselves to learning and built this sanctuary themselves! The meditation hall and garden held events and gatherings throughout the week for their larger community, composed of dozens of non-resident mindfulness practitioners.

From the very start, I was curious how just the four of them were able to care for the gardens and support such a thriving mindfulness center. During our week-long stay in Meppel, the residents warmly invited us to all their communal activities, including a biweekly resident meeting not normally open to guests. We met in Joan and Rudi's dining room behind sliding glass doors that overlooked the sunny garden patio. Between us at the table was a steaming pan of homemade pizza, six mugs, a pot of tea, and a vase of handpicked yellow daisies sprinkled with other wildflowers. A large, rainbow-colored peace flag draped over one wall and a calligraphy composed in Dutch hung on another: "Peace in oneself, peace in the world." Before any business began, Joan invited three sounds of the bell, and we sat silently, breathing together for several minutes. Peace in oneself was not merely a slogan in Meppel; it is a practice that cares for communal harmony.

Digging into the pan of pizza, we chatted lightheartedly for several minutes before diving into the agenda. Vimh, the facilitator this week, began: "Item number one, resident outing. So will August be another day in the garden, or are we going out this time? I think it's Greetje's month to decide." Greetje responded, "We were working here last weekend, but I can't think of anywhere else I would rather be." She laughed. "I would like to stay here if that's what others want as well."

Greetje explained to me and Vanessa, "We set aside one day each month to have fun together, just for the four of us. We learned a while back that we really need that time for just us who live here. We're always doing so many things with the rest of the community, but we were neglecting each other. This helps us appreciate each other more, I think." Vimh added, "Sometimes we go off site, to a museum or a park. Each month, one of us gets to decide. In the summer, though, we often stay here and garden most of the day, as we all really enjoy that. As you can see, the garden is wonderful right now." His eyes lit up as he told me how blessed and proud they felt about their Sangha garden.

Joan chimed in, "We like to have a nice time together. Our outings are very fun!" She radiated a smile even more telling than her words. Rudi raised his eyebrows and nodded in excitement to add full consensus around their community playdates. Joan later showed us some photos they had taken of each other while riding tandem bikes together to the park; the four of them may have been on the older side of life, but their faces looked as happy as children!

The Meppel community does what most other centers need to do in terms of regular meetings, administrative committees, relationship and communication circles, work periods, and meditation practice, but within their busy community schedule they prioritize sacred time together. A monthly outing may seem like a small event, but they were emphatic about how significantly it shaped the quality of their friendships, which were the very core of the larger Sangha. They regarded themselves as a kind of family whose happiness is worth treasuring by having fun together. Prioritizing fun is where self-care and community-care collide with big, childlike smiles.

## Play for Kids, Play for Adults

Every community I visited, whether solo or during my travels with Vanessa, carried its own mix of play and practice. Where the majority of practitioners are young adults, play and joy seem to be more prevalent. This is partly why young adult mindfulness communities have been so successful and growing steadily around the world. Their playfulness and joy are contagious! In communities run by older individuals, practice often dominates play.

Are you part of a community that likes to play or to practice more? That's the Zen *koan* for every community. Young adult communities are masters of play, but are they also grounded in depth of practice? Communities with more seasoned practitioners may touch greater depths of peace and insights, but does their rigor lose the spirit of playful connection?

Decades of research confirms the value of play not merely in childhood but throughout life. Play among adults is documented to relieve stress, improve brain function, stimulate the mind, boost creativity and vitality, and improve resistance to disease. Fostering empathy, trust, intimacy, and compassion—play improves relationships and connections with others, making it a tremendous asset for communities. When we play, we keep relationships fresh and resilient, and we learn how to cooperate positively and differently with others.[25] Because play holds so much potential for community-wide joy, it is essential for communities of all ages and stages to learn how to incorporate a healthy amount of play into their repertoire.

To some people, even those who have been practicing for many years, the playful side of mindfulness practice may appear confusing or even superficial. I had heard many criticisms from older meditators over the years that the Wake Up movement is all about socializing and having fun, but lacks real substance. When I was younger, I sought advice about this from an older friend and senior Dharma teacher, John Bell, who offered his reflections: "Many longtime meditation practitioners and even Dharma teachers feel uncomfortable around young people and are skeptical of their ways. They don't understand them. Why? It's because they haven't healed the child in themselves yet." As a young adult myself at the time, I felt moved to hear John share so honestly about his peers as well as deeply encouraged by his witnessing of the innate strength and virtue in our young people's communities.

In my work as a child and family therapist, I have repeatedly witnessed the miraculous power of play to heal deep emotional wounds, both within and between children and parents. Parents often feel intimidated and paralyzed by the prospect of following their child's lead into PicassoTiles, Play-Doh, or in a dollhouse, as if they're entering a foreign country where they don't speak the language. Play is in fact the language of children and creativity, their kingdom. After much encouragement, when the parent finally gets on the floor, the child becomes their teacher, and they rediscover their forgotten pleasure of being purely engrossed in curiosity, imagination, and joy. They rediscover the freely creative child within who innately knows the art of play.

During the last few years, I have tried to bring these gifts of young adult communities to all-age Sanghas. My friends and I organized a series of retreats in London that were open to all ages but facilitated by and mostly composed of young adults. We still enjoyed sitting and walking meditation in the morning, talks, mindful sharing, and other foundational mindfulness practices throughout the day, but every morning after Noble Silence (a period of nourishing silence beginning before bed and ending after breakfast), we gathered outside to enjoy at least thirty minutes of pure play—basically recess all over again! Remember how fun recess used to be? In a supportive school environment, it was often the best twenty to thirty minutes of my day! In our retreats, people rediscovered the lost art of communal play, and let their inner child and young spirited teen run free again. I have a metaphorical back-pack full of my favorite communal games, but I also ask partici-pants to share the games they remember and love the most, further sparking communal creativity. Depending on the ages and physical abilities of retreatants, we experimented with different forms of tag, imitation games, icebreakers, and musical games. If some people couldn't move very easily, we also offered seated or standing games so that everyone felt included.

Both young and older adults frequently shared with me how much the playful spirit of these retreats impacted them. A woman in her early forties expressed during our New Year's retreat, "My goodness, I haven't played like that in forever! I was feeling quite intimidated at first, but then the game of tag just took over and I was running around like everyone else!" One young adult wrote about the connecting power of combining practice, silence, and games together: "I feel like it brought us all closer as a family. People I'd never met before became my amazing friends and family in just a few days—flipping fabulous!" Another first-time retreatant said, "I was new here and felt some social anxiety. The songs and games each morning brought a really positive atmosphere and helped me to come out of my shell. It set a positive tone for the rest of the day."

When people release their self-consciousness into the spirit of play, they relearn laughing, running, jumping, and singing with the energy and lightness of a child's heart and soul. Then when it comes time for circle sharings in groups of ten or twelve, people already feel a greater depth of safety and trust, and they can speak more vulnerably and courageously about the deeper suffering hidden in their hearts. It's as if people are saying, "You already know me now—I'm a fun and joyful person that you like to play with. Now I trust you and don't feel afraid to share my suffering as well."

The young adults also benefit tremendously from the presence of older adults in these retreats. Just as young and energetic saplings need the shade, stability, and strength of older trees, young people take refuge in the wisdom and compassion of older, more experienced practitioners. For example, my friends Patricia, in her early fifties, and Joe, in his late thirties, were not in the Wake Up eighteen to thirty-five age range, but we co-organized retreats for many young adults. On multiple occasions, I encouraged struggling young women to connect with Patricia. "She's a good listener and has lots of experience with mindfulness. She loves spending time with young people, so perhaps you can ask her to go for a walk together." Joe, on the other hand, is like an older brother for countless young adults throughout London, even spearheading a residential mindfulness community with several of them. I watched Patricia and Joe naturally build informal mentoring relationships with countless young people at our retreats.

## It's Simple

If we want more joy and playfulness in our community, we can grow it. Just like growing an orchard, we have to plant the seeds and water them often. Take a step back for a moment and consider the level of joy in your own community. Perhaps it's only at 25 percent capacity, or maybe you're at 50 percent of what feels possible. Either way, how much do you wish for your own relationship and community joy to increase? It's not hard work—it just takes some gumption, creativity, and courage to light the sparks.

## THREE SIMPLE STEPS TO CONSCIOUSLY FOSTER JOYFUL CONNECTIONS IN YOUR COMMUNITY

**First**, think about what you want to do the most—what is your dream of doing something fun with those you love? Maybe you love hiking up to a cliff with breathtaking views or having bonfire dance parties at the lake. Whether it's visiting an art museum with adults, go-kart racing with kids, or having a barbecue cookout for everyone, do what you want to do first!

**Second**, get your people together. Meppel's formula is to do something fun every month. It sounds simple, but someone needs to speak up for the joy we all wish for; someone needs to wrangle the herd together. During the winter months at Morning Sun community, we enjoyed weekly game nights—someone hosts and picks the game, someone else brings snacks and beverages, and everyone else just brings themselves.

**Third**, and this is key, give everyone in the community an opportunity to share what they wish to do. This allows people to learn from and grow with each other. Perhaps you like circle dancing, our friend likes anime movies, and I like butterfly exhibits. A given activity may not be fun for everyone at first, but exploring new activities as a community is a fabulous way to get to know each other better. Most importantly, everyone gets a chance to express what is meaningful for them. If you gather once a month, eventually everyone gets to do something they like.

There is no limit to things that can foster joy in our communities. Whether we grow playful qualities and joyful relationships within our beloved Sangha or family depends on us. The good news is that we don't need to choose between practice and play; if we look deeply, they are one and the same.

# CHAPTER 6

# SHARING SILENCE

*Close your eyes, fall in love, stay there.*
—JALAL AL-DIN MUHAMMAD RUMI

*Silence is essential. We need silence just as much as we need air, just as much as plants need light. If our minds are crowded with words and thoughts, there is no space for us.*
—THICH NHAT HANH

Brother Phap Dung invited the sound of the small copper bell for us to stand, another bell to bow to each other, and a last bell for a bow in gratitude to our ancestral altar. A bright violet orchid with a dozen blossoms sat on the small wooden altar, its stem and petals climbing upward and almost touching a calligraphy in Thay's signature penmanship that read, "Enjoy your tea." It was a rare treat to be in the venerable tea room that evening in the monks' hamlet, and we had just finished a deep listening session, called a "Dharma sharing," with several monks. As people began to leave the tea house, I overheard a young man ask Brother Phap Dung a question: "I'm trying my best to build a weekly Sangha where I live and I'm curious—what are the most important things to know about doing this well? Brother Phap Dung was a master of Sangha-building, and my ears were magnetically drawn to hear more, so I quickly shuffled over to their conversation.

When Brother Phap Dung was a young boy, he and his family immigrated to the United States after the war in Vietnam. He grew up in Los Angeles, attended the University of Southern California, and became an architect for several years before ordaining as a monk with Thich Nhat Hanh in Plum Village, France. Due to both his Vietnamese roots and Southern California youth, Brother Phap Dung had an unusual ability to seamlessly sow seeds of beloved community in the Vietnamese and non-Vietnamese monastic and lay communities wherever he went.

Brother Phap Dung first offered a few words about the crucial importance of building friendships in the Sangha. Then he shared, "There are many ways to build harmony and siblinghood. But at the heart of the Sangha is your meditation practice. There is something magical that happens when everyone is sitting and breathing together in silence, in stillness, in the dark." The spacious quiet between Brother Phap Dung's words seemed to magnify them. "In that silence, you touch a space of togetherness and connection on a deep level of consciousness that you can't describe. It's what so many groups and organizations lack, that deeper connection below the surface of the mind. People are hungry for that deeper belonging." Brother Phap Dung, as if he was letting the question gather steam once again. He continued, "No matter who you are, whatever your backgrounds and identities, in that deep silence, you touch something profound together, like tree roots in the forest touching their true earth nature. There's no replacement for sharing silence together, breathing mindfully, and savoring your lives in each moment."

## A World Desperate for Silence

Among the various practices to nurture a Sangha, the power of silence is foremost —the invisible glue holding everyone and everything together. As Brother Phap Dung extolled, silence taps into the rejuvenating sources of our physical and mental well-being, not simply within us but more importantly, between us. Silence is the hidden beams, the quiet forces holding up the integrity and strength of our beloved community home.

It's no secret that we inhabit a world that lives the antithesis of silence. Tens of millions of Americans, especially those in urban areas, suffer from a variety of negative health outcomes from noise pollution, including heart disease, hearing loss, and various mental and emotional effects.[26] Inside people's homes, the average US adult watches 304 minutes (over five hours!) of television per day. But television is just one slice of the pie; people around the world spend an average of 7.5 hours each day on various forms of media, with Americans averaging even more. The hours spent consuming media increase every year. Devoid of quality human interactions, such media addiction feeds alienation, restlessness, and isolation, sending individuals and families into a loud yet lonely abyss.

True silence is medicine for our time. How can we consistently tap into sources of quiet rejuvenation, connection, and peace, both within ourselves and with one another? Lao Tzu famously said, "Silence is a source of great strength." But when practiced in community, silence becomes an even greater strength. Communities practicing mindfulness generate a depth and quality of presence far more powerful than any individual can touch alone—it comes from the silence between us, like an invisible web linking people's hearts and minds on a level that words cannot reach.

In every mindfulness center we visited, silence was an indispensable part of communal life and practice, although practices varied considerably. I'd like now to explore the benefits, methods, and stories of how mindfulness communities harness the power of silence together, offering ways for any community of friends to strengthen their quality of presence, joy, and connection together.

## The Dawn of Silence

Every morning at Blue Cliff Monastery in upstate New York, where I lived for three months one winter, the community rises under serene stars and cold bright moonlight before quietly entering the Great Togetherness Meditation Hall for seated meditation. The slow, collective quiet in the monastery's early morning hours feels like the aural equivalent of soft candlelight upon awakening, not rushed, nor too bright for the senses. The gentle footsteps of monks and nuns, the unfurling of winter coats, the reliable creak of doors, the rustling of meditation cushions, the security of one's breath, all become a gentle pre-dawn symphony, steadily rousing our groggy minds out of slumber and into a peaceful and alert abiding. There are no words, no conversations, no unnecessary greetings; just a silent trust in each other's presence while welcoming the wordless unfolding of dawn that speaks of past ages, long before humans uttered their first words.

This way of listening, of wordless being and voiceless communication, is in our bones, hearts, and cells. Our animal ancestors lived and communicated without words before language finally blossomed in our neocortex. These exquisitely quiet early morning hours of course do not guarantee perfect peace, whether living in a meditation community or not. The absence of external distractions may even highlight internal storms or forgotten sufferings waiting for their chance to be heard, learned, and embraced.

One morning, a flurry of anxious thoughts swarmed my internal landscape like a family of mayflies, constantly buzzing inside, unwilling to settle down, bugging me for most of the sitting period. My lower back grew tense and my mind impatient as the forty-five minutes crawled to a close. And yet, the silent tenderness of the room encircled my restless nervous system.

As meditation ended, I pushed through the glass doors to leave the hall and greet a bright winter blue sky above me, a thinly frozen lotus pond before me. Surprisingly, my mind felt as clear and sharp as the thinly crystalized pond and as spacious as the vast sky. The Sangha was no longer around me, yet its silence had penetrated every cell of my being. I turned the corner and with effortless focus beheld a theater of golden sunrise beams dancing through a dramatic horizon of bursting white clouds. Underneath the tumultuous surface of my anxious mind, the collective silence had created a space of clear, gentle awareness.

## Practice: Touching Silence

In the midst of busy and noisy lives, most of us crave moments of peace and silence. Touching silence within ourselves is something any of us can cultivate wherever we are. But silence is both a tricky concept and an elusive experience, not merely an external or individual phenomenon. The dictionary defines silence as "the complete absence of sound" and "the fact or state of abstaining from speech." These are two different concepts—one refers to sounds in general, the other refers to the noise of our words.

In nearly all daily life, one may touch slivers of silence, but complete silence is nearly impossible. Even if you live in an electricity-free cabin in the middle of the woods (as I did for several years), you won't find silence. You may not hear engines roaring, refrigerators buzzing, television blaring, or sirens wailing, but you will still hear the wind coursing through white pine needles, black-hooded chickadees chirping, or the sound of boots crunching through freshly fallen autumn leaves. Even in the middle of Antarctica, as Erling Kagge documents in his book of few words, *Silence: In the Age of Noise*, silence is a myth. In fact, one hears the subtlest of sounds with even greater intensity: grating skis on ice, fluttering wind across snow, even breath moving through your nostrils. The less distraction and noise, the more you hear.

Silence's second definition, the absence of words, is just as elusive. Even if you separate yourself and stop talking all day long, you'll still hear your stream of inner dialogue. The ever-flowing river of thought runs day and night, from the time we wake up to our last conscious moments before sleep. This internal noise can be just as loud as a noisy conversation or a blaring television. How can we touch the deeper silence and peace that our heart longs for?

When we stop talking out loud, we can begin to touch another kind of silence: the silence of meditative concentration. When we focus on or listen deeply to an object, such as one's breath, an inherent silence and stillness begins to emanate from within us. Although it is much easier and more powerful to experience silence in the company of meditators, we can still touch some slivers of this silence alone.

Let us experiment for a moment—whether closing your eyes or leaving them open, focus your attention on an object: a stone, a blade of grass, the sky, the moon, your body, or your breath. Listen deeply to its essence and the silent song of its being. What do you hear? Listen to the silent emptiness of the object in this very moment. We can experiment with all sorts of phenomena—even if you are on a busy street in the city, try stopping for a moment and listening deeply to the silence within you: the space between this thought and the next, the hum in the depths of your heart, or the quiet rhythm of your breathing. Whether you are alone in the forest or in a crowded city, close your eyes for a few moments, tune into the quiet spaciousness of your breathing, and as the beloved poet Rumi invites us, "Listen to silence. It has so much to say." Now, what do you hear?

## The Benefits of Silence with Your Sangha

If you find it difficult to deeply enjoy this silence by yourself, you are not alone — it is much easier to practice within a supportive community. When we sit, walk, or eat quietly and mindfully together, the silence within and around us strengthens like an invisible force. My friend and meditation teacher Jonathan Borella captured this idea beautifully during a mindfulness retreat: "The sound of one person talking is not very loud. But when three or four people are talking at the same time, the noise becomes much louder. The same is true of silence. When we sit alone, we may touch a little silence. But when many of us sit together, our collective silence also becomes much 'louder.' That is the gift of practicing together."

The silence of a group is like a fresh breeze coming off a deep lake on a sweltering summer afternoon. The cool air gently caresses your skin, lifts the sweat off your face, and invites your whole body to surrender to ease, relief, and calm. Practicing silence with a community can be the most luxurious oasis in the world.

Every Sangha we visited during our tour integrated silence into their community life in unique ways. Jonathan Borella and My Tong, whom I've known since they were young adults, cofounded Sugarplum Sangha, a mindfulness retreat center in Ukiah, Northern California. Before the pandemic, their meditation center was thriving with people of all ages. During the many months of social distancing, their leadership team launched initiatives for people around the world to touch the gifts of silence in community. Jonathan wrote, "These times of social distancing and online gatherings affirm an often unacknowledged yearning for silence supported by community and collective space holding. Retreats are not an end in themselves; rather, they are a means for touching deep silence held in a collective space."

At Honor Oak Sangha, the small residential mindfulness community of five young adults in London with both crunchy and smooth peanut butter, Ramanprit shared the gifts of each morning's communal silence. "We enter the breathing room together before speaking, and stay silent. There's something that's very precious about joining together in stillness and silence that we bring from the quiet night into each morning. I feel such solidity arriving and sitting together to breathe as one body."

As Ramanprit describes, waking into wordless communal experience fosters a subtle yet powerful internal shift from individual to collective consciousness. In the early morning hours or at night before sleep, when community members breathe in meditative awareness, a transformation occurs. It's like random clouds floating in the sky—drawing near each other, they steadily merge while slowly, effortlessly dissolving feelings of loneliness and alienation. This profound experience of togetherness is one of the greatest gifts of mindful community life.

Intersein Practice Center in Lower Bavaria, Germany, has morning meditation similar to Oak Honor Sangha, but their evening sittings were a novel experience to me. They have "open sitting," in which residents and guests all begin the meditation together and then people may leave at any moment after. It feels like a "choose your own adventure" book I used to read as a child. If I am feeling tired, I can leave after five minutes. If I want to watch the sunset, I can walk mindfully outside. Or if I'm feeling invigorated by the collective silence, I can keep sitting with others for an hour or longer. People at Intersein love this freedom and autonomy in their practice. Open sitting encourages everyone to simultaneously show up together in community and to listen with respect to their own body's needs, inspiration, and wisdom.

## THE BENEFITS OF REGULAR DAYS OF MINDFULNESS (QUIET TIME TOGETHER)

Hosting days of mindfulness is like throwing a party for your friends in silence. Among the countless benefits of practicing silence in community, here are some quiet jewels:

**Attention to interpersonal communication.** In the absence of noise and talking, I more easily tune into the subtle currents of communication I am continually sending and receiving from others. Unconscious gestures, micro-movements, and even my very thoughts and feelings all offer silent vibes, whether positive or negative, to those around me. If I am aware, I can work with them constructively. Wordless communication points to the heart of my relationships with others.

**Greater attention to self-care.** In silence lies a spaciousness to be oneself. My deeper physical and emotional needs come to the surface, whether it's need for rest, nature, exercise, physical nourishment, or something else. This awareness helps revitalize my overall health and well-being, which is crucial in community life. Silence itself is a vital nourishment for individual and communal vitality.

**Emotional availability.** When I'm not talking or thinking about what to say, I listen more attentively and curiously to my inner streams of consciousness, and greater compassion unfolds naturally toward my suffering. The more tuned into myself I am, the more emotional availability naturally flows out to others like a lake overflowing with abundance into streams below. What my community needs most is for me to be emotionally available to myself.

As a fairly strong extrovert, silence has not always come easily to me. Mountain Lamp Community in Deming, Washington state, where I lived and worked for a year and a half as a temple keeper, held "days of quiet practice" and weeklong retreats in almost complete silence every month. Initially, spending a whole day or week of silence in community was at once rare, awkward, disappointing, stunning, and blissful. When friends arrived, I so badly wanted to catch up! I felt lonely and craved the social connection. Shutting my mouth all day felt like such a bummer. And yet, as the days of practice unfolded, I cherished the moments together even more intimately. Each drop of quiet connection sank into my bones. I listened more deeply to the subtleties of others' moods, facial expressions, and body movements, the silence allowing me to pay loving attention in ways I had never before recognized. By the end of each retreat, I felt alive, refreshed, and ready to communicate what was most important to my heart rather than simply chattering to fill some inner void.

## Noble Quiet and Meditation

Finishing a busy day at work, what I often want the most is just to breathe in silence with nothing to do, nowhere to go, and no one to talk to. In that space, I can release the tension and fatigue that has stored up in my body and mind. Enjoying breathing silently, by myself or especially with others, often becomes the most satisfying moment of my day. Renowned meditation teacher Deepak Chopra wrote in his classic spiritual guide *The Seven Laws of Spiritual Success* that one can access limitless creative potential and wisdom through daily periods of silence, meditation, and time in nature. Chopra encourages his students and readers to periodically withdraw from speaking and mentally "noisy" activities such as social media, books, television, or music. He welcomes students to make a daily commitment of silence:

> I will get in touch with the field of pure potentiality by taking time each day to be silent, to just Be. I will take time each day to commune with nature and to silently witness the intelligence within every living thing.[27]

Most meditation centers in the Plum Village tradition observe a period of "noble silence," "noble quiet," or "sacred silence," typically at the beginning and end of each day. This is not the heavy or punishing silence you may remember from sitting in after-school detention. Rather, this silence encourages tenderness, ease, and acceptance in order to replenish our wellsprings of joy and freshness. Such silence invites the chatter of the mind to quiet so that you can touch the meaningful truths of your day.

When my friends and I started to build Greatwoods Zen, our new meditation center in Charlotte, North Carolina, I asked several monastic friends and Dharma teachers from the Plum Village community for advice. Sister Tham Nghiem encouraged me to "Follow a schedule of practice that is appropriate for you. You will be doing so many things, lots of service, and the schedule will give you energy. Sitting, mindful walking, mindful eating, listening to Dharma talks, the schedule supports your practice and gives you positive energy." Each of these activities is infused with silence and meditation.

Some couples and families I know take an hour of "noble quiet" together every day before bed or upon waking so they can tune into their own needs and internal landscape. Phones go downstairs and computer screens shut down. Every family or mindfulness center has their own agreements. In some places, whispers or quiet conversations are welcome; in other centers, total silence is the law.

## Finding the Silence in the Busyness

Perhaps you have doubts about your capacity for daily silence "I'm too busy with work, friends, and family obligations. I don't have time for daily meditation and silent time in nature," I hear many people say. Given the several hours of average daily screen time, replacing thirty minutes is a possible alternative. Just last month, I caught up with an old college friend who told me that after a period of intense stress and depression, she resolved to start meditating for thirty minutes every morning and evening. At first, she could barely find the time, given her full-time job and responsibilities caring for two school-age children. But during her meditations, she realized that television, Facebook, and other social media were draining her energy, so she cut those out. She told me, "David, now I meditate for forty-five minutes twice a day and I've never had so much free time for me and my kids in my life!

Perhaps your life is similarly filled with child care, a full-time job, and other responsibilities; if thirty minutes of daily silent practice is not doable for you, then what is? When would silence be most rejuvenating and peaceful to support your busy day? I invite you to reflect with your partner, family, community, or by yourself and then to commit to a period of silence and meditation each day. Withdraw from screen time and even books. Make a commitment for at least two weeks together, and notice how it affects the quality of relationships with each other and yourself.

I once heard a story that shows no amount of responsibility precludes having time for silent meditation. During the thirteenth century in Vietnam, a prince had a deep hunger to learn and practice Zen. Instead of assuming his royal duties, he wished to live in the mountains where ascetic life flourished. However, his country was facing both internal divisions and an imminent Mongolian invasion in the north.

The prince was an intelligent and capable leader who loved his people dearly. At the age of twenty-one, the young prince became King Tran Nhan Tong and promised to unify and strengthen his country.

To make a long, dramatic, and heroic story fairly short, with his father's guidance, the young king guided his military against naval and cavalry offenses, saving their country from imperialistic domination. Instead of following his monastic dream, King Tran Nhan Tong continued to strengthen his country's security over the next fifteen years. But his desire and commitment to inner peace never wavered, so the king compromised by meditating silently every day during his royal tenure. It may be hard to believe, but among all the responsibilities of leading a country, this young king still practiced meditation for twenty minutes, six times a day! Although this took up much precious time, the king was able to respond to difficult decisions with greater insight and compassionate solutions for his people. Hopefully, the story of this king's practice inspires you to find time to practice, too.

## Drops of Silence

At this very moment, I am sitting in the White Crane Hamlet dining hall at Blue Cliff Monastery, and the clock chime has just sung its tune, which goes off every fifteen minutes. My fingers stop typing, my eyes release their tense fixation, and my body recognizes its stiffness, slowly and naturally softening into the chair. I realize I have been sitting for over an hour, so I stretch, stand up, make some oolong tea, and enjoy a few minutes of not working—a simple, yet satisfying source of delight I can enjoy as many times a day as I wish. These drops of silence, sometimes inspired by bells of mindfulness like a clock chime, remind me to become my best self again. They take almost no time at all, infusing silence effortlessly throughout the day.

Almost every community we visited used intentional bells of mindfulness, whether it was an activity bell outside, a clock chiming in the kitchen, church bells, or a phone or computer app. When the bell sounds, everyone puts down what they're doing, stops talking for several moments, and pays attention to what is happening within and around them. While pausing, you notice the quality of your conversation, relax your anxious shoulders, listen to the house wren singing nearby, or smell the lavender blooming in the garden. You let go of your thinking, feel the air flowing into your lungs, and hit the reset button on your life.

For those new to this practice, it may feel awkward and uncomfortable when everyone in the room stops what they are doing—as if everyone is playing a secret game of freeze tag. But practicing in community is a perfect way to train in the practice of stopping in the midst of daily stressors. Nowadays, you can easily install a bell of mindfulness on your phone or computer. The Plum Village app is a great support for this practice and can be flexibly timed according to your schedule and preferences. I can't tell you how many times I was ready to say something very stupid and problematic, feeling overwhelmed with stress-filled anxiety or lost in a psychodrama story, when suddenly a "Ding! from my app stopped me mid-sentence and helped me to realize I was breathing; slowly, the tension in my body relaxed, and I could gratefully reassess what the situation was asking of me.

By oneself, it is easier to ignore the bell or chime going off. But when everyone in the room pauses to breathe and recollect themselves, this collective habit of stopping increases exponentially every time we do it. As each person in the community stops and tunes in like this throughout the day, a collective harmony and attunement unfolds in the Sangha. Instead of moving around as separate individuals, consistently stopping and breathing together builds a collective rhythm and connection. It is a communal dance of mindfulness set to rhythms of bells and silence throughout the day.

## The Silence of Buddhas

Thich Nhat Hanh wrote one last book before a stroke in 2014 moved him into sacred silence for the rest of his life. As if it were a premonition, the book was titled *Silence: The Power of Quiet in a World Full of*

*Noise.* But even before Thay lost his capacity for speech, I had never seen someone embody silence so profoundly. In the early 2000s, I was traveling with Thay and a large delegation of monastics during the annual tour of retreats and public events across the United States. One day during a large retreat in Colorado, a few hundred people were conversing in the dining hall during an early afternoon break after lunch. The hall had become quite noisy with so many people talking at once. Suddenly, in a matter of moments, the conversations in the entire hall came to a halt. It was uncanny how abruptly the congregation shifted from raucous conversation to total silence. What had happened?

Following the eyes of two friends across from me, I looked over my left shoulder and saw the source: Thay and two attendants had just walked through the main doors, taking slow and mindful steps through the hall. Thay smiled as cheerfully and peacefully as a child riding a carousel, waving casually at the assembly, and then continued ahead. He walked as quietly and freely as a cloud floating through a mountain forest. He had not uttered a word, yet his practice was so revered and influential that the entire hall closed its doors of words. Within a few minutes, Thay had left the hall and people's voices naturally picked up again, yet in a quieter and more conscious tone than before.

The Buddha was certainly not a fan of frivolous speech; he consistently praised silence and admonished the monastics' habits of idle chatter or speaking carelessly. In his teaching about the four opposites of right speech, the Buddha grouped idle chatter with lying, divisive speech, and harsh or cruel speech. In the gang of negative speech, idle chatter is among terrible company! The Buddha once offered a teaching to a group of lay friends about the value of developing wholesome habits of speech and reducing the harm of frivolous speech. He encouraged them to reflect,

> *If someone were to address me with frivolous speech and idle chatter, that would not be pleasing and agreeable to me. Now if I were to address another with frivolous speech and idle chatter, that would not be pleasing and agreeable to the other. How can I inflict*

*upon another what is displeasing and disagreeable to me?' Having
reflected thus, he himself abstains from idle chatter, exhorts others
to abstain from idle chatter, and speaks in praise of abstinence from
idle chatter.*[28]

The Buddha's ancient wisdom can also be summed up rather succinctly by the comedian Will Rogers, who said, "Never miss a good chance to shut up. "

Idle chatter fills the empty space between us with distraction and meaningless words. It parallels the same sensory overload of screen time and social media that numbs our capacity for more nourishing means of communication and contact with nature. Mindful silence, on the other hand, offers space for communication to fully ripen with purposeful and loving expression. In order to truly express oneself, one must first master the art of refraining from words.

How can we communicate most deeply with our beloved community? Kahlil Gibran wrote, "There are those among you who seek the talkative through fear of being alone and there are those who have the truth within them, but they tell it not in words."[29] To quietly enjoy a red rose sunset with a friend, sip a cup of tea together in pre-dawn candlelight, or stand at the edge of a pond while watching the light silently dance upon its rippling waters—worlds can be communicated between us without a single word exchanged.

What else can one say about silence? I'm afraid I have said too much already.

# CHAPTER 7

# SHARING APPRECIATIONS

*If the only prayer you ever say in your entire life is "thank you," it will be enough.*

—MEISTER ECKART, THIRTEENTH-CENTURY
DOMINICAN FRIAR AND MYSTIC

*We should study how loving speech has power to transform the world.*

—DOGEN ZENJI, THIRTEENTH-CENTURY
ZEN BUDDHIST MONK

During a question and answer session, a woman once asked Zen Master Thich Nhat Hanh, "What is the most important quality a Dharma teacher should have? The entire meditation hall, filled with almost a thousand people, was powerfully silent. I could practically hear the wheels of inquiry turning in people's minds: "Wisdom? Compassion? Insight? Knowledge of the sutras?" So many qualities seemed important, but which was most essential? Thay breathed with ease, no sense of rush visible. He looked out at the audience with a sly half-smile, the sparkle in his eyes revealing some magic. Finally, in a beaming response to the woman, he said, "A good Dharma teacher should be a happy person." The audience laughed with lightness and admiration at such a simple yet wise answer.

So, what makes a happy person? One unmistakable quality is the ability to deeply appreciate oneself, those around them, and life. A happy person appreciates blessings as much as hardships, recognizing both the roses of one's life and the compost that feeds those roses. They know how to dwell in gratitude for the myriad miracles surrounding them at any moment, be it a flaming sunrise bursting through a cloudy horizon, a cup of steaming oolong tea in one's two hands on a frigid morning, or the precious silence of the Sangha after meditation—all sources of appreciation I am soaking up right now as I pause from writing for a few moments. In this very moment, what is a source of happiness and appreciation in your life, right here and now? Please take a moment to stop, put down your book, look around or look within, and let these sources of appreciation crystalize in your mind. Happiness is that close.

If there is just one single thing that can substantially raise the level of happiness in any community, be it a family, group of coworkers, classroom, or Sangha, it is the art of mindful appreciations. These are the open windows that bring raw sunlight and a fresh breeze into the soul of our community home. While a mind of gratitude begins within each of us, creating a collective atmosphere of appreciation is much more than an individual effort—it invites the whole community to flourish. The fruits include greater harmony, conflict prevention, more relational resilience during times of disagreement or conflict, greater trust and bonding, increased joy, and more fun being together! Of all my communal living and Sangha experiences, I was the happiest where I felt most valued by others and expressed my appreciations freely.

It may sound simple, but creating a communal culture of appreciation that genuinely uplifts and empowers every member takes intention, creativity, and perseverance, especially during challenges and times of conflict. But if you can succeed, the rewards of an appreciative community are exponentially greater and longer-lasting than one person can ever achieve alone. We will soon dive into strategies, creative exercises, and stories of growing a thriving culture of appreciation. But first, let us hear what the research has to say about this topic.

## The Value of Appreciation

Over the past few decades, a steadily growing mountain of research has been affirming the personal and relational benefits of practicing appreciation and gratitude. Gratitude is the state of thankfulness for life in general or for a particular gift, whether human or not. "Gratitude comes from the Latin word *gratus*, meaning "pleasing or "thankful." Appreciation is like gratitude's fraternal twin; it is the enjoyment and recognition of the benefits someone or something has offered. It a "thankful recognition," often the expression of such feelings of thankfulness. Gratitude is the soil from which appreciations bloom.

Leading research teams have found that when people—adults and adolescents alike—regularly cultivate gratitude and appreciation, they experience a whole multitude of emotional, psychological, and even physical benefits. These include better social integration, lower levels of envy and depression, better sleep, lower blood pressure, and more effective exercise. Gratitude interventions promote more emotional resilience in the face of both daily and traumatic stress than any other positive psychology intervention designed to foster well-being.[30]

In fact, gratitude has the highest correlations with mental health and life satisfaction of any personality trait—more so than even optimism, hope, or compassion.[31] Research also consistently draws out the vast implications of gratitude for friendships and romantic partnerships. Those who habitually express appreciation tend to listen more deeply and respond more proactively to the other person's needs.[32] In this way, gratitude strengthens these relationships when it's expressed explicitly as appreciation for the other person.[33] If gratitude and appreciation are so beneficial on personal and interpersonal levels, imagine the impact of cultivating gratitude on a community-wide level, allowing the collective consciousness of appreciation to become the daily social norm.

## Mind Is the Forerunner

Given the overwhelming rewards of appreciation on both individual and communal levels, how does one cultivate this art of living? The Dhammapada, a distillation of the Buddha's teachings offers a strong lead: "Mind is the forerunner of all actions. All deeds are created by mind. If one speaks with a corrupt mind, then suffering follows, just as a wheel follows the hoof of an ox carrying a cart. If one speaks or acts with a serene mind, happiness follows, as surely as one's shadow."

As the Dhammapada illuminates, gratitude is an inside job. The art of appreciations for oneself or others begins with mindful attention in daily life. If one is consumed by judgmental thoughts all day long, then expressing appreciations toward others on the spot will likely be challenging, if not impossible. Intentionally noticing when people say or perform even small acts of kindness or beneficence in the subtleties of daily life is the bedrock of an appreciative mind. The consistent observation of these acts steadily builds up over time in memory and emotional regard as the ground of appreciative relationships.

Who is the most important member of your community? Yes, you are! If you want to raise the quality of happiness in your community, then offering appreciations toward yourself is a solid step forward. This can be difficult, especially if we are feeling down about ourselves or have a habit of criticizing ourselves instead. But let us be straight—until we can sincerely and consistently appreciate ourselves, it will be difficult to sustainably offer gratitude to those around us. Our inner reservoir must be steadily fed by underground streams so that our pool of communal joy and gratitude will remain abundant.

## The Gratitude Well

Most mornings after breakfast, I pour myself a pot of oolong tea and journal about what I feel grateful for, including several appreciations about my own efforts. To some, this may seem self-indulgent or self-absorbed. But for me, the fruits of this daily practice are fourfold.

**First**, when I feel the joy and lightness of appreciating myself, I naturally want to extend this out to others.

**Second**, appreciating my own efforts fills a tender spot in my heart that can otherwise be a gaping hole of lacking self-worth. Without appreciating myself, I'm more likely to crave external praise and acceptance from others and I will continually do things, such as accomplish big projects or shape my appearance, to get people to tell me I'm wonderful and good enough. While I wish to be receptive to others' love and appreciations, I don't want to depend on others' praise to feel accepted, valuable, and worthy. Offering appreciations regularly to myself gives me the inner flexibility to appreciate others freely without needing something in return.

**Third**, when I am used to appreciating myself, I tend to feel more comfortable, at ease, and receptive to incoming appreciations without deflecting or minimizing them. Receiving appreciations can feel uncomfortable and even overwhelming at times. The habit of appreciating oneself opens up this channel toward greater ease and familiarity.

**Fourth**, appreciating qualities in myself is a way of practicing humility, through honoring and expressing gratitude toward my ancestors, various teachers, and friends who have bestowed many gifts upon my life. Right here within me is a vast community of people to thank for this life.

Another way to cultivate appreciations is to write down positive memories at the end of the day. This practice has helped me understand my interpersonal relationships more fully. Interestingly, the more that I reflect on someone's beneficial actions, no matter how easy or difficult I find that person, the more that I begin noticing their kind words and personality traits in daily life. These people are behaving more or less the same, but I wasn't recognizing them before—the difference is my attentiveness. Whenever I feel irritated with a community member, I intentionally try remembering things that

I appreciate about them. Sometimes this is a breezy task and I immediately feel flooded with gratitude and joyful memories. Other times, I have to really work at it before the gratitude well starts pumping out some drops of appreciation. Whether the person is more or less easy to get along with, the key is that the gratitude well begins within me, no one else.

The shadow side of expressing appreciations is speaking the words on the outside but not really feeling them on the inside. Then it's just an empty bag of words, a mere ghost of appreciation. I distinctly remember a few occasions when someone called me out on this. My friend Matthias once said to me when we were in Athens, "David, you shared this appreciation about me a few days ago, and while I do appreciate your effort, I didn't really get the feeling from you—it felt disingenuous to me. I thought it would be important to tell you this." I respected my friend's honesty. Upon reflection, I did in fact feel very thankful for his helpfulness the previous week. But when I spoke to him, I was feeling quite exhausted as well as anxious about an upcoming appointment, so I was not present enough to convey the heartfelt energy of gratitude to him. Now, I try my best to wait until I am fully available to genuinely express an appreciation toward others so that we can both feel it and enjoy it.

## The Power of Collective Appreciation

Individuals can cultivate an appreciative mentality, but when a family or community practices this together with you, it's easier and more powerful. For example, if everyone in your family, workplace, or community shared three appreciations every day toward others—imagine how seen and valued everyone would feel! This is the great power of community, of our environment; the collective consciousness of the people surrounding us has a tremendous influence on how we think, perceive, feel, and act in every single moment.

Throughout the years I studied with Thay, I repeatedly heard him teach, "Environment is very important for our happiness." The

Buddha also repeatedly spoke to this truth with teachings on community, friendship, and collective consciousness—our environment is always watering seeds in our minds at every moment, thereby impacting the quality of our life. In Buddhist psychology, our mind is likened to a field that holds many kinds of seeds: seeds of joy, compassion, determination, and gratitude as well as seeds of anger, despair, envy, and sadness. At any moment, a seed in this store consciousness of our mind may be watered by the environment around us or within us and sprout up into our awareness. If I were to write about the oceans being polluted and killing sea life, you might experience the seed of despair rising up in your mind consciousness. If I were to write about how hundreds of young people are working together to clean up plastic debris in the ocean, your seeds of gratitude and hope may sprout.

The practice of attentively observing and feeding particular thoughts and emotions is referred to as selective seed watering. Mindfulness practice helps us to water beneficial seeds like gratitude, appreciation, and compassion in our consciousness and to intentionally not water seeds that can cause more suffering like envy, jealousy, or anxiety. Our seeds are watered by ourselves, by our inner dialogue and consumption, but they are also heavily watered by our environment. Think about how much your family, friends, and colleagues water your seeds every day. Our happiness and suffering largely depend on which seeds are watered by the people and environment surrounding us in every moment.

The Buddha emphasized that one's closest friends have the most influential impact upon the success of our mindfulness practice because they are watering our seeds every day, whether beneficially or not. When a community intentionally focuses on gratitudes for one another, it's like turning on an appreciation sprinkler system! Even if one person feels shy or uncomfortable receiving or expressing appreciations, the collective energy still soaks that person's mind with the water of loving appreciation. This is creating a culture of appreciation, and it becomes as normal and nourishing as the air you breathe.

A friend who is a Dharma teacher in California once told me that every day before leaving work he writes an email to someone, thanking them for something, even if it's small. I felt inspired to try this at the community mental health clinic where I worked, as it was a demanding work environment and my collegial relationships were feeling very stressed and uncomfortable. No matter what was going on, this practice became a hopeful way to end my day. I didn't always know how it landed for others, but I always felt better after the email! It took only a couple of minutes, yet the consistent focus on appreciating my colleagues and dwelling on the joys of our work together transformed our relationships over and over. My office became a joyful place to come to every day, and the positivity broke through the stress, allowing our friendships to flourish. Finally, on my last day of work before moving, my colleagues surprised me by holding a circle to water my positive seeds; they appreciated me by saying that I was the most appreciative person to work with! We had created that culture of appreciation together.

In your current daily life, does your family, workplace, or friends water seeds of kindness, respect, gratitude, and appreciation within you? Or do they water seeds of criticism, doubt, or anger? What about your partner, children, colleagues, or Sangha friends—are you watering their seeds of appreciation every day so that they bloom like a flower? These are important questions to honestly ask ourselves to see where we can grow. Whatever degree of appreciation exists in your family or community, how can you strengthen your capacity for watering seeds of mutual appreciation and positive regard?

A community needs just one person who can set a tone for everyone else, consistently illuminating others' unique gifts, goodness, and strengths. Their loving speech will spread throughout the community, igniting people's inner sparks of feeling seen and loved. Is there someone like this in your community already? If so, you can join forces together, like the Care Bears, a cartoon I watched while growing up. They teamed up together to shoot love out of their chests and heal those around them. It was very inspiring community practice!

If you do not have someone else to team up with yet, maybe you can be the person who starts things off. You may be surprised how much one person's efforts can raise the quality of mutual regard and happiness in your community. You can be the appreciation inspiration for others.

## Flower Watering

Thich Nhat Hanh invented the term "flower watering to describe the art of appreciations. In order for a dahlia to grow, it needs sunshine, earth, water, compost, and air, among other elements. Similarly, for a human heart to grow, it needs to be seen, encouraged, loved, and valued. Flower watering is intentionally recognizing and celebrating the most awesome qualities in others—their strengths, unique gifts, deep aspirations, or contributions to others, for example. When someone waters my flowers, it feels like a light being shone on the buried treasures in my heart. When such appreciations are expressed publicly, it feels like ten stadium spotlights all beaming down on that inner golden treasure chest. Flower watering circles toward both myself and others have been some of the greatest joys in my life of community building.

A standard form of flower watering is when a group gathers together and each person is invited to share their appreciations for others, themselves, or the community as a whole. Everyone gets an opportunity to water flowers in the community. But there are many other ways to practice the art of flower watering, depending on your communal configuration, creativity, and inspiration. For example, yesterday a group of us had our first meeting as a laypeople's Care Taking Council at Blue Cliff Monastery. My friend Sophie was facilitating, and by the end of the meeting, there were some noticeable disagreements and hints of frustration about scheduling decisions. So, Sophie decided to end the business logistics and pick them back up next week. People started preparing to leave, but Sophie said, "Oh, we're done with the business, but we're not done with our meeting—let's end by sharing appreciations! People put their coats down and settled back into their seats. Still enthusiastic, she continued, "Now, take a moment to think of one thing you appreciate about the person to your left. We'll go clockwise when people are ready."

We took a minute to reflect, and then Sophie started us off. Soon we realized that no one could share just one thing! The memory of a slightly frustrating disagreement was long gone; only the spontaneous joy of our budding friendships was alive. We were still getting to know each other, and I was blown away by my neighbor, Cathy, and her appreciations for me. "David, it's really apparent what an amazing listener you are and the empathy you have when people are sharing a difficulty," she said. The tension in my chest relaxed and opened up, and my face felt warm under the group's glowing attention. Then it was my turn. "Alex, I am really inspired by your capacity to reflect back another person's views with such care and solidarity while at the same time expressing your different views and needs so easily. What a rare and precious skill that is in community life."

The whole exercise took less than ten minutes, yet by the end, people's faces beamed with joy, tenderness, and cheerful intimacy. What a drastic change in the group from just minutes before. Even though we didn't make any big decisions that evening, we became better friends and a more trusting group. It made our whole time together worthwhile.

At our retreat center in Charlotte, North Carolina, we often start or end meetings with a round of appreciations to bring a flavor of lightness, joy, and friendship that not only cuts through work-related stress and heaviness, but reminds us why we are there in the first place! Each person is invited to share one or two appreciations about others and one for themselves. For people who are not accustomed to such open and direct communication, this exercise can feel vulnerable or awkward at first, but it invariably creates a genuine intimacy and positive regard for each other. It always surprises me how joyful, easy, and impactful this simple exercise is, often a highlight of my day. I also know that if my colleagues or team members are more bonded and joyful, we will be able to work more efficiently and harmoniously together.

## Birthday Flowers

One of my favorite forms of flower watering is when everyone focuses on just one person, like during a birthday gathering or before someone moves away. After dinner or while eating cake, we go around the table and each person shares what they love and appreciate the most about the birthday person. I can distinctly remember the facial expressions of friends who received flower watering for the first time during their birthday—more radiant and joyful than I had ever seen them. Hearing what your whole group of friends cherish and admire in you can make you feel like it is the best day of your life. In our young adult Sangha in Bellingham, Washington, a few years ago, we had a birthday flower watering session for our Sangha sister Kali. She looked more timid than excited when we started. But by the end of the evening, her eyes were overflowing with light and elation. When I asked her how she felt, she could only say "Oh my goodness, I've never experienced anything like that! Several days later, she wrote me a letter, stating that she was still feeling high from the experience and that this was one of the most special gifts of her entire life. This practice became a ritual for our Bellingham Sangha. Every birthday, we had full permission to release any obstacles to loving appreciation and freely express the depths of friendship, care, and joy we felt for each other.

Flower watering is a deeply healing and transformational practice for both individuals and the whole community. When one person shares what they love and respect about another's personality, values, and actions, everyone else is invited to see through that person's eyes. Thus, one person's view instantly transforms the community's perceptions about another person, shifting the collective belief about who that person is. When several people share about one person, it illuminates qualities, strengths, and gifts that others could not see before, perhaps not even the person themself.

Several years ago, my former partner and good friend, Andrea de Cleyre, received a birthday flower watering in our local Sangha. I also invited her closest friends and family who lived far away to write, draw, or creatively express what they appreciated about her, and we presented the collection of offerings on her birthday. She was so moved by the out-pouring of love that she enthusiastically attempted to offer flower watering during her best friend's birthday party a month later. Her friend Will was a magnificent community builder, having founded a thriving ecovillage in Southern California. Will had never experienced a birthday flower watering before, but he was up for the experience, and of course, he loved it, saying that it was one of the best birthday gifts of his entire life.

Just a few days later, this beautiful young man died in a motorcycle accident. Will's mom told Andrea later that week, "I'll be forever grateful to you, Andrea, for giving us all the chance to appreciate my son so fully like that before he died." In her grief, Andrea felt immeasurable gratitude that she and Will's community could appreciate him like that while he was still alive. Too often, people receive such out-pourings of appreciation at their funeral; there's no reason why we can't enjoy this gift while we're still here, celebrating our life right now with the people we love the most. Indeed, it's rare to be appreciated and loved so openly and publicly. Practicing flower watering, we don't have to wait until someone dies—we can freely express our gratitude while still blessed to be alive together.

## Building a Community Culture of Appreciation

Flower watering fosters harmony and joy in communal relationships, which naturally reduces conflict and supports easier reconciliation. A dear friend of mine in the Netherlands said she learned the absolute necessity of flower watering as part of an organizing council for young adults. After working together on some large projects over a few years, a young man in their group one day said that he did not feel appreciated or valued by anyone, his friendships felt hopeless, and the damage between him and the community felt irreparable. He left and never returned, which was a terribly painful loss for everyone. In their grief over the community rupture, their group decided to implement flower watering regularly into their culture so that no one would ever feel this way again. Now before they work on any service project together, they begin with twenty minutes of flower watering to inspire joy and support in each other. She said that her council relationships bloomed brighter than ever before, they attracted more members, and the work felt lighter and more harmonious together.

Flower watering can also highlight landmark events or transitions, so the community can honor and celebrate closure together. Every summer at Morning Sun Community, several volunteers come to live, practice, and work alongside residents for one to two months. To celebrate the end of our summer program one year, a participant enthusiastically invited us to try an "appreciation waterfall." This was a more intense watering exercise than the gentler garden hose style we were used to. Here, someone sits or lies down in the middle of the group and closes their eyes, if they wish. For the next ninety seconds, everyone in the circle shares as many positive qualities and gratitudes they can think of, all at the same time, literally making a waterfall of appreciations! When you're in the middle, you can only partly make out what people are actually saying, but you can really feel that it is all great stuff! Being under this cascade of loving, joyful, and caring attention is such a rush. As a lover of actual waterfalls, I would definitely say this experience is comparable to being under a real one! At Morning Sun, we don't use drugs recreationally. Why would we? We get natural highs from experiences like appreciation waterfalls instead.

While these practices appear harmless and well-intentioned, it's still important to be careful about introducing new group exercises. At Morning Sun, we found that this intensity of group attention can be quite uncomfortable, intimidating, and even scary for some people. One participant in our summer program excused themself, stating that they preferred not to be "steamrolled over or drowned" by an onslaught of appreciations. We never know people's degree of sensitivity, introversion, or even past trauma that may arise in group dynamics. It is important to explain any of these exercises beforehand, offer comfortable ways to opt in and out, and to openly converse about how to support people's diverse needs for safety, support, and choice during group activities.

---

## FLOWER WATERING AS A REGULAR PRACTICE

Flower watering has been one of the most powerful practices that I have experienced in community life, healing and transforming a myriad of communal and familial relationships. But like any mindfulness or positive psychology practice, it is most effective when applied regularly. The trick is to make flower watering a systemic part of your individual and community practice. Even if it's just five minutes of reflecting on gratitudes during breakfast, sharing a small round of appreciations at the beginning or end of a meeting, regular birthday flower watering, or a monthly flower watering circle in your family, these small habits will steadily grow into a transformative culture of appreciation. The fun part is tailoring these practices to the unique shape, fit, and flare of your community. Whether you are part of a residential, spiritual, friendship, or professional community, you can experiment and adapt these practices to what your group is ready for. Make it your own flavor, play with different styles, invite new approaches, and watch your community of friends bloom right before your eyes.

---

## The Healing Power of Appreciation

Perhaps you're thinking, "Yes, it's easy to practice appreciations with people you like and everything is all hunky-dory. But what about someone who's really difficult or I just don't like? I shouldn't fake appreciations, right? Why not just tell them how I actually feel? Martin Luther King Jr. wisely said, "A second thing an individual must do in seeking to love his enemy is to discover the element of good in his enemy. And every time you begin to hate that person and think of hating that person, realize there is some good there and look at those good points which will over-balance the bad points." As the Dhammapada similarly reminds us, gratitude and appreciations are an inside job—it begins within us.

My experience is that when I am really pissed off with someone, my first instinct is to think that I cannot, do not want to appreciate them, not even one bit. But this habit is actually a choice. My capacity to appreciate actually depends on whether I am willing to try it or not. When I make the effort, I'm always surprised. Once I break through the thick crust of criticism, judgments, or defensiveness, I typically find a whole hidden treasure chest of appreciations. Flower watering doesn't mean I no longer feel any judgment or resentment. Rather, an appreciation expresses the truth that I am more than my hurts and criticisms, and the other is more than their negative qualities. We are all complex beings with many seeds of life in our hearts.

Appreciations and gratitude have a healing and transformational power for the giver, receiver, and witnesses. No one is left out; all three are intertwined. Appreciations can grow toward anyone, even those we do not like, because we are transforming our perceptions of others as well as ourselves through this practice. Writing down a few appreciations has a remarkable power to wither away old internal stones of resentment, envy, and bitterness. Even a few drops of light can shift my negatively colored mind from midnight black to twilight blue or bright indigo. And that is already a gift to myself.

Perhaps because of the suffering I experienced as a young adult myself, I still feel called to build community with young people. One of the most pervasive sources of suffering I see in young people is feelings of self-criticism, unworthiness, and doubts about being good enough. Like a tower of building blocks, their social identity is built upon feelings of shame, self-loathing, and despair. Seeing the positive qualities, skills, jobs, or positions others have often magnifies their feelings of inferiority. They are hungry to feel seen and valued for their gifts, presence, and specialness in their community. Starving from a lack of wholesome attention, they crave the status, popularity, and external appearances of others. If only they had the teaching position that so and so has; if only they played guitar like so and so; if only so and so were not here to take all the attention, then they would finally feel true belonging and happiness with themselves. These patterns of jealousy and resentment are normal, occurring in healthy communities, and whether people are seasoned mindfulness practitioners or not.

When I lived in the monastery in my early twenties, I was often sizing myself up against other aspirants and young monks, judging, criticizing, and secretly competing against them so I would feel as good as them or better. Academic culture, sports, toxic masculinity, and our society's overwhelming individualistic drive nurtured these competitive and critical attitudes in me, such that I didn't even recognize them as negative habits at first. I still feel compassion and gratitude well up in me as I remember my unskillful interactions and the young men who put up with me during these early Sangha years. The older monks patiently guided me to look with eyes of interbeing toward my brethren, as if I were looking at myself. Seeing our mutual dependence on each other in community life sparked seeds of compassion and gratitude. Now, twenty years later, my Sangha siblings jokingly call me a "professional flower waterer." If such drastic transformation is possible within me, it is surely possible for you too.

Flower watering may appear as a light and superficial practice, but it is not. Cultivating a mind of appreciation is one of the most powerful methods of healing these individualistic and contentious tendencies that isolate and pit ourselves against others. Deeply appreciating and illuminating someone else's most radiant virtues, especially in front of others, can singlehandedly topple towers of criticism and defensiveness by replacing the foundational blocks with appreciation and self-worth. When someone feels deeply seen and valued in front of others, their social regard does a cartwheel, and the tendencies to criticize and resent others tumble down. It may seem like magic, but I have seen it happen many, many times.

Psychologists have discovered that when we express positive traits about others, people tend to ascribe those same traits to us. Thus, it doesn't make much sense to routinely judge others negatively, as those words just fly right back at us. Instead, witnessing and sharing about another's wonderful qualities or actions actually reinforces those same virtues in us.

Lying at the root of envy or competitive resentment is often an unexpressed, yet tender admiration for the beautiful qualities others embody. When observing another's esteemed qualities, I may initially believe that such gifts are outside of me, only found in others, which feeds feelings of inferiority, loss, and craving at the root of envy. Appreciations offer the shortest distance to actually embodying these qualities myself. When I begin to genuinely accept my appreciation for another's gifts instead of feeling resentful or envious, their positive qualities start to grow within me. The cloud of separation between us dissolves as the "other shifts from being a threat to a resource, from my competitor to my friend, and from an outsider to my community.

When I was living in our service-based mindfulness community in Athens, we had flower watering circles regularly, and my friend Phillip experienced a remarkable shift from envy and jealousy to appreciation and companionship. He put it like this, "When I was first living here, I was like, "Man, who's this guy Dylan? He's better at guitar than me, he knows more songs, he's better looking, and he's a lawyer to top it all off. Now, after we've been living together these last months, I tell people, 'Hey, you've got to meet my buddy, Dylan! He's amazing at guitar, he knows tons of songs, he's super good-looking, and if you can believe it, he's a lawyer too!"

## Gratitude to Teachers

In the Buddhist canon, there is a phrase that is often shared, "Never miss the opportunity to show gratitude before teachers and friends."

When I was a young monk, a few times a year I had an opportunity to have tea with Thay. I never knew when this would happen, as Thay had hundreds of monastic students and was often meeting with politicians, spiritual leaders, business executives, as well as writing books and giving talks; but Thay always made time for his monastic students, especially during important moments.

One day, I had my last cup of tea with Thay. While living in Plum Village, I developed a serious condition of anemia, which affected my physical health as well as my emotional well-being; after consulting with a doctor, I asked the older brothers to return home to my family in the United States to seek medical attention and care for my health. I didn't know if I would be returning to Plum Village. Before leaving, I went to Thay's hermitage in Upper Hamlet, where he stayed during most winter retreats. I asked Thay's attendant, a young Vietnamese monk, Brother Forest, if I could see Thay sometime before I left. He asked me to wait and after about fifteen minutes, the brother returned and said. "Okay, come now." *Oh, you mean right now?* I thought nervously, with surprise. The brother ushered me into Thay's room, where Thay was putting on his long robe, and his attendant started preparing a pot of tea for us. Although I knew that returning home was the right action, I also felt sad and confused about leaving the monastery, ambivalent about my monastic aspirations, and had some fear that I had disappointed my teacher.

There were two dark brown cushions facing each other. Thay invited me to sit down, and we drank our tea silently together for a few minutes. The warm roasted aroma of oolong tea, its earthy and comforting flavor, and the smooth glass tea cup heating my palms relaxed the jitters of sitting across from my esteemed and noble teacher. In recent years, a few Western monastics had left the monastery on a bitter note and never returned, so my impending departure was touching a tender spot in the monastery. Thay asked very openly, "So, you are leaving soon? After I nodded, he asked again, "And are you uprooting yourself now from the tradition?" I was surprised by both the question and his directness. "No, not at all, Thay," I responded

sincerely. "I'm returning home to take care of my health." Even though
I questioned my monastic life, I knew this Sangha was my home and
that I would never leave. Thay seemed satisfied with my answer and
after a pause, he asked, "So, you are happy to leave, then? I responded,
"Yes, Thay. But I didn't think I would be leaving so soon," with a touch
of frustration in my voice. My mentor had bought my plane ticket
without consulting me on the dates, and I would be leaving just before
the monastic ordination ceremony of several aspirants I had grown
close to, which was upsetting me. Thay seemed to understand, and his
face softened slightly, knowing where my heart was.

Finally, I was ready to share what I had come for. Even though I was
normally very nervous while talking with Thay, the words poured out
easily, clear and straight from my heart. I had reflected on them often
over the last several days. "Thay, I just wanted to share with you that
even though things have been difficult for me here with my health and
all, I always felt your compassion and support for me this whole time.
You've always been there for us, like a father. And I just want you to
know, I really appreciate that." It was true, especially during my most
difficult moments: whenever we gathered to listen to a talk, I felt Thay's
unswerving compassion and love beaming through the meditation
hall as if he were directing one hundred percent of his compassion and
grandfatherly wisdom toward me. Throughout my time as a monastic,
no matter the difficulties I faced, I always felt supported by him.

After I spoke, I looked up at Thay, who was staring a few feet
ahead, but clearly taking in the moment. His eyes turned from a
serious focus to a gentle warm glow that grew more luminous every
moment. It seemed that his whole being, every cell of his body, was
opening up, softening, and brightening at the same time. His face
looked like an unfolding lily flower moving from its closed posture
in the early morning hours to unfurled petals radiantly reflecting the
first beams of morning sunlight. I had never seen someone respond in
such a sensitive, organic, and free way to words of appreciation before.
After what felt like several minutes but may have been just moments
later, Thay said in a more familial and light tone of voice, "Well, Phap

Cuong, as you go home, sleep a bit more, eat a bit more, and rest well. Return to your right thinking, and then you will know what to do. The brothers at Deer Park are there for you too. And you are always welcome back here."

# CHAPTER 8

# THE MAGIC OF APPRECIATIONS AT MORNING SUN

*When we focus on our gratitude, the tide of disappoint-
ment goes out and the tide of love rushes in.*
—KRISTIN ARMSTRONG

*Gratitude is the wine for the soul. Go on. Get drunk.*
—JALAL AL-DIN MUHAMMAD RUMI

The morning of arrival day for our first retreat in our new meditation hall at Morning Sun, I went down to see how our construction
had turned out. "Oh, my goodness!" I muttered in disbelief. The table
saw and chop saw were still out, piles of fresh sawdust covered the
floor, two-by-fours and siding planks stretched across one side of the
room, and abandoned screws and wooden scraps of various shapes
and sizes lay shamelessly scattered on the floor. "What a disaster!" I
complained, aghast. *How will orientation be held here tonight?* I had been
working all the previous afternoon on retreat schedules and programming, and apparently there were just not enough hands to go around.

Last fall, we believed we would have easily finished our new retreat
facility by this spring, so I enthusiastically organized a mindfulness
retreat for educators in June. However, the New England winter
buried us in snow longer than usual, and construction overall took

much longer than expected. We were, in fact, a group of meditator volunteers led by one skilled builder, not a tribe of carpenters. By the time May rolled around, we were far from finished. The external siding was partially completed and the rooms were built out with wooden beams, but there were still no walls anywhere—no sheetrock, plaster, floors, or paint. We pleaded with our community for help and over a hundred friends came to volunteer with us on the weekends while a small handful of us worked tirelessly throughout the week. By the beginning of June, we had miraculously finished bamboo floors, walls, and plaster in most of the bedrooms, but there was no meditation hall, kitchen, or electricity, and the septic system and well were still being installed. Meanwhile, the number of registrations for our educators' retreat was showing it would be our most popular retreat ever!

So here we were on the final morning with all available hands on deck, desperately trying to assemble the last puzzle pieces of this meditation center before people arrived. I stepped into the kitchen to clean up the air compressor, its long tentacle hoses snaking around the room between hand drills, nail guns, and other tools. Stepping around, I realized there were no still no bed frames assembled and only one sink and toilet installed out of three! Witnessing the compounding messes and unfinished work was overwhelming, and my worries began spiraling out of control: *Could we still finish? Where would people sleep? What will people think when they see this mess after traveling all day? Maybe we can still cancel the retreat? Yes, we'll cancel everything, and I'll send out a quick email to everyone so we can avoid disaster, that's a great idea.* As if snapping out of a dream, I remembered people were not only driving here; they were flying in from Colorado, Mexico, California, Canada, Florida, Michigan, and all over the Northeast. They were already in mid-air or on the road by this hour; their destination: Morning Sun. My mind swirled with fears: so much to do and so little time. The air hoses in my arms seemed to wrap around me in tighter circles. Feeling anxiety closing in, I stopped everything and put down the tools. I felt the soles of my feet firmly upon my sandals, supported by the solid concrete floor and earth underneath. The cool morning air entered my nostrils in quick breaths. Slowly, the air sank deeper into my chest, and my belly softened and relaxed with each breath out. My racing thoughts slowed, my chest loosened, and ease gradually descended back into my body. *Others are responsible for cleaning up this mess*, I thought. My job was to check in with our volunteer team and coordinate registration.

Heading upstairs, I saw Jonathan carrying out some wooden two-by-fours, his face looking noticeably dimmer than in past weeks. Instead of the bright spark of enthusiasm he usually carried, his eyes looked sullen and his face fatigued to the point of sulkiness. I peeked in the bathroom, where Willow was fixing cabinets. She worked steadily, but her spirit was grayed over, lacking joy in the handiwork she usually delighted in. It was understandable—we had been working overtime the last few weeks, trying to finish before today's deadline. Our weekly days of mindfulness transitioned into working meditation, and several of us skipped our day off to finish the bedrooms. We had the determination of a colony of beavers, inspired by our community-building dreams. But right now, people's spirits were dried up.

My heart dropped seeing Jonathan, Willow, and others looking defeated. I went to Fern, our community's spiritual anchor, who was outside discussing the meditation hall with Candace. "Fern, our volunteer team is looking exhausted. I'm really concerned about them, especially as they are also staffing the retreat. Can we take some time to support them?" I know when Fern is really listening to me because she doesn't agree or disagree. Rather, she pauses in contemplation, often looking into the distance. Finally, she said, "Yes, I can offer something during lunch when we're all together."

We ate in silence for ten minutes, resting our minds amidst the flurry of tasks. After everyone had finished, Fern led us in a loving-kindness practice for fifteen minutes, gently guiding us in gratitude and compassion for ourselves and all our efforts. After the meditation, I felt more rested and ready to get back to work. But Fern was just getting started! Her eyes were calm, her body unhurried, and her soothing voice encouraged us to stay present, dwelling in the peaceful eye of the storm. With serene confidence, she said, "We've all been working so hard the past weeks and we've been doing such an amazing job. Now, we may be feeling tired, even exhausted. At times like this, we need to return to the depths of our peace and joy as a Sangha—this is the most important offering for ourselves and those who are coming. We don't have to do this alone; we can help support each other. Each of us is a gem in the Sangha, and we can help each other to shine more brightly. Let's practice appreciating each other, one by one. Since we have limited time and still things to help with today, two people can share for each person." I felt relieved and excited that we could shower our volunteers with abundant appreciation, yet I was also worried we were taking too much time, knowing the mess inside the hall would not clean itself up. Still, I trusted Fern's guidance and went with it.

Eight of us sat together under the northern shade of our new building, the "Barn," resting our bodies on the grass for a well-deserved break together. One by one, we each indulged in the glorious spotlight of the Sangha's loving attention, receiving heartfelt words from two inspired friends. Five minutes is a relatively short period in normal time. But under a cascade of loving gratitudes and golden acknowledgments, each minute transforms into an epoch span of glowing inner experiences.

I still remember having shared for my friends, Lark and Angelica: what I said and the looks of their affectionate faces—luminous eyes and bashful yet beaming smiles as we showered them with appreciations. And I still remember Anne and Fern's tone of voice when they spoke to me—sincere, sweet, and grounded in their lived experiences with me. I actually remember very little of the verbal content compared to the intimacy of the group experience. There is something indescribable, even magical, in being truly seen and celebrated for one's inner light in front of others. It is one of the most healing and joyful gifts I have ever experienced in community.

We traded about sixty minutes of work time that afternoon for this appreciation and rejuvenation circle. During this hour, it felt like we were transported to another world, one where exhaustion and hopelessness were no more than remnant notions of the past. Yes, we still had an overwhelming amount of work to do before guests arrived; and yes, we were all still fatigued. But people no longer looked emotionally beat. The complaining, weary, and hopeless faces were replaced by a new buoyancy, support, and trust in each other and our communal journey.

After the gathering, I quickly sequestered myself to finish the rest of the retreat's registrations and scheduling documents. I felt grateful for Fern's guidance, yet I still questioned in the back of my mind, "Was this really the best use of our time? People would be arriving shortly—how would everything play out?" Time, of course, would tell.

By 5:00 p.m., I finished the retreat registrations and scheduling and called Fern to check in. "Hey, are you guys almost finished down there? How's it going?" I asked enthusiastically.

"No, it's a disaster down here, David," she exclaimed, talking to people in between. "It's chaotic—people are arriving, and no one was assigned to cook dinner, which is already forty-five minutes late. I'm searching for soup ladles. And no one has been able to move in yet because the rooms aren't ready." Perhaps because of Fern's earlier meditation and appreciation circle as well as having finished my own tasks, an abiding calm washed over me, and I no longer felt panicky about our retreat. Instead, I picked up the printed schedules and came down to help right away.

To my surprise, the meditation hall was totally transformed! The heaps of sawdust, tools, and debris had all disappeared. Instead, curving rows of orange meditation cushions lay in front of two dozen white chairs, all facing a sublime altar. Sheetrock still lined the ceiling and three walls, but the altar wall was a warm, smooth, and bright lemon color with arrangements of white daisies, violet lupin, and yellow lilies from our garden. *Thank goodness!* I rejoiced. *At least one thing around here looks like a retreat center!*

While people were finishing dinner, Fern and I convened in one of the unfinished bedrooms that still had tool boxes and extra sheetrock. "Great job on throwing dinner together, Fern—at least they're all eating now and the meditation hall is amazing! It's beginning to look like a meditation center, almost!" We both laughed to each other and to this ridiculous start to the retreat. Then I asked, "So we're almost an hour behind schedule and will need to start orientation soon—what's left?"

Fern counted off, "We still have two toilets and one sink upstairs to install, and all twelve bed frames to assemble. Michael is almost finished with the last electrical hookups and can help us." I responded, "I know you and Michael are supposed to offer orientation, but I'm sorry, I don't know shit about toilets." Fern offered, "Okay, Michael and I can lead the team upstairs while you hold orientation down here with our guest teachers, Valerie and Richard." "Yes, that seems best," I responded. "At the end, you can come down and meet everyone. But we need those beds and toilets!"

Both Fern and I thanked our volunteers profusely, "You guys are amazing! We couldn't do this without you!" Then I added cautiously, "Just please try to tiptoe around up there, because we'll all be meditating down here!" They laughed and rolled their eyes as if nothing about our situation could astonish or faze them anymore. But there was lightness in their laughter now, and I could tell we were having fun again.

I started orientation with a guided meditation. Amidst our meditative silence, I subtly heard the floors creaking upstairs as our ninja volunteer team tiptoed around. *Thank goodness they're not too loud,* I thought. But soon enough, sounds started growing, coming from various directions above: shuffled footsteps, an unmistakable drilling, a thud in one corner and then another. One moment it was here, another moment there. A bit later we heard some heavy, bulky sounds that were surely toilets going in. I nervously opened my eyes to observe how our new guests were handling it all. A few started looking around in a kind of bewildered curiosity. I imagined them asking themselves questions like, "What the hell is this place?" Or "What kind of mindfulness operation are y'all running here?" It was a bizarre start to the retreat, to say the least. But I kept on breathing through it, not feeding unnecessary worries and trusting in the moment. It would be whatever we made of it, whether precious or pathetic, amazing or embarrassing, an experience of growth or failure— the choice was ours.

In the end, no one got up and left; they followed our lead and breathed through it with us.

After the meditation, I needed to address the elephant in the room—the particularly noisy one stomping around upstairs. I shared, "Meditation is about being present in this very moment. Whether the conditions are more or less favorable, what's important is whether we are watering seeds of appreciation or suffering in each moment." I was truly speaking from the heart as flashes of this afternoon rolled across my mind. "During the meditation, you may have heard some noises upstairs—well seriously, how could you not have heard them?" I asked with a smile, which broke the ice with a few chuckles. "Well, we were still putting together a few last nice touches. We thought having some beds and toilets might give that extra special something you all could appreciate." Now people were laughing, which breathed a sense of relief into the room. I continued, "In fact, we have a team of volunteers working hard for us, right at this moment. Can you guess who is installing these toilets for us? Morning Sun was founded eight years ago by Michael and Fern, who were monastic disciples of Zen Master Thich Nhat Hanh. They are senior teachers in our tradition, and lead retreats around North America. They also led construction on this new building. Tonight is a special occasion, for we have world-class meditation teachers installing toilets and beds for you!" Altogether good-humored and appreciative, people clearly looked excited to meet Fern and Michael.

When orientation finally came to a close, Fern knocked on the door and entered slowly. "Excuse me for interrupting," she said in her typical angelical and optimistic voice as if something special were just about to happen. "I wanted to let people know that your beds are made, the bathrooms are finished, and you can now start moving into your rooms." People cheered, the joy and relief in the room palpable.

I went outside to lend a hand, but our volunteers were already on it. Their energy had turned 180 degrees from this morning. Each was beaming smiles and caring eyes toward our guests, offering to carry luggage up the stairs, and wishing everyone good night. After the last retreatants were settled in, our team gathered in the kitchen to celebrate. Upon seeing them, I burst open with joy, "Wow, you guys were amazing! Can you believe it—we did it!" Angelica asked, "Could you guys hear us up there? We were tiptoeing all around, but you had to have heard us, right?" We all burst out laughing, trying to muffle our exuberance so as not to disturb our guests. Harry said, "Yeah, those toilets had to be loud. But people will really appreciate them in the morning!" Jonathan chimed in, "Well, it was pretty fun actually working like a stealth team up there with Michael and Fern." Angelica beamed, "And it was so worth it, seeing how happy people looked at the end."

Building the Barn was one of the biggest challenges I have ever faced in my life of community building. Yet, by all accounts, the retreat was extraordinarily successful. Some guests shared that it was the best retreat that they had ever experienced. As for our residents and volunteer team, we invited everyone to enjoy a week of lazy rejuvenation to recoup our energy afterward, with barbecue bonfires at Blueberry Pond and daily excursions to a local swimming hole.

# CHAPTER 9

# SHARING CONFLICT AND RECONCILIATION

*Difficulties are meant to rouse, not discourage. The human spirit is to grow strong by conflict.*

—WILLIAM CHANNING

*There is no better place to learn the art of loving than in community.*

—BELL HOOKS

As I was writing this very chapter, one of the most difficult conflicts of recent years spontaneously erupted with a longtime community member. It reminded me how painful, gut-wrenching, humiliating, scary, and humbling conflict can be. The conflict touched old wounds, and for days I felt consumed with fury and hatred for how this other person "made me feel." I wanted it all to go away, and I wished that final spark had never ignited. I wanted the other person to go far away; I wanted these painful feelings to go away; I wanted to run away. On the one hand, I could have done just that—walk away from it all and find another community that I felt would respect me better, see me, and treat me the way I deserved. But on the other hand, even as such tempting thoughts arose, I knew they were pure folly—I would only be running away from myself.

My community and my mindfulness practice held me to a much higher standard of integrity than that; I knew I could muster up some faith, slowly turn toward the pain, surrender to my own unskillfulness, and face the shadows that lay between us with kind eyes. Instead of further running, hiding, fighting, or numbing—our typical nervous system responses to perceived threats—I heeded the call to listen deeper, to "sit with my shit," as they say in Zen circles, and humbly accept my suffering with greater self-compassion. Moment by moment, breath by breath, the knots within me revealed themselves, and oh so slowly, they softened and loosened. Coming back to myself again and again, the pitch-black forest of our conflict began to show colorful traces of dawn.

There comes a moment in every conflict when I finally no longer wish for it to never have happened. Each painful encounter teaches me something invaluable about myself and my relationships; I receive an unforeseen gratitude gem for its healing force. Previously my worst enemy, the conflict becomes the unlikely yet heroic teacher that helps me and my relationships grow stronger, wiser, and more trustworthy than was previously possible.

No matter where we go, what partner, family, or community we commit to loving, we cannot escape the fact that conflicts are waiting for us. It is part of our human nature to struggle, wrestle, and suffer with one another while working out long-standing habits, unskillful communication patterns, and old relational wounds within. Sometimes we'll be personally embroiled in a heated dispute; other times, we'll experience friction on the periphery of others' entanglements. The old saying "You can run but you can't hide," coined by heavyweight champion Joe Louis, is not only for those in the boxing ring— it's for each of us. In *All About Love*, bell hooks captures this timeless tension between breaking versus holding the pain of conflicts: "When we face pain in relationships, our first response is often to sever bonds rather than to maintain commitment."[34]

We all know what this running tendency feels like. But wherever we go, however we try to ignore it, the seeds of conflict continue right here within us, following us like a shadow throughout our lives. When we finally stop running, our capacity for community grows like seeds that sprout only in the midst of fire. Conflicts are the essential fertilizer for our spiritual growth. Conflict, too, is community life. Community means sharing the wholeness of our lives together, pain and conflict included. They are just as important and meaningful to share as joy, appreciations, and friendship—the pain and suffering tenderizes our hearts and minds, preparing us to better understand, compassionately support, and humbly love one another.

Many of us search for an ideal community, a family that we choose. My longtime mentor, Brother Phap Dung, once told me, "What people are really looking for is a community who can accept and embrace them just the way they are, including all their garbage." Maybe our search for happiness is that simple—a family or community that truly accepts us, as we are. Are you part of a community, a chosen family, where your inner smelly compost can be received with the safety and trust you need? Or are you still looking for that precious container of friendships? A safe and healing community is one of the greatest treasures we can receive and cocreate alongside others.

Our community may well be the perfect garden for us, but we still have to turn the smelly compost over and over ourselves. Are you ready to dig in? Then how does one skillfully transform these inevitable conflicts so our community grows closer together rather than more distant? When community bonds eventually rupture, how do we learn to break open together, instead of apart? Whether in community or family life, we must choose to work together in order to work things out. If you truly feel your community is not safe or skilled enough to do this work, you might actually need to search for another that is. Human suffering is relational, and to heal at the roots, we need safe and supportive relationships that can embrace our seeds of suffering over the long run.

The good news is that we have tried and true mindfulness practices to methodically work through relationship difficulties and even prevent future ones from occurring. Like the intricate plumbing system of a home, the daily practice of tending to communication blocks, flushing out old hurts, ushering in new understandings, and washing our relationships clean is the source of well-being in any family, tribe, or community home. The following three chapters are dedicated to the art of sharing conflict and reconciliation as a community. The stories, insights, and practices are offered to support our families and communities to transform bitter speech, conflict, and distrust into more skillful, safe, and loving relationships. This chapter will help you understand the universality of conflict and how to avoid its pitfalls in community life. Recognizing and transforming the roots of conflict within is the first crucial step to healing those around us. The following chapters will then explore ways to nurture the seeds of reconciliation within oneself and constructively engage conflict and build relation resiliency.

Often called "the father of American psychology," William James wrote, "Whenever you're in conflict with someone, there is one factor that can make the difference between damaging your relationship and deepening it. That factor is attitude." Conflicts are inevitable; pain is inevitable; yet reconciling is optional; healing is optional. The choice is ours.

## The Power of Collision

The word conflict comes from the fifteenth-century Latin, *con* meaning "with" or "together," and *fligere*, meaning "to strike or dash down." Thus, *confligere* means "to strike together," or "to bring into collision." In this light, conflict is the result of two forces crashing into one another, perhaps painful and fierce, yet also creative and intimately connected. This is where the magic lies—where there is conflict, there is connection. The collision exposes the tender parts of one's being, revealing hidden vulnerabilities, helplessness, fear, humiliation, anger, or despair. Practicing mindfulness in community means consciously choosing not to ignore or abandon these exposed hurt feelings. Rather, the pain of conflict and the love of the relationship serve as motivations to dig even deeper into ourselves, to a place where the pain can be met by the equally strong forces of acceptance, compassion, and forgiveness within us. Thus, each conflict becomes our unlikely yet golden encouragement to touch the most compassionate parts of ourselves, both forcing and allowing us to become the kind of friend, spouse, parent, or coworker we dream of being.

I witnessed Thay masterfully open the door from conflict to compassion during a question and answer session in Plum Village in 2014, shortly before the stroke that left him unable to speak again. A woman explained that her spouse recently had an affair, and she struggled to know how to deal with overwhelming feelings of betrayal, rage, and despair. At first, Thay looked at her silently with eyes that were bottomless wells of compassion. Then he shared, "Where there is betrayal, there is fidelity. Where there is anger, there is compassion. Where there is despair, there is hope." Thay was flipping the situation upside down so that the woman could see her life through the lens of interbeing. Because she was feeling the immensity of betrayal, she had the opportunity to more deeply understand the nature of fidelity within herself. Thay did not give concrete advice to either reconcile or break off the relationship. Rather, he encouraged her to see the interdependent links between her suffering and the happiness she truly longed for. By mindfully embracing betrayal and rage, she could cultivate the power of fidelity and compassion. This is the opportunity that every conflict can offer if we open to it.

## The Universality of Conflict

I think most people imagine Buddhist and mindfulness communities as places filled with calm and compassionate people who get along peacefully all the time, free from the relationship strife that plagues everyone else in society. Before starting our global tour of mindfulness communities, I certainly carried a childlike naivety that at least some communities were more or less immune to major conflicts, that Sanghas with a strong enough practice could transcend typical human bickering and disputes. Sure enough, though, everywhere we visited, people unfailingly shared about their community's trials and tribulations of conflict and disharmony. Whether currently embroiled in a dispute or reflecting on past turmoil, person after person proved that conflict was as common as weeds in a garden. Hearing about and directly witnessing communal stories of rupture, repair, and renewal has illuminated the power of communal resilience in the face of conflict.

At one meditation center in Europe, a senior student was extremely upset with the two founding teachers and spread rumors throughout the community before encouraging others to depart with him for good. Many decided to leave, and the two founders were heartbroken by the resulting fallout. Nevertheless, the founders committed themselves to rebuilding the community from the ground up with just a small core group. They reflected on the causes of the conflict and restructured the community into a center that flourished to be even healthier than it had been before the falling out.

At another practice center, two long-term core members became severely at odds with one another, eventually entangling every other core member in the dispute. Despite attempts to reconcile, the drama dragged on for several years. During my month-long stay, a five-day-retreat took place with all the community leaders present. In the midst of the retreat, the core members collectively decided not to leave until the conflict was finally laid to rest. They sat in the meditation hall and listened to each other for hours, until every last person felt adequately heard. Toward the end, the senior teacher firmly stated, "This is your last chance to speak, to feel heard and understood. Afterward, we agree to never bring up this conflict again with each other. We must heal and put this conflict to rest once and for all; if not for us, then for the sake of future generations of practitioners." The community wholeheartedly committed to laying the conflict to rest as well as to having regular reconciliation meetings moving forward.

Such conflicts happen even in the most outstanding meditation communities. Even if we feel despair, anguish, and grief in the midst of conflict, remember: you are still in the company of great teachers and sages. No one is immune to conflict; however, resilience exists for those who practice courageously and perseveringly. Although you may be in the midst of a valley, new beginnings and friends can lie just around the bend.

## A Community without Conflict?

Toward the end of my and Vanessa's research year, I noticed one community that appeared to be the exception. *Wow, there are no real conflicts here! How do they do it?* I wondered. Their strong practice must keep them joyful and immune from such struggles, I thought, marveling at how harmony had prevailed throughout the community's eight years.

We returned to visit this community the following summer. A week before arriving, the founding teacher confided in us that a painful conflict had just erupted, and two residents had left for good. Her voice was calm, kind, and non-blaming, yet still revealed her shock and heartbreak. "We've never had this happen here before, and we are still accepting and embracing this painful situation. We wanted to let you know directly." She spoke with tender humility, and I appreciated her open communication with us.

As the story unfolded, I learned that a community resident had been suffering from cancer for two years. The severity of her illness, the toll of treatments, and the stress on her child were overwhelming her husband and the two other residents who had been living in the same house, helping care for the child. Amidst this ongoing crisis, tensions accumulated, and eventually a conflict erupted between the husband and the two other adults. Previously benevolent relationships drowned in stress, animosity, fear, and irritation. The community was shocked and dismayed by how quickly things escalated. Some members tried to intervene by mediating a Beginning Anew practice to repair the situation. But the community did not practice reconciliations regularly, and there was not enough trust or familiarity with the process for the parties to come together—it is difficult to build a shelter during a storm. The relationships at this point were exhausted, and faith in each other broken. The two residents felt the best recourse was to leave all together.

While the stress of life-threatening illnesses can overwhelm any community, conflicts of course happen even between physically and emotionally healthy members in well-built communities. The point of admitting these challenges—to owning up to the fact that even peaceful-minded people will argue and fight—is not to forecast doom on your beloved community. On the contrary, being conscious and candid about this truth offers two powerful and uplifting insights. If we are receptive, conflict can be a (perhaps bitter, but not unexpected) medicine.

The first insight is that the refuge of reconciliation takes time to build. Individuals and communities unfamiliar with the art of relational repair are most vulnerable to the consequences of conflict. Ignoring the inevitable tensions of community life is like watching a snowball slowly roll down the mountain, gaining speed and power until it eventually knocks over everyone and everything. Regularly caring for the tiny conflicts of daily living is the key.

The second insight is that we are not alone in our conflicts. Conflict is normal—your community is normal. Conflict is a healthy stage of growth, even in the best of friendships and the most upstanding of communities. About ten years ago, I enjoyed a small group conversation about community life with Brother Phap Huu, the abbot of Upper Hamlet in Plum Village. He shared with us, "Thay was just saying the other day that every community has compost. No Sangha is without it. Compost is part of the path. It helps us to grow and to know how to cultivate our happiness together."

In the midst of conflict, it is easy for me to feel ashamed, think poorly about my own or my community's practice, or feel angry and remorseful that the difficult situation ever happened. These are common mental traps based on the illusion that conflicts are the exception to community life rather than the norm. Keeping in mind what other healthy communities have faced and overcome nurtures the long view of true communal growth and healing.

When I notice myself thinking negatively and suffering during a conflict, I may say to myself, *Yes, this is painful and hard, David, and that's okay. Conflict is a natural part of relationships and community life.* I may add, *This conflict will help me to learn greater compassion and humility. What else is this teaching me?* Remembering these simple truths helps me to feel more at ease, hopeful, and gentle toward myself and others while increasing my ability to learn. The next time that you're in the midst of a conflict, I invite you to try reminding yourself of these truths. For example, *This conflict is upsetting and hard; yet it is natural, even in the best of communities. It's a part of every close relationship, and even essential for our growth.*

How does it feel to say that to yourself? How might you feel saying this to the one you are struggling with?

In the thick of interpersonal challenges, I remember the wise words of my teacher, Zen Master Thich Nhat Hanh: "We can never find a perfect Sangha. An imperfect Sangha is good enough." What is most important is to use the imperfect elements to grow stronger, training ourselves to be more accepting and understanding of ourselves and each other. A mentor and dear friend of mine, Karen Hilsberg, recently celebrated her local Sangha's twentieth anniversary. She dedicated a poem that included these words:

> *The tree of Sangha is deeply rooted and strong.*
> *A healthy manifestation of the Three Jewels.*
> *But look closely and we see the disfigured branches, pest-eaten*
>     *leaves, and imperfections*
> *That create a real, living, breathing, authentic community.*

Make no mistake—the ugly, broken, and messy parts of ourselves and our community are exactly where the real growth takes place. The imperfections invite us to become more authentic, loving humans together. Alone, we're not confronted with our shortcomings; community reflects back to us our hidden blemishes, what we don't want others to see but are unwilling or unlikely to face ourselves alone. In community, we learn to accept ourselves before others, creating the soil bed for self-forgiveness, belonging, and deep rooted maturation to thrive. If we run away from the messiness, then we miss the source of both our own and our community's greatest treasures.

My longtime friend, monk, and Dharma teacher, Brother Phap Lai, once shared personally with me about his years as a young monk, "It wasn't until I saw the slimy underbelly of the Sangha that I really grew to love it deeply." By seeing and understanding the Sangha's less glamorous sides, Brother Phap Lai also found true belonging for himself in the community. Acceptance is the foundation of true love.

## Corrosive Elements of Community

While conflicts are a natural process of community life, if we are not diligent and careful, our thoughts and words may destroy the sacred temples of our lives. The ethical foundation of the Plum Village tradition is the Five Mindfulness Trainings, and the fourth training encourages us to "reconcile and resolve all conflicts, no matter how small." I used to wonder why we can't let some things slide here and there, but I've since learned the big cost of that approach. When people avoid caring for small conflicts, bigger tensions build up, and each person becomes like a hose that is slightly turned on but closed at the end. The emotional pressure increases until the hose starts leaking and spraying out the sides with anger, criticism, misunderstanding, and blame. Then everyone gets wet.

One of these leaks is "speaking about the faults of others in their absence," as described in the Fourteen Mindfulness Trainings of the Order of Interbeing. In middle school, we had different names: "talking smack behind their back," "talking about you without you,"

---

* In fact, from this conflict, the Buddha developed a series of teachings and practices to promote harmony and humility that have become the foundation for Beginning Anew, the powerful reconciliation practice developed by Thich Nhat Hanh in the Plum Village community, which we will explore in the following chapters.

or simply, "talking shit." Many of us have strong habitual responses during conflicts, wanting to explain ten reasons why the other person has said or done something terrible and twenty reasons why what we have done is right. It's okay to think and feel this way initially—it's normal. But left unchecked, repeatedly criticizing others in their absence can do incredible damage to community relationships. Sadly, I have seen this uncurled pattern of gossip and division play out again and again in communities throughout my travels and home Sanghas. I believe it is the most corrosive element in community life, steadily and quietly tearing apart the threads of trust, safety, and integrity in the social fabric. People leave, and entire communities separate at the seams because of this small, hardly noticeable habit. Moreover, negative speech often hurts the speaker the most. Community life can be challenging enough already; by speaking about others' faults, we are pretty much begging for trouble.

The truth is no one is ever truly separate from each other in community. We live and breathe as one body of interconnected relationships and neural networks. What we say, think, and do affects everyone, whether they are physically present or not. If we are serious about building beloved community, we must offer vigilant awareness to this all-too-common, pernicious habit. Each of us has the power to offer safety and respect through moment-to-moment awareness of our thoughts, speech, and listening. Sometimes I catch myself right before a judgmental, unkind, or uninformed thought sneaks out my lips. Other times, I realize the mistake just after blurting out some negativity. No one is perfect in this game. That's why we call mindfulness a "practice."

I have experimented with different mindful speech practices to avoid talking negatively about community members in their absence. One strategy is to consciously consider someone's well-being when conversing about them. I think to myself or say out loud, "I'm aware Julie is not here right now, and I want to respect her as we talk about her." Or I will say out loud, "Since Sam is not here right now to respond, I will think about this and talk to them later." These simple reminders immediately help me better discern whether my speech is gossipy and complaining or constructive and compassionate and whether there is someone who should be included in the conversation moving forward.

Sometimes, it is helpful and necessary to talk about others' difficulties when they are not present. In this case, I may say, "Since we are talking about Julie right now while she's not here, I would like to speak with respect and compassion as we offer support to this situation." Caring for community asks for this vigilant respect and verbal awareness day in and day out. During conflict, sometimes we need to talk about the person we are quarreling with. This helps us to responsibly process our "shit" so we may avoid "talking shit" later. I find the safest approach is to confide in friends who are not related to the conflict at all in order to avoid creating triangles of negativity within my community. I regularly reach out to friends, therapists, or family members who can shine a light on whatever turmoil is happening without feeding the drama and hurting my community.

By the end of our research tour, the votes were unanimous: every community—large or small, seasoned or inexperienced, younger or older—checked off the conflict box. The question is not whether these relational collisions will come into your community life or not, or even when they will come. Conflicts are brooding every day, in small unresolved exchanges and in old, unhealed relational patterns, whether above or below the surface of our awareness. The real question is how we can turn toward and embrace conflict without fear in order to avoid common pitfalls that tear communities apart and move toward healing and reconciliation together.

## The Journey of Reconciliation

The journey of reconciliation is like hiking in the mountains. While living at Morning Sun Community in New Hampshire, I often hiked in the White Mountains, a geologically old range with steep ascents, breathtaking ridge lines, cascading waterfalls, endless glacial boulders, and mesmerizing peaks. It is not easy hiking by any means—moving slowly and steadily, you bring your body up to the mountain peaks and then carry yourself back down, again and again. At the same time, you go through mental and emotional ups and downs. When climbing a steep trail, thighs and calves burn, the chest bursts for more oxygen, sweat pours through your clothes, and it can feel like you will never reach the top. But if you keep on moving, one foot in front of the other, one breath at a time, and take short breaks to rest, eventually you find yourself nearing the long-awaited peak. You see the horizon bending over the path and suddenly, pure relief, exhilaration, and joy take over. "My goodness, we are almost there…. We did it! What a view!" The pain of the climb feels totally worth it: you are stronger and more confident in yourself than before you began the journey. You look into the distance with astonishment at the many peaks and valleys you transcended.

The journey's highs and lows, sweat and bliss, happinesses and suffering—it's all interrelated; each depends on the other. Mindfulness practice includes recognizing the interwoven, interbeing nature of all things so that we don't get lost in the ups and downs. Just so, every community goes through many peaks and valleys of conflict and reconciliation. No community stays on plateaus forever. Conflicts are the arduous uphills of community life, and they are the path to peaks of communal harmony and compassion. Journeying through conflict strengthens community bonds and helps individual members heal and grow in ways that are impossible alone.

But if you try to climb a steep mountain without regular training, you will likely fall far short of the top. I have witnessed many conflicts where people give up because the ascent looks too steep. It's not because the mountain is actually too high, but because they haven't trained by climbing smaller mountains already. There is no confidence and experiential faith in the reconciliation practice or in themselves. If you live in a family or community, you can use the small conflicts of daily life as a training ground to strengthen your reconciliation skills.

In my years of living in and visiting communities worldwide, I have observed a secret ingredient to communal harmony and reconciliation. Can you guess what that is? I invite you to pause, take a few breaths, ponder this question, and take a few guesses. I'm curious what your experience tells you. In my experience, the secret sauce of community reconciliation and harmony is consistency. The art of relationship building and conflict transformation needs sustained and ongoing practice, both individually and collectively, for people to learn, strengthen, and develop trust in each other and the process.

Reconciliation is not merely a destination—it's a process of exercising our muscles. In the steep ascents of community conflict, the muscular fibers of reconciliation and harmony get flexed, stretched, and regularly torn apart. Each time they tear, an opportunity to heal and bond together even more strongly arises. With each hill you climb together, your confidence and trust to overcome even bigger peaks grows. When you train often in conflict reconciliation, your capacity to cross over many mountains and valleys of communal challenges will be unsurpassed. No canyons will be too wide and steep to cross and no peaks too high to summit; your confidence and trust in yourselves and each other's capacity will lead the way.

It may sound like common sense to make time for consistent reconciliation meetings each month to strengthen a community's relational well-being. But what is common sense is not always common practice. This is our choice. There are many tools at our disposal to regularly nurture reconciliation and trust in order to care for and prevent unnecessary disharmony. We will dive into these skills in the following chapters, starting with the key process of Beginning Anew.

# CHAPTER 10

# BEGINNING ANEW WITH ONESELF

*The question is whether we are practicing loving ourselves. Because loving ourselves means loving our community.*
—THICH NHAT HANH

*People come here to find a group of people who love one another. They don't come here merely to see you as individuals; they come to see you as a community of love. If they are going to find grace and help, it isn't so much from each one of you as an individual, but from the grace that is present in a community of love.*
—THOMAS MERTON

The ability to live in harmony often eludes us. In a world filled with strife, hatred, and war, is there any more pressing question for humanity than how to heal old conflicts, live peacefully among our neighbors, and partner together despite tensions? We may feel a deep wish for peace in the world, but until we can successfully transform conflicts within ourselves and our closest relationships—our friends, family members, neighbors, and coworkers—it is naive, if not ridiculous, to expect political groups, nations, and religious factions to do the same. We must begin anew within ourselves and then radiate this peace out to our closest relationships and widening community. The next chapter expounds the four components of the reconciliation process called

Beginning Anew using descriptions and stories of how communities, families, and friends use the practice in real life. But first, we will share the groundwork of Beginning Anew within oneself.

## Step One(self)

Beginning Anew is an inside job. Healing relationships has little to do with what others say or do. The true heart of reconciliation is within us. It is a relief to finally realize that the gateways to peace and reconciliation have been right here all along. Thay often said, "Brotherhood, sisterhood, and siblinghood always begin with oneself. Compassion always begins with oneself. The question is whether you are practicing." Our tendency is to focus on what others say or do, but turning the spotlight around is how real transformation takes place.

Most of us feed the mind of conflict in the following six ways:

1. We focus on others.

2. We blame others.

3. We praise ourselves.

4. We deny personal responsibility.

5. We share criticisms.

6. We ignore or run away from the situation.

Beginning Anew counters each of these tendencies by offering alternative responses. As such, a reconciliatory mind can be summed up in these six alternative ways:

1. Instead of focusing on others, we embrace our hurt feelings and reactions.

2. Instead of blaming, we express vulnerability and hurts honestly and compassionately.

3. Instead of praising ourselves, we appreciate others.

4. Instead of denying responsibility, we acknowledge our own contributions to the conflict.

5. Instead of sharing criticisms, we seek emotional support.

6. Instead of running away, we ask for support.

How would your relationships be if you responded in these ways during conflict? Pretty darn amazing, I bet! The goal here, though, is not to be perfect. Rather, our aim is to be kind toward ourselves whenever we notice the habitual self-protective and defensive tendencies that fuel the burning conflicts within. Once aware, we can pause, soften, and patiently, tenderly listen to ourselves. Then we can more easily take slow and gentle steps toward a reconciliatory mind. It is not easy work. But it *is* easier than endlessly staying in our habits of conflict.

## Resolving Conflict from Within

Both the Buddha and his foremost disciples consistently offered teachings to help people identify and transform the roots of conflict. Mahamaudgalyayana, one of the Buddha's greatest students, encouraged his younger brethren to discern what intentions and behaviors make them difficult to be around. He likened a practitioner to a young woman looking in the mirror. If she sees a smudge or blemish on her face, she doesn't start rubbing the mirror to clean her face. Instead, she wipes her face directly to remove the dirt and filth. If the woman looks in the mirror and sees no blemish, she rejoices—her face is clean and bright. Just so, when a practitioner recognizes that no negative qualities are appearing, they delight in their wholesome state of mind.

Every one of us has such personality blemishes: defensive judgments, blaming others, superiority complexes, irritable outbursts, and many other unskillful tendencies that cause ourselves and others to suffer. When we find ourselves in conflict, can we look in the mirror to account for our own blemishes and contributions? Focusing solely on others' faults is merely scrubbing the mirror. Mahamodgalyayana encourages us to find our true power of harmony from within. Otherwise, we will repeat the cycles of conflict and suffering in situation after situation, relationship after relationship.

Removing blemishes is everyone's work, even seasoned Dharma teachers. About twenty years ago, I heard a teaching from Sister Annabel (Sister Chan Duc), one of Thich Nhat Hanh's two most senior disciples. In an angelic yet grounded manner, she shared, "With mindfulness, I notice when I have judgements about other people. I've realized that if I let these judgments continue in my mind, they will bring suffering to my community. So, when I notice them, I stop, come back to my breathing, and embrace my judgmental thoughts and feelings. I breathe with them tenderly and compassionately, helping them return back to store consciousness." I felt very moved to hear such an esteemed, wise teacher share so humbly about her own judgments and how diligently she cares for the roots of conflict in herself.

In her book *All about Love*, bell hooks similarly and bluntly writes: "Two things that are very bad for community making are judgment and blaming." It can be so alluring to focus on others' deficits as the cause of our suffering. But Sister Annabel's insight was clear—the roots of conflict lie in our mental state, not the objects of our judgment and blame.

If we take a moment to reflect on the conflicts in our lives, what blemishes do we see in the mirror? How can we care for them before the next argument or dispute rolls around?

## Rain before Rainbows

When I was aspiring to be a monk in Plum Village, I learned a gatha, or meditation poem, for watering the garden. You breathe in while reciting the first line, and breathe out with the second. It goes, "The rain of compassion and understanding/Can transform the dry desert into a vast fertile plain."

Being in a difficult conflict can feel like walking through a scorching desert. We desperately want to get out of the sun, but we can't find any shade. Often, we try to solve the problem by hashing things out with the other person right away. If I am still feeling upset, angry, or defensive, things almost always get worse. How many times do we have to learn that lesson?

What we really need is the rain of compassion to relieve the suffering inside ourselves. Self-compassion is the bedrock of making real peace with others, and mindfulness is the foundation. When I touch the deep well of compassion within myself, my pain is relieved, and I no longer depend solely on others to unburden my pain and justify my anger. Practicing self-compassion involves three steps. First, recognize how you honestly feel in your body and mind, allowing whatever is alive in this moment—be it rage, numbness, indifference, pity, judgment, annoyance, skepticism, disgust, fear, or anything else. I find it helpful to place one hand on my abdomen to feel the steady flow of my breathing and then, once my attention is stable, to allow the difficult sensations to be fully felt with my whole awareness. Focusing on the breath and bodily sensations helps disengage from obsessive thinking while embracing the roots of difficult feelings. Second, bring to mind that suffering and imperfections are part of being human. Everyone suffers; everyone endures conflict at times; everyone gets angry and makes mistakes. Recognize that you're not alone—it's okay to suffer. Last, treat yourself like a real friend. How would you treat a beloved companion going through a similar difficulty? Try to treat yourself the same way, with loving attention and nonjudgmental understanding. Whenever the fire of afflictions, practice stopping, pausing, breathing, and embracing the difficult feelings with all the kindness in your heart, again and again. Practicing in this way, compassion will permeate your heart and peace will descend upon your soul like a cool summer rain.

Some years ago, I had a serious conflict with a fellow community member. For weeks, I was so furious and resentful that I could not look her in the face. Every day, my mind ran circles around the mean things she said to me, what she was telling others, and how unfairly blamed and criticized I felt. The fire of anger consumed me from morning to night. Feeling exhausted and desperate to relieve myself from this bottomless well of suffering, I redoubled my efforts to compassionately come home to myself. Every time I noticed I was jumping back on the fury train, I paused what I was doing, closed my eyes, placed my hand on my abdomen, and allowed myself to feel the raging fire of resentment and fear burning in my core. Gentle breaths and tender pauses felt like cool misty raindrops slowly dripping onto the wildfires within. Whenever I noticed thoughts racing like the wind and my heart pounding with adrenaline again, I disengaged from the heady windstorm and took shelter in my breathing belly.

Several days later, I woke up before dawn and settled my groggy mind and body onto the meditation cushion. As I listened to the rhythm of my breathing, I realized something inside felt different. *Oh, I'm not seething with anger this morning. Actually, I'm mostly just feeling really sad. I'm the one who is suffering here.* The lightning clouds storming my heart for weeks had finally burst open. Raindrops streamed down my cheeks like an old creek flooding dry, barren soil. After some time, the clouds dispersed and patches of blue sky emerged. It felt like waking up from a dark dream to realize how much I was the one needing loving attention—not others. The other person's behaviors mattered so little to me now, compared to my own well-being. I had truly come home.

During my years at Deer Park Monastery, I studied with a remarkable Vietnamese Zen teacher, Thay Phuoc Tinh. He once shared in a talk, "Life is really all about learning how to laugh and how to cry." I was surprised to hear about crying from such a masterful teacher. Apparently, he had to learn how to cry, too. Crying is an indispensable mammalian emotional faculty that is largely lost in our present culture of masculinity. As a teenager growing up in the United States, I must have unlearned how to cry. I have never seen my dad cry, and he once shared with me that he never saw his dad cry either. Actually, I don't recall seeing any man cry while growing up. I learned instead to develop steel armor against emotional vulnerability, shield attacks to masculinity, and suppress weak feelings. Such armor, of course, comes with a significant loss. To reclaim access to the intimacy of their inner life, men especially need to relearn the cleansing and rejuvenating power of tears. The art of grieving is married to the art of happiness. Crying opens the floodgates of self-love, submerging a wounded heart in the soothing waters of tenderness and compassion. For myself, crying is often the best preliminary work for a successful reconciliation. So, before any significant reconciliation, let loose some of those bags of tender saltwater, even if just a drop or two. Remember, the way out is in.

## Listening Deeply

Crying, self-compassion, and self-reflection are all forms of cleaning up our own emotional living space. Once we've swept, mopped, and generally tidied things up inside, more room opens up for others. Herein lies the last key to reconciliation, which has little to do with what we say. Rather, it's how we hold space for others' experiences. If you are not ready to truly listen, then don't kid yourself—the work of Beginning Anew with yourself is unfinished. But when your presence is pure, listening deeply can be the lifeline of friendship, even during hard moments.

Thich Nhat Hanh frequently encouraged us to wholeheartedly listen with just one intention when someone is angry and suffering: giving the other person a chance to empty the suffering in their heart. You don't say anything, especially not to correct criticisms or mistaken views; you can share later when they are more receptive. For now, you just listen with 100 percent of your being so they can feel relieved. This is a superhero practice—powerfully effective but also deeply so difficult, especially when someone is blaming or criticizing us. Just listening to understand has saved so many moments of friendship for me. And it's not just for the other person—under the shell of their words of frustration, a sweet fruit of insight may be ripening for us both to hear.

# CHAPTER 11

# BEGINNING ANEW IN COMMUNITY

> *We have to consciously study how to be tender with each other until it becomes a habit because what was native has been stolen from us.*
>
> —AUDRE LORDE

The art of reconciliation has many forms, colors, and designs to choose from; the following chapter explores the practice of Beginning Anew, a signature practice of the Plum Village tradition taught by Thich Nhat Hanh and Sister Chan Khong over many years. In her memoir *Learning True Love*, Sister Chan Khong writes, "After many years of working with Beginning Anew in Plum Village, both with monastics and laypeople, I have seen it work. Palestinians and Israelis, couples, parents and children, brothers and sisters, monks and nuns have all practiced Beginning Anew there. It is part of the heart of Plum Village, and I believe it is one of the key practices that helped turn our dream of Plum Village into a living, breathing, thriving reality."[35]

Beginning Anew is both a concrete reconciliation method for families or friends and a daily life practice to embody gratitude, humility, and compassion. There are four main components:

1. sharing appreciations,

2. expressing regrets,

3. voicing hurts,

4. and asking for support.

The tradition is to begin by placing a vase of flowers between two people or in the middle of the group, a reminder that each of us is a uniquely beautiful flower that needs love and attention to bloom brightly. Whoever wishes to speak may pick up the vase, place it in front of them, and begin with "flower watering" (sharing appreciations). When that person speaks, the others listen with wholehearted attention.

Beginning Anew can be applied in a wide range of forms. For example, you can practice the four steps weekly or monthly with your housemates, partner, family, or community. You can also practice on singular occasions when conflicts need more caring attention. For more serious disputes, it can be helpful to invite a third party experienced with this practice to listen, offer empathy to both parties, and mediate the sharing.

In my travels to various communities, I was surprised by how many experienced difficult conflicts, yet so few practiced reconciliation regularly. Just a small handful of communities in the Plum Village tradition practiced Beginning Anew on a monthly basis. People were familiar with the practice and believed it was valuable, but what is common knowledge is not always common practice. The wisdom of reconciliation is in its practice, not its concept. Beginning Anew is much more than mere conflict resolution. It is an art of relational cultivation that needs tending to regularly if not every day, similar to growing a garden. Instead of waiting until the weeds have ambushed your beds, Beginning Anew, like any reconciliatory method, is most effective when practiced regularly to steadily water the good seeds between one another, strengthen relational roots, and care for withering or ailing relationships right away. With regular Beginning Anew practice, individuals tend to begin applying each of the four elements to various relationships in their life, helping daily interactions feel more invigorated, supportive, and renewed. I have witnessed and experienced this often in community life, and it has been one of the greatest gifts of healing in my life.

Now, we will dive into a few real stories of Beginning Anew as if we were sitting at the community table ourselves. Then we will explore each of the four steps in detail with explanations and examples of how the practice is realistically expressed and embodied through myriad communal relationships.

*** 

While visiting communities around the world, Vanessa and I immediately fell in love with the close-knit connections at Meppel mindfulness community in the Netherlands. Luckily, their monthly Beginning Anew landed on the first weekend of our visit, and they were delighted for us to join them that afternoon. A vase of fresh wildflowers, mostly yellow daisies and purple lilacs freshly cut from their meditation garden, sat on the dining table with us. Greetje poured sweet and spicy herbal tea into each of our clay-fired mugs. Wim was facilitating and started off the meeting: "Today we speak in English, for our guests, but also because we like it very much," he said with a warm grin. "Most of the time, we only have nice things to say. But sometimes, you know, we have to say some difficult things too. So just be prepared," he said, looking over at us as we chuckled together. The atmosphere was relaxed yet increasingly focused. Wim concluded, "We will start with ten minutes' silence, just breathing together." Wim invited three sounds of the bell, and our small community sipped our tea, savored the warm family vibes, and contemplated silently. Another bell sounded, and then each person began to share appreciations, one by one.

Greetje thanked Joan for clearing some brush and weeds in the garden; Wim appreciated Rudi for taking care of the chicken poop this month in his place; Joan celebrated everyone for gardening together the last few weeks and expressed her gratitude for realizing her dream of living in such a kind and supportive community; Rudi said he loved their playful beach outing together last month. This went on for about ten more minutes until everyone seemed satiated with appreciations. Then Wim spoke again as facilitator.

"Now people can share apologies or hurts if you have them." After a minute of silence, Rudi spoke, "Wim, I really like working in the garden together. And I know I like to do my own thing that is different from others' ideas. But last week, and this happens sometimes, you told me not to garden my way and to do something else in the garden too strongly. And that makes me upset when you don't listen to my ideas. I would like you to let me do my own garden ways sometimes too." Although there was some tension in Rudi's voice, Wim listened calmly, looking directly at him and nodding every so often. Everyone was quiet after Rudi shared; there was no discernable urgency or distress. Eventually, Wim responded: "Thank you, Rudi, for telling me how you feel. I also very much like working in the garden with you. And yes, I know I have the habit of telling people what to do sometimes, not very kindly, and being strong in my ideas." He continued, "I'm sorry I hurt your feelings. I will try to stop and breathe more if I am feeling some frustration, especially during the garden. Yes, we have some areas that we agree on for gardening, and in other areas, everyone is free to do as they wish." Joan and Greetje listened serenely, almost undetectable smiles on their faces as the men made their peace.

Several minutes later, Wim closed the sharing with three more sounds of the bell. Greetje turned to me and Vanessa and asked, "Was that okay for you two? We have some difficulties sometimes, but it's normal for us," she said warmly. She added with a lighthearted laugh, "If we don't talk about it, it gets worse, I'm afraid!" Vanessa and I felt awed by their tiny community's powerful trust and ease. Even with two new guests, they were able to speak vulnerably and comfortably in each of the Beginning Anew steps. Vanessa shared, "You all clearly have something very special here. Thank you so much for including us. We are learning so much from you." Vanessa's words, sharing that their intimate ways together had a small yet meaningful ripple into our world, landed like sunshine on their peaceful faces.

\*\*\*

At Morning Sun Mindfulness Community, we regularly faced the public, but during Beginning Anew sessions among the residents, we faced each other in the naked honesty of our interpersonal lives. It always felt like we were meeting as a true community in the sincerest way possible. A unique power was forged between us as we leaned into the uncomfortable intimacy of our beautiful yet messy lives together. When we turned back toward the public during retreats, our community radiated a genuine closeness and trust. People coming from outside could feel it; you cannot fake this kind of love.

Beginning Anew happened every second Thursday of the month. From May to September, we usually circled up on the beach of Blueberry Pond. Those facing the water enjoyed the golden orange rays falling behind the circle. The other half watched the same rays bouncing off the luminous faces of our Sangha siblings. From fall to spring, we lit the wood fire stove and some candles on the altar to keep us cozily connected. Such beauty nurtured joy and safety in each moment of our shared circle.

Each Beginning Anew was unique because a different resident facilitated according to their personal inspiration; we were not afraid to experiment with the traditional form. The first few months we started meeting regularly, we only did flower watering! It was so much fun, feeding our joyful togetherness. A few months later, Joaquin gathered us in groups of three to share the first two steps: appreciations and regrets. On yet another occasion, Honey Bear boldly and skillfully invited us to focus on expressing hurts and requests with one another. Another month, we gathered silently and wrote Beginning Anew love letters to someone special in our lives. We didn't read or share the letters with each other, but the group energy supported us in looking deeply at our lives to see where reconciliation was needed.

I remember coming home late one evening and joining a circle of eight residents already twenty minutes into their sharing. There had been so much negativity among staff at the mental health clinic where I worked that I was feeling exhausted, frustrated, and a bit hopeless. Upon entering the candlelit meditation hall, I saw people looking sweetly into each others' eyes while sharing appreciations or hurts. One resident, Sam, expressed gratitude for Lorraine's gorgeous centerpiece arrangements every Sunday. He then shared humbly about speaking his views too quickly to her one day instead of taking more time to listen to her. With open caring eyes and a deep, soft voice, Sam respectfully added that he was holding onto a hurt—she had criticized him a few times about not helping her more in her garden. He conveyed that he was already overwhelmed by his job and volunteer work; her garden wasn't his responsibility, and that was bothering him.

Lorraine waited a few moments and then responded, "Thank you very much for your honesty, Sam. I would much rather know when I do or say things that hurt people. I will think about what you said and try to be more careful with my words in the future." They looked each other in the eyes and smiled, and then it was over. Peace, gentleness, and respect infused the entire room. I sat, stunned by the dramatic change in my environment: in a matter of minutes, I traded a mental health hell realm for a heavenly friendship realm where hurts could be magically expressed and transformed into love. The communal kindness settled into my soul like a fresh breeze and my heavy mental fatigue drifted away effortlessly.

Whether in New Hampshire or elsewhere, I have seen communities everywhere reap the fruits of compassion, healing, and joy from this practice. Beginning Anew has been one of the most powerful blessings in my life in community; I hope you have the chance to explore it in your most cherished relationships as well. As we dive into each of the four steps in greater detail, I invite you to consider: What forms of Beginning Anew feel the most authentic, meaningful, and fun for you to try? Only you and your community will know what works. Consider relevance to both your communal or family culture as well as the suffering in those relationships—how can you apply Beginning Anew in genuinely supportive and uplifting ways? You can test out different approaches and enjoy the fruits of reconciliation right at home.

## The Healing Force of Appreciations

Whereas the foundation of reconciliation is an open heart, its cornerstone is an appreciative mind. As such, appreciations are the first step of Beginning Anew. As we saw in previous chapters, appreciations may appear lightweight, yet they have a mysterious power to open the door to greater respect, generating joy and healing old wounds. As Mary Poppins sings, "A spoonful of sugar helps the medicine go down." In this case, appreciations are both the sugar and the medicine! They are my go-to medicine whenever I feel irritated or resentful toward my partner, family, or community members. When I finally remember to consider what I cherish about them or how they have supported me in difficult times, my anger transforms almost instantly. It feels like jumping into a cool lake on a blistering summer day—the heat of resentment immediately washes away, restoring balance and clarity to my attitude.

When do you know that it is time to finally reconcile with someone following a conflict? A good indicator is your readiness to offer sincere appreciations; otherwise, you probably aren't ready. This first step of Beginning Anew is also the most important; ideally one should include at least four or five times as many appreciations as hurts. Taking time to share the full depth of one's appreciations provides a foundation of joy and respect, making the next, more vulnerable steps much easier.

When first practicing Beginning Anew as a community or family, it's okay to just focus on flower watering. If you've never tried appreciating one another for a full sixty minutes, I highly suggest you try—it is really fun! Feel free to experiment with different ways of making this practice enjoyable, engaging, and healing. Fern led our practice one evening as we gathered on beach chairs and wooden benches in front of Blueberry Pond, the clear blue waters and shiny green lily pads reflecting the golden rays of the slowly setting sun. Fern gave each of us some paper and pens and informed us that we would be writing an appreciation letter to the person on our left. She invited us to close our eyes in quiet contemplation for several minutes before writing all the qualities and gifts we treasure about this person. After about fifteen minutes, she surprised us with the task of writing another letter to the neighbor on our right. Upon finishing both, Fern surprised us again by inviting everyone to read their letters out loud to the group. Fern really earned our flowers that day. I remember the affectionate, glowing eyes of those hearing their letters and the beaming smiles of their neighbors—it was an unforgettably intimate evening in community.

These are my experiences of communal healing through the power of appreciation. But please don't take my word for it—experiment with this practice yourselves. When you are feeling resentful or angry with a friend or family member, try writing down ten things you appreciate most about them. Notice what happens. You may still feel some hurt inside, but has your attitude toward them shifted at all? Is there perhaps more openness, ease, calm, and, well, appreciation?

## The Power of Regret

In Beginning Anew, expressing regrets follows appreciations like rainbows after a gentle rain. Regrets or apologies are the truce that make the whole sky and earth beautiful again, no matter the night's previous storms. After sharing appreciations, offering apologies is the next natural medicine to clear any obstacles between affectionate minds. As such, it is the second foundational step of Beginning Anew. In *Life's Little Instruction Book*, H. Jackson Brown Jr. beautifully captures the essence of Beginning Anew's first two steps: "Never forget the nine most important words of any family: I love you. You are beautiful. Please forgive me."

Saying one's regrets out loud can deescalate tensions in almost any difficult situation and can transform our most undesirable behaviors and attitudes into new sources of relational trust, healing, and compassion. Conflicts may bring me to my knees in humility and regret. But from there, closer to the earth, I learn to love myself and others deeply and differently. We don't need to throw out the mistakes and conflicts of our lives, just the old habits that no longer serve us.

Some people are uncomfortable with feeling or expressing regrets because they are afraid of being trapped in a cage of guilt over the past or being too exposed by acknowledging mistakes in front of others.

But regrets help us learn from and transform the past into a more beautiful present and a stronger future. The word itself helps me to remember this—if I made a mistake, then I can "re-get" it the next time! This is the epitome of the Beginning Anew practice—there is always a chance to learn and love again, differently. Especially in community life, we grow up together, one mistake at a time.

## Self-Acceptance

The first and most crucial component of expressing regrets is self-acceptance. Once I've been able to acknowledge the suffering I've caused, I can begin offering myself slivers of self-compassion and forgiveness. By making peace with myself, disclosing errors to others becomes easier, less threatening, and even relieving. I no longer need to carry around the burdens of defensiveness, angry pride, or guilt.

Acceptance also waters the seed of humility, which is the heart of reconciliation and one of the greatest virtues in community life. Not everyone possesses this gift, yet anyone can learn it. Humility has the power to dismantle unlimited walls of pride and superiority-inferiority complexes and create emotional safety for ourselves and numberless beings. By respectfully laying down our natural human messiness in humble acceptance before ourselves and others, what conflicts can emerge? As a young man raised in the United States, I associated humility with weakness, passivity, and inferiority. However, true humility is anything but weak. It takes courage, integrity, and strength to accept and disclose one's unskillful qualities, learn from mistakes, and reap the wisdom.

## From Regret to Wisdom

Perhaps the best way to convey the power of this second step in Beginning Anew is through stories of my own community blunders that later revealed themselves as blessings in disguise. Several years ago, I was trying to advocate for more diverse leadership in my local Sangha's

Care Taking Council (CTC.) Being a White, straight man with some good intentions and much less skillfulness, things went awry very quickly. I had been aware of our CTC's homogeneous White racial identity for a few years and tried talking to the community founders, but the conversations were going nowhere. Feeling frustrated and determined to change things, I decided to share my desire for a more diverse CTC that better represented the spectrum of people and diverse strengths in our larger community. During a Sangha-wide meeting with everyone present, strands of frustration and criticism weaved into my tone as I called on others to take action. I believed I was being helpful by using my privilege as a White-presenting person to help address these leadership-level inequities.

After I finished sharing, Melonie, a Vietnamese American woman and regular facilitator, quickly responded. "David, I am feeling quite triggered by what you are saying. In so many nonprofits and Sanghas I am the only woman of color in the room. So, everyone asks me to step up and fulfill those seats, again and again. I'm tired of that. You don't think our CTC cares about us, but they do. And we already have some BIPOC facilitators here in our Sangha. So, let's focus on how good that is. And another thing: Ryan is taking Vietnamese classes, and that helps some of us feel more at home here—he's trying to meet us on our level. We need more support like that, if you want to know. "

My sister's fiery response was the last thing I had anticipated. I felt shocked, confused, ashamed, and unable to process my feelings on the spot. I mustered up a superficial public apology and then left the meeting early.

Over the next few days, I called friends who were well-versed in cultural humility. About a week later, I felt ready to ask Melonie to go for a walk together, an invitation she warmly accepted. We met at a nearby trailhead and walked for about fifteen minutes over a forested ridge filled with beech, poplar, and white birch trees before reaching a small peak with a rocky cliff edge that offered an expansive view to the south. We perched ourselves on a semi-smooth slab of granite rock, looking over the green undulating canopy that stretched for miles beneath us. Using the granite as our tea table, I poured two steaming cups of chai from my thermos. We agreed to sit silently for several minutes together to ground ourselves and absorb Mother Earth's exquisite beauty. This gave me time to calm my nerves and muster the courage to bring up last week's uncomfortable exchange.

With the warm cup of tea in my hands, I eventually asked, "Melonie, I'm wondering if there is anything you would like to share about the Sangha meeting we had a few weeks ago?"

Melonie responded, "Yes, thank you for asking, David." She contemplated for a minute and then said, "I think it was your tone of frustration and criticism that watered my seeds of feeling triggered. For a topic like that, I would rather people ask me what I need to feel supported in the Sangha than try to push through their agenda. Because then it feels like I'm just a sign of diversity for people. I think we can build a more diverse Sangha by focusing on supporting those who are already here, asking us how we are doing, and celebrating what we do."

Melonie finished talking, but her words seemed to hover in the air between us like a misty fog. I sipped my tea while savoring the crisp forest air and silence following her sharing. After one or two minutes, I turned to her and said, "I can better understand why my words were upsetting, and I'm very grateful for you telling me. I feel some regret for not talking to you individually or in a small group before blurting this out in front of the whole Sangha. I think that approach would make it easier for all of us to better understand the issues. Also, I notice a pattern in myself that sometimes I feel doubtful authority figures will really listen to me unless I share in a strong way. I'm sorry my angry and critical tone was triggering for you."

I paused to drink some tea and consider what else to share. I continued, "I also hear you, Melonie, about feeling pressure as one of the few leaders of color in our Sangha and perhaps feeling tokenized in our community or elsewhere. I really appreciate you sharing that so I can keep learning to be a more skillful friend to you and others moving forward."

"Thank you, David," Melonie said, a grin on her face. She added, "I'm also sorry, David, for being upset and angry with you during the meeting. That is something I want to work on, not to be so triggered during meetings. "

"Thank you for sharing that, Melonie," I said, "but I also hope that you feel comfortable being frustrated and upset sometimes; you deserve the space and support to feel whatever you need to feel. It must not be easy being one of the few women of color in our community and constantly dealing with these issues." I noticed a subtle sigh of relief in Melonie as she looked out over the forest; I knew our reconciliation was complete.

I never intended harm or even knew that Melonie was triggered by my words until she spoke out. Nonetheless, she suffered from my ways of thinking and communicating. Every person is a unique universe of experiences, perceptions, cultural conditioning, sources of power and privilege, and relational habits. Even if I am trying my best, it is inevitable that my actions or speech will hurt others. Hurts are unavoidable; conflicts are unavoidable. Yet learning is possible; reconciliation is possible. The choice is ours, and we can choose to take responsibility for our mistakes.

## Sharing Hurts

After expressing regret, the third step is owning our hurts and sharing about them with respect and kindness. Conflicts expose our tenderness, our wounds. But this can be a gift, if we allow it. Beginning Anew offers us a path back home to heal both fresh sores and old hurts within us and between us. During difficult conflicts, flower watering is not enough. We also have to let our beloved partner, friend, or community know when we are hurting and trust their willingness to love. But most of us never learned how to safely share about and entrust our pain to others. Typically, when my feelings get hurt, my first instinct is to recoil and hurt the other person back—maybe you can relate? Most people act out their hurts either by getting angry and accusatory or by suppressing their resentments and withdrawing in silent fury. As we know very well, both options cause a fair amount of collateral damage.

There are two kinds of hell. Most people are familiar with the fiery one, loud with rage, resentment, and blame. But perpetual silence around conflict is the "cold hell" and just as terrible. Such isolation and withdrawal freeze the heart, ices communication, withers relationships, and destroys the needed warmth for intimacy to survive. Respectfully and sincerely letting our loved ones know we are in pain is the key to melting the ice. Sharing our hurts in the context of Beginning Anew invites us into a middle way between the extremes of suffocating suppression or overwhelming rage. But this is not an easy task. It takes vulnerability, courage, and skill to voice one's hurts while not further perpetuating anger, blame, and isolation. Even when doing our best, sharing hurts can still be messy.

How can we safely and skillfully deliver the message of hurt feelings when the terrain is filled with emotional landmines? Here are three strategies that have guided me through countless interpersonal difficulties:

1. Sharing in a way that lets love in

2. Accepting the other's weaknesses

3. Asking when is a good time to talk.

The first point invites us to speak in ways that both acknowledge our pain and let love in. The key is expressing the hurt with genuine vulnerability. This disarms people's fears of criticism and invites their compassion for your shared suffering to grow. For example, you can approach someone by saying, "My friend, I feel nervous to share this with you, but I'm suffering with something you said to me last week. I hope that you can hear me, because I care about you and our friendship." This nurtures compassion, trust, and appreciation in the other, inviting them to hear the hurt feelings more easily. Although working up the courage to share a big hurt can feel gut-wrenching, finally communicating with our friend or beloved can produce the same intensity of relief and joy. The reward of a harmonious and renewed connection is worth all the effort it takes to get there.

## Accepting the Other's Weaknesses

During my early twenties, when I first started living in a monastery, I put all the monks up on lofty pedestals and glorified their perfect behavior. Meanwhile, I attributed any relationship difficulties to my own faults. I realized over the years how far off my projections were, and how unskillful some of the monks could also be at times. No matter who you live with or spend time with, everyone has weaknesses and suffering that propel them to act in unkind, inconsiderate, or unwise ways. Yes, even monks and nuns, even Dharma teachers—everybody.

The question is whether we can first recognize and then accept others' limitations while not heaping all the blame onto ourselves. Dumping all the blame on ourselves or shoving it solely onto others are two extremes that deny our nature of interbeing; every situation has myriad causes and conditions. Sharing regrets acknowledges our contributions toward others' suffering, whereas sharing hurts respects that our pain is partly caused by others. Acknowledging both allows for a true reconciliation.

When I find myself angrily in conflict—feeling hurt, ignored, disrespected, and so on, there comes a point when I recognize my own agency and feel willing to accept another's unskillfulness and forgive everyone involved, including myself. In his sermon "Loving Your Enemies," Martin Luther King Jr. says, "Forgiveness does not mean ignoring what has been done or putting a false label on an evil act. It means, rather, that the evil act no longer remains a barrier to the relationship."[36] Similarly, the intention of Beginning Anew is to communicate our pain to our friend or beloved so the wounds are no longer obstacles to loving connection. I may not condone the behaviors or let them continue hurting me, but I do accept the limitations of their emotional and spiritual development, just as I accept my own. From such acceptance, I can communicate my hurts or grievance with clarity, compassion, and strength.

## Find the Right Time to Share Hurts

When is a good time to share hurts? Personally, I am way more equipped to listen deeply to someone's suffering when I am prepared ahead of time. I may take several minutes to breathe and center myself beforehand or make silent intentions to help the other person suffer less and be truly there for them, just as if I were suffering. A few minutes of mindful breathing and grounding with this intention can make a phenomenal difference. At times, I have said to coworkers, friends, and family members, "I have something to share that is important to me and a bit difficult. Is now a good time for you to talk, or would you rather me share another time?" In all honesty, they may not want to hear about your hurts, either now or later! They may think, *Well, now is a bad time, but later will be worse!* But at least they can have a say in the matter, which already strengthens an atmosphere of safety and respect. The important message is that you are offering consideration, care, and choice in the midst of a vulnerable situation.

Mutual agreement of when and how to talk about a conflict is perhaps the most important factor in a successful reconciliation. Have you ever experienced someone dropping a grenade of grievances without warning? It can feel both shocking and overwhelming; it's hard to listen to someone's pain when you're thrown off-center. One time, a neighbor and Sangha member invited me over for a walk and tea without disclosing her intention of sharing grievances. I responded, "Oh, that sounds nice. But I'm making dinner, so why don't you come over and enjoy some stir fry with me? She came over, and we chatted amicably before dinner. After the meal, when I was ready to say goodnight, she said, "By the way, I have something to share with you," and then proceeded to share a ball of fiery grievances that had grown throughout the year. I was shocked by the onslaught. *Seriously,* I thought, *who comes over for dinner and then shares a bunch of angry resentments without warning?* I was caught off guard and suffered while listening to her. Her communication damaged my sense of trust and safety in our relationship, and it took several weeks before I felt safe enough to talk again. She later apologized for her explosive speech without warning and promised to do differently in the future. With the support of another community member, we reconciled the conflict and reestablished peaceful terms.

Sure enough, a few months later, another problem arose between us—I will be honest, it was not an easy friendship! This time, though, she said, "David, I really do care about you as a friend. And what you said has upset me and I feel really angry. Can you listen to me now?" I could see she was trying to communicate differently with me, even though she was really angry. I agreed to come back a few hours later with the support of a mutual friend, which was very helpful. Honestly, though, it was not easy to listen to her this time either! However, because of her different approach—because we agreed about when and how to talk about the conflict—I was able to center myself and listen with more compassion, as much as I could muster. I really heard her this time. Underneath her rage was a deep, old pain that I was unknowingly and unskillfully triggering because of my blind spots as a cisgender man. We met again a few days later, and I reflected back all that I had understood. My friend responded that she had never felt so heard by a man in her whole life when she was angry. By expressing her consideration and patience for me, she had invited deep listening and compassion back into our friendship.

## A Real Family

Sharing hurts in a community or family context can be done very creatively and compassionately. I would like to share a story about this practice from when I lived in an intentional community in Europe. It was Alejandro's turn to lead Beginning Anew, and he called me a few days before; I was in charge of organizing. "Honestly, David, I'm not a big fan of Beginning Anew. Yes, it has its strengths and drawbacks. But what are your thoughts about me leading a little differently? I want to focus on the third and fourth steps, and I have a different method to share." Alejandro was skilled in nonviolent communication and a seasoned mindfulness practitioner.

So, I responded, "That's amazing, brother, it would be a gift for us to learn from you. If nothing else, your different approach may help us understand what we're still uncomfortable with." This is the magic of community—diverse gifts and methods of community building can manifest unexpectedly. Why limit ourselves to what we already know?

Alejandro started our gathering with ten minutes of meditation and reflection. During the silence, he shared in a warm and tender voice, "Dear friends, I invite you to listen to see if there is some grievance or hurt that has not yet been expressed but wants to be heard. No pressure, just listen." After the meditative reflection, he spoke to our group with familiarity and encouragement. "Dear community, we are like a family here, or at least, that's what I think our aim is. Tonight, we have a chance to share openly with each other, not letting obstacles remain between us. This is a safe atmosphere to share and be present for one another. We will practice sharing hurts or grievances and asking for support. To begin, I will invite us to say the following phrase three times together, 'I see your practice supporting me, and I support your practice.'" We spoke the mantra in unison. It was grounding, affirming, encouraging, and even celebratory. Alejandro continued, "I invite each person to start and end their sharing with this phrase. Now I welcome each of us to share any hurts with someone else in the group. The rest of us will listen."

After a few people had already spoken, I felt my heart beating faster, urging me to speak. Earlier this year I had written a Beginning Anew letter to Stefan, one of our founding teachers, but we never talked about it. I felt the burden still weighing on our friendship and working relationship. Our communication had become distant. I bowed in and looked toward him. "Stefan, I see your practice supporting me, and I support your practice." Then, totally unanticipated, we both started grinning widely and joyfully at each other. It was like the curtains hiding the intimacy between us had drawn back, nothing obscuring our genuine love and friendship. Some moments later, I resumed, "Stefan, I feel uncomfortable not sharing my depth of appreciations for you first, but I'm giving this method a try. I'm still bothered that you invited me to participate in the Care Taking Council and then after a few months of attending, I stopped hearing about when the meetings were taking place. It seems you didn't want me there anymore. I wish you had communicated directly with me that you didn't think I was a good fit. I know you are extremely busy with large family and work responsibilities. But it still really hurt, because I need to feel like I matter to you, our communication matters to you, and that my contributions matter too."

At this point, the listener has an opportunity to empathetically reflect back what they heard, and ask if their reflections were accurate. The one sharing hurts may say "yes" and "thank you," or they may further clarify how they actually felt. There can be a back and forth exchange until the person feels adequately heard and understood. The listener can then share their personal response to the grievance. Stefan began responding, "David, I remember reading this from you in your letter, your beautiful long letter to me last summer, which I so deeply appreciated. I know that communication between us, and the lack thereof is something that you've brought up other times as well. Something that I've been realizing with raising my children is ..."

I thought that I knew what Stefan was going to say—that raising children is so time- and energy-consuming, he didn't have the emotional bandwidth for much else, that he sometimes drops one of the many balls he is carrying, and he's very sorry for all that. However, that was just my story about Stefan in the moment—my wrong perceptions of him. What he actually said was, "David, I'm slowly accepting in myself that communication with others is just something that doesn't come easily for me. And I'm sorry that this unskillful quality in me has been so hard for you while living here." I was shocked and moved to hear Stefan speak to me with such humility, bare honesty, and care. My face felt like a thin earthen surface barely covering a geyser breaking through from underneath. The room was dark, lit only by candles. Could others see the streams flowing down my cheeks? The well of old hurts had finally poured itself to the surface, clearing out and cleaning everything inside.

Through the tears, I could see Stefan not merely as a teacher, founder, and administrative leader, but as a human—one with weaknesses, limitations, and tender humility. I could see him now as a real teacher—not someone who maintains flawless behavior, unfettered speech, or impeccable virtue. Rather, someone who acknowledges and embraces their shortcomings as a full human being. Stefan and I both overcame our communication shortcomings that evening by sharing our utmost vulnerability and trust. In lowering ourselves in humility, we raised each other up even higher.

## Asking for Support

The last major step of Beginning Anew is asking for support. This exercise in humility comes very naturally after the third step of sharing our wounds. Whether from one's partner, family, colleagues, or community members, requesting help can feel vulnerable or even terrifying. At the same time, acknowledging one's needs and identifying support is no less than an act of personal empowerment and liberation—it transforms feelings of isolation, helplessness, and pride into friendship, humility, and gratitude for the interdependent nature of human relationships. Marshall Rosenberg, the founder of nonviolent communication, famously expressed that the number one reason people's needs are not met is *unclear requests*. By naming and voicing what we need or wish for the most, whether to others, one's higher power, or to ourselves, we are opening the doors to receiving what we need most.

The art of identifying and voicing one's needs is an enormous skill set in community life, where it is easy to feel lost in a sea of competing demands, voices, and relationships; one's needs easily become drowned out. It takes courage, trust, and humility to place ourselves at the center of our lives and to feel worthy enough to ask our friends, family, and community for the nourishment we need and deserve. This practice slices through our society's deeply ingrained messages that we must overcome hardships and succeed in all endeavors by ourselves alone—"pull ourselves up by our bootstraps," as the saying goes, yet an impossible task.

Asking for support is also a true gift to others. It teaches them how to best love us. It is like giving our beloved a recipe for our happiness. Instead of playing a guessing game, they can love us in the ways we most need and want. In return, we offer our happiness—the most precious gift of all.

At the same time, telling someone what we need or want is an invitation, not a guarantee or entitlement. What others can or are willing to offer may look different. If you have asked for support, you have done your work; now let go. So often, the act of asking for support, even before any concrete action takes place, already relieves much suffering. Just feeling heard, understood, and known in our community is powerful medicine. Releasing expectations can help avoid narrow thinking about how such support may eventually be offered or unexpectedly show up. Trust that your needs will be met when life conditions and timing are favorable.

Asking for help reestablishes bridges of compassion and connection during reconciliations as well as during the heat of challenging moments. Both community life and romantic partnerships offer ample opportunities to ask for support, partly because it is so easy to feel vulnerable, hurt, and afraid in our closest relationships. One of my former partners was very gifted in this art of loving speech, much more than myself. If we started to argue, she would wisely and openheartedly ask, "Can you please just stop, listen, and be there for me right now?" Her humility and loving speech reassured my reactive brain that we were on the same side, that it was safe to trust each other in the midst of a painful and frustrating exchange. My triggered defense walls could then go down and the caring forces within my fortified castle felt safe enough to come out again and reconcile.

In my work as a child and family therapist, I hear many men, and especially fathers, say that the most difficult task for them is asking for support. In *The Will to Change*, bell hooks writes, "The reality is that men are hurting and that the whole culture responds to them by saying, 'Please do not tell us what you feel.'"[37] From an early age, boys and men are encouraged to suppress their feelings and deal with them on their own—the antithesis of asking for support. This emotional isolation creates untold hardships not only for individuals, but for whole families and communities.

As a cis man, asking for support has not come easily to me. Flower watering, I've got down; apologies, covered; sharing hurts, I have learned. But asking for support, that's another beast! I experienced this pitfall recently with my partner. The two of us went on an ice skating date, and while showing off my teenage skills, of course I took an embarrassing fall. I got up just fine, but my neck and shoulders cramped up that night. The next morning, my partner said she would be happy to give me a neck massage that night. We both arrived home late and by the time we were in bed, she didn't think the injury was bothering me anymore, so she went to sleep. Instead of asking for the long-awaited neck rub under her healing touch, I started feeling frustrated and resentful. The coveted massage became a symbol for her loving care, what I wanted so much but could not ask for myself. I didn't want to ask, I wanted her to ask me. Though she was tired, if I had just asked, she would have surely sat up and soothed my tender neck. The minor hurt was tumbling downhill, and a childish voice inside of me was beginning its tantrum, saying, "You said you would massage me, but you didn't. You don't care about me; you don't consider my needs." The reinforcing loop of resentment and blame moved me further away from the love I desired.

I sat up in bed and followed my breathing to steady and calm my tumultuous mind. My partner noticed I was awake and asked, "Are you okay, honey?" I lit a candle on my nightstand and then honestly revealed that I was upset with her for not giving me the message she had promised. She listened patiently, especially to the pride and fear in my childlike, masculine heart. After listening, she said, "Sweetheart, I didn't think your neck was bothering you anymore." Then she requested, "You need to ask me for what you need. I think this is difficult for you. You can ask me, but I won't ask for you." So, I asked her sweetly for the long-awaited massage. Just moments afterward, we both fell into a deep sleep, the tension in my neck partly gone but the ache in my heart totally dissolved.

## Appreciation Sandwich

There is one last, optional mini-step to properly finish a Beginning Anew session—a final flower watering. It's like finishing a meal with a cup of honey-ginger tea—one or two gratitudes helps digest the full meal of reconciliation. These closing appreciations are literally "reminding" our minds that wellsprings of love and gratitude are still surrounding any hurts.

Neuroscience research tells us that it takes five positive interactions to make up for a single negative interaction. A friend of mine, Dr. Rick Hanson, is a neuroscientist and meditation teacher who famously summarized the human brain's natural negativity bias: "The brain is like Velcro for negative experiences, but Teflon for positive ones."[38] Dr. Hanson encourages people to "take in the good" by frequently sharing positive experiences. Flower watering is just that—training awareness to see the good in each other more than what is missing. It is not enough to focus only on our suffering.

## Letting Go

With many conflicts, Beginning Anew helps restore harmony and ease, and the friendship bounces back even stronger than before. But not always. Even if we practice every step of Beginning Anew wholeheartedly, there is no guarantee things will be all hunky dory again. We cannot predict or control how others will respond, whether they will offer sincere reconciliation themselves, and whether the friendship will bloom again. How the relationship unfolds depends partly on us, but largely on countless circumstances beyond our control. Sometimes, Beginning Anew salvages the relationship, but the tender wounds still need to lie dormant for another season or two. Silence may be the most healing step.

While living at Deer Park Monastery many years ago, two of my friends, a laywoman and a nun, had an ongoing conflict. The lay woman invited the abbot, Brother Phap Dung, to facilitate a Beginning Anew and the nun accepted the invitation. After it was over, the laywoman confided her suffering to the abbot: while she had sincerely expressed every step of Beginning Anew, she felt the nun had offered no genuine appreciations or apologies. Brother Phap Dung told her, "The Beginning Anew is finished, and you have both shared to the best of your ability. Now, it's time to let it go. Practice putting it down. This is the practice." His firm, clear, and compassionate guidance helped my friend stop the conflict from running on and on in her mind. We are responsible only for our own honest inner work. That is enough to be happy about. The rest is letting go.

## Beginning Now

Many of these stories show that we don't need to live in a community of jerks to experience difficult relationships. We can live next door to Dharma teachers, bodhisattvas, and beloved friends, and still encounter hard times. But if you can reconcile tensions and heartbreaks with those you live and work intimately with, then you will be able to do it with anyone. Conflicts are like different colored threads that are slowly sewn into a unique tapestry of community relationships over time. The more diverse the skillfully woven and lovingly tied threads, the stronger and more colorful the communal quilt. Gathering together every month in the spirit of Beginning Anew will naturally weave the precious skills of reconciliation into the heart of your daily lives. You can start with others or you can start with yourself. But be sure to start now.

# CHAPTER 12

# SHARING RACIAL HEALING AND WHITE AWARENESS

*Each of us has anger, hatred, depression, racial discrimination, and many other kinds of garbage in us, but there is no need for us to be afraid. In the same way a gardener knows how to transform compost into flowers, we can learn the art of transforming anger, depression, and racial discrimination into love and understanding.*

—THICH NHAT HANH

*This is the most precious gift true love offers—the experience of knowing we always belong.*

—BELL HOOKS

It was June 2020, just after the murder of George Floyd, and several residents of Morning Sun Mindfulness Community had just participated in our nearest Black Lives Matter protest in Brattleboro, Vermont. Decompressing over lunch, Albert Karcher, a Filipino-German-American friend, and I fell into conversation about the ways in which violent social discrimination had the power to tear apart our sense of safety in community, not only at the national level but also in our own small intentional communities.

"How's your book coming along, David?" I put down my food and confided, "Well to be honest, I'm at a crossroads. It feels wrong to write about communities without speaking to racism and Whiteness.* But I still have so much to learn myself." I could feel Albert's listening antenna tune in, his eyes kind and calm yet sparking with interest. I continued, "So, I feel hesitant to write about racial healing, especially as a White-presenting man, not to mention a straight, cis, US-American one." Albert nodded and chuckled, affirming this dilemma. I concluded, "What I really need is to keep listening to other teachers and working on myself."

Albert laughed and said, "Yes, we all need to keep learning and listening, that's true; there's no end there." I felt relieved, knowing Albert understood me. Then he added with a touch more assertiveness, "But David, you don't have to run away from all those privileges. With your community leadership and writing, you can use your privilege to support others on their path of White awareness." He added, "Besides, White people really need to educate and support each other more."

Albert's insights spoke to me. If I neglected this crucial realm of community-building in my book, I would feel like a coward. But if I did address it, then I would surely feel like a fool! Competently addressing this infinitely complex and painful topic was well beyond my knowledge and experience. Yet the benefit of being a fool is greater potential for learning. There was no turning away.

Yes, I accept I may never fully understand or be completely competent in antiracism work. But I can still take the next step forward in learning. It's the same for all of us: if we want to build a community that feels truly welcoming, safe, and collaborative for diverse groups of people, we must first step into the unknown, vulnerable, and often

---

* I have chosen to capitalize "White" as a racial identity, just as other racial identities are consistently capitalized. Many prominent teachers of racial healing believe that it is crucial for White people to recognize and embrace their own racial and cultural identity as a foundation for addressing the roots of racism, healing racial wounds, and engaging skillfully with members of other racial groups.

confusing territory of our own racial identity development. This is true not only for communities in the United States, but also for their European counterparts, which have their own histories of intergenerational violence and colonization, not always along visible racial lines.

The following two chapters offer stories and practices for White people to build communities of resilience, racial healing, and inclusivity together. I focus on White awareness as a path of inclusive community building because, as a White-presenting person, it has been my experience of healing ancestral pain and racism. TFor those who identify as BIPOC, I understand that stories of a White person's racial ignorance, defensiveness, and self-centered thinking may be unpleasant, all too familiar, and unhelpful to read, and I request your understanding in advance. For my White siblings, my hope is that sharing these stories of community growth and my own personal journey through ignorance, vulnerability, and mistakes will humbly support you and your community on this path of inquiry and compassion.

Becoming intimately familiar with our own racial identity development is the foundation for developing greater individual and communal allyship. How can I be inclusive toward others if I have not yet embraced the ancestral wounds and hidden gems of my own heritage? In order to strengthen our community's capacity for safety, inclusivity, and diversity, we must begin with ourselves.

## "Qui suis-je?"

The first meditation retreat I ever attended took place at a centuries-old Christian monastery in the French Alps that had been revamped into a Buddhist retreat center. A French lama was teaching, and since I was new to this scene, I was very impressionable. I only remember her saying one thing, which she obviously found important because she kept saying it over and over: *"Qui suis-je? Qui suis-je?"* "Who am I? Who am I?" For over twenty years, this question has followed me like an echo in a glacial valley, growing ever louder on the path of spiritual inquiry.

Albert and I had first met a number of years ago at Morning Sun. One evening, as he and I walked to a hilltop overlooking the amber-lit forests, enthusiastically sharing some ideas about creating more inclusivity in our Sangha, Albert casually yet confidently mentioned, "Well, the most important step for anyone working to build a more inclusive community is to better understand their own identity and heritage." The same bells went off, *Qui suis-je? Qui suis-je!* No one had asked or invited me to explore my own racial identity while growing up. I had one Chinese grandparent, but I looked White like my other grandparents of European ancestry. As a kid, if anyone had asked me what my race or ethnicity was, I suppose I would have said I was "normal." That's how blind I was growing up regarding race and Whiteness.

Some months after walking up that hill with Albert, I met someone at a mindfulness retreat who would soon drastically influence my understanding of my own racial identity. Sandra Kim, a Korean American antiracism teacher, was passionate about integrating mindfulness to support racial healing for both BIPOC and White folks. I asked Sandra if she was interested in teaching a mindfulness-based White Awareness retreat that a few friends and I were willing to organize.

Following George Floyd's murder, White people everywhere in the United States and abroad were desperately seeking ways to understand and respond to the systems and ways of being that had led to it. The labyrinths of race, identity, and privilege are complex and overwhelming for people to navigate alone. But as a Sangha—coming together with intention, cultivating an inner strength of awareness, relating to one another compassionately, and held by the guidance of a skillful teacher—people could learn to find the answers both within and with each other. Sandra loved the idea.

## A White Awareness Retreat in Vermont

Even though I helped to organize the retreat, Sandra and Sister Ocean, a Canadian nun who was assisting Sandra, provided the teaching and overall leadership. Too many times, I had witnessed teachers or facilitators trying to lead conversations about racial suffering and inclusivity when they were actually quite inexperienced; they had more learning and healing to do first. I didn't want to be in roles that limited my capacity to dive inward and learn with space and freedom. This was a good move because the retreat was much more challenging than I had anticipated.

During the first two days, Sandra broke down the foundations of Whiteness and White supremacy. I intended to be completely receptive, so I was continually thrown off by my own defensiveness. Questions and thoughts continually stood up like walls: *Why does she keep saying "White supremacy?" It's not like we're a bunch of racists here. Is she actually saying that we're White supremacists? Isn't that kind of extreme? Whiteness was invented? That's weird—how could Whiteness be invented? Is she saying again that we're the racist ones? Hello, we're the allies here!* Skepticism, confusion, irritation, feeling misunderstood and judged—you name it, I felt it. At the same time, I judged and criticized myself for being defensive at all. For two whole days, I watched these walls painfully rise up and slowly fall back down, again, and again, and again. I was clearly suffering and confused when confronted with the roots of my own racial identity.

Sandra taught about the roots of Whiteness by exploring its historical foundations of classism, oppression, and exploitation. From its inception, Whiteness in the United States was weaponized to divide poor people from joining forces. For example, Bacon's Rebellion in Virginia in 1676 marked the earliest known period in colonial America when the word "White" was used to distinguish privileges for indentured servants or poor farmers with European heritage over "Blacks." The colonial lawmakers knew that if poor "Whites" and "Blacks" continued joining forces, they would be done for—game over. So, they sowed seeds of hate and division. White indentured servants and farmers were given more power as landowners and impunity to punish Black slaves, whereas Blacks became hereditary slaves forever and could never employ Whites. Previously, White servants were at the bottom of the rung, in dire poverty, along with Black servants.

Race was used to make Whites superior, so that these poor Whites were no longer the lowest of the low.

This and other historical lessons helped us see how closely bound White privileges and thinking are to oppressing Black, Indigenous, and other communities of color today. It may appear on the surface that privileges and discriminatory thinking are unrelated. Yet they are like the left and the right, codependently manifesting. It is often difficult for those in the dominant group to acknowledge that oppressing one group serves the privileges of another. The identities, attitudes, and privileges that White people carry today originated hundreds of years ago to intentionally foster competition, superiority and inferiority complexes, and perceptions of otherness between poor workers.[*] Sadly, most of us never recognize these original forces that continue to imprison our minds within walls of discrimination. This historical knowledge offers empowerment, individually and collectively, to free our minds from social and economic manipulation into othering and believing different racial communities are superior.[†]

What a task, teaching about White toxicity to a room full of White people. To this day, I feel such compassion and gratitude for Sandra's brave presence and compassionate dedication. She was the perfect teacher for the job, and it was the perfect job for such a teacher. She held back no truth-telling punches. She wanted us to really get it, even if the medicine was bitter at times. She had no problem challenging

---

[*] A superiority or inferiority complex is the perception of being greater than or less than another. It is fueled by a comparing mind, and is the root of divisiveness and feelings of separation. The concept of otherness refers to seeing someone as different from or outside of one's own social or group identity. In her blog, The Other Sociologist, Dr. Zuleyka Zevallos writes that while dichotomies of otherness are natural in daily thinking, perceptions of otherness can strengthen social identities that represent a hierarchical social order, in which particular groups are seen as superior or inferior to others.

[†] This is why Dr. Martin Luther King Jr. launched the Poor People's Campaign shortly before he was assassinated: to reignite this ancient struggle to unite diverse groups of poor and oppressed people into powerful solidarity.

our beliefs about ourselves and classic White patterns of thinking. At the same time, she beamed kindness and luminosity through carefully delivered stories—little narrative nuggets of compassion that enthralled the room. I still wonder how much energy it took from her as a teacher of color to offer so much wisdom and compassion to this predominantly White audience. What I remember and treasure most is the unmistakable feeling that she trusted me. Even if I was a straight White guy who didn't totally get it, afraid and intimidated by White supremacy's thick shadows, she believed in my capacity to wake up to my own racial conditioning and my calling toward true allyship. That was her deepest gift, continuing to influence me well after the retreat was over.

## Looking Within

During the first few days of the retreat, my head was altogether drowning in grief about what we were learning, swimming with new insights, and swirling with confusion about both racism and my own racial identity. I often found myself frustratedly asking myself, *Why have I never learned this shit before?* Fortunately, the morning and afternoon meditations were a reliable source of peace and resilience where I could find clarity and compassion within myself each day.

One afternoon's sitting meditation period was particularly powerful. The gentle stillness of my surroundings—quiet friends sitting nearby, the knotty pine paneled meditation hall itself—helped to soothe my restless thoughts. Throughout the day, unresolved questions had been repeatedly splashing in the turbulent waters of my mind. *If Whiteness was just "invented," a construct used against us, and if I'm not White, then what am I?... Who am I really?* I invited my mind to dwell more deeply in the bones and flesh of my limbs, the soft rhythm of my breathing, and the tender spaces of my heart.

During the meditation, I felt a powerful visceral embodiment of Whiteness, like a cloak covering my whole body, emanating from my skin, dimly glowing around me. This invisible yet tangible mask coated my whole being, particularly my face. It covered me, yet it was not me. I could see through it, feel its superficial nature, yet I couldn't simply shake it off. I had been unknowingly wearing this cloak for so long—my entire life, perhaps—that I had somehow forgotten who I was underneath it. *But if I'm not White, if Whiteness is a myth, then. . . .* The ancient koan arose from the depths of my heart: *Who am I? Who am I?* The more I listened, the deeper the question echoed in the caverns of my bones, flesh, and blood. Deeper than the discourse of Whiteness, deeper than how others saw me, the question beckoned and rang like a great bell in my consciousness.

From the silent spaces of my chest emanated a blooming constellation of ancestral heritage, cultures and ethnicities all wrapped together in a single flourishing bouquet—Irish shamrocks, Chinese chrysanthemums, Italian lilies, as well as Scottish, English, and German flowers of all sorts. I felt the rich beauty, complexion, and strength of all my ancestors still living, flourishing, and cross-pollinating within me. I was not only White—I was a rich assembly of ancestral cultures, lands, and tribes. Whiteness had flattened and masked my ancestral origins into a single layer. I could now see it for what it was, as the knots within me slowly and effortlessly untied themselves.

The retreat with Sandra embodied the power of mindfulness in community, where the heavy emotional content could be steadily and compassionately digested within a safe, caring, and spacious container of support. It drastically changed the ways that I regarded being White, and how White supremacy had infused my life and worldview. Previously, I had always regarded racism as something outside of *me*, present instead in those I regarded as terrible people: KKK members, neo-Nazis, the radical right, and so on. I was the least likely suspect! *I was a good White person, an open-minded and supportive friend.* The retreat pulled back the curtains so I could peer deeply into the myths of Whiteness, its intrinsic roots of superiority, and the layers of fear, indifference, and wounding that had been passed down for generations.

I had seen through the illusions of Whiteness, but I could not yet escape its destructive realities. I was just waking up to it more fully. Whiteness was still sewn into every fiber of my life, relationship, and world. My journey into White awareness was just beginning; it felt encouraging yet depressing, exciting yet scary, overwhelming yet empowering. Upon coming home from the retreat, the next step was the most important: building community where racial healing could continue.

# CHAPTER 13

# THE POWER OF RACIAL AFFINITY CIRCLES

*Without community, there is no liberation.*
　　　　—AUDRE LORDE

*How can we sustain ourselves for the long haul? One thing I have learned is that we need a community of support. We all need community to give us energy, to strengthen our voice, and to offer constructive criticism when we stray off course. We need to speak up against racism and other forms of oppression, but we do not have to speak alone.*
　　　　—BEVERLY TATUM

*Ally is not an identity; it is a practice.*
　　　　—PAUL KIVEL

How can White people, as individuals and in communities, embody true allyship? As the White Awareness Retreat with Sandra revealed, we can't learn about and embody antiracism on our own. We need the support, motivation, and guidance of others to mirror our blind spots, compassionately recognize the roots of our racial conditioning, and learn to develop true allyship from the inside out. Just as it takes a village to raise a child, it takes a community to raise an ally.

Whereas the last chapter focused on individual racial identity development, this chapter's purpose is to support White people's community journey: from avoiding to embracing the topic of racism, from White isolation to supportive affinity groups, and from White-dominant thinking to more racially conscious community building. The primary vehicle of this work, the practical way in which people can grow their awareness, is through mindfulness-based racial affinity circles.

Similarly to the last chapter, I am speaking primarily to other White folks given my experience of community healing as a White-presenting person who is still learning, growing, and often stumbling through this very challenging and infinitely complex topic. We will explore the real struggles and accomplishments of initiating and maintaining racial affinity groups that help members embrace the seeds of internalized racism within their own hearts and minds. Collectively and compassionately embracing the suffering of our racial heritage paves a hopeful, redeeming, and bright path for our descendants.

## Race in the Sangha

Ruth King, a seminal thought leader in the intersection of mindfulness and racial awareness, writes, "Racism is a heart disease. And it is curable." As a global heart disease, no spiritual community, including Buddhist, mindfulness, or compassionately oriented groups, is immune to racism or other forms of discrimination. The emergence of non-Asian or convert Buddhist traditions in North America and Europe have predominantly White congregants and are situated within a White-dominant culture. My experience is that most of these communities, including my own, are still in the very early stages of their collective racial identity development and healing.

My spiritual tradition has roots in Vietnam, and our monastic community is predominantly Vietnamese, whereas the lay community in North America, composed of several hundred local mindfulness groups, is heavily White. In 2017, the ARISE Sangha (Awakening through Race, Intersectionality, and Social Equity) did a demographics survey for North American Order of Interbeing members, comprising the core community of ordained lay members in the Plum Village tradition. Of the roughly four hundred order members who responded in the United States, 84 percent identified as White, 6 percent were of Vietnamese heritage, 3 percent identified as Latinx, and just 1 percent were Black.* About 11 percent identified as LGBTQ. In terms of age, only 11 percent were under forty-five years old, and 70 percent were between the ages of fifty-six and seventy-five. Over one-third had incomes higher than $80,000. These numbers were not a big surprise, but confirmed with hard data what we had already experienced—our Sangha community is a predominantly older, White, heterosexual, and middle-class group of people.

Why don't more BIPOC practitioners feel supported to practice and take refuge in this core community of ordained members? There is not one answer to this question—rather, it is a koan, a Zen riddle for each of us to sit with and reflect upon. Many BIPOC friends throughout the years have openly shared with me that they do not feel at ease or supported in their local mindfulness groups. On the one hand, they love the Sangha, the teachings, and the practice with all their heart. On the other hand, they grow tired of continually brushing up against White-dominant spaces and feeling solely responsible for making the Sangha more inclusive to other practitioners of color. As White people, what can we do? Simply smiling more or being nicer to friends of color is not going to cut it. We have to try something new, something revolutionary, within the roots of our individual and collective conditioning. As a community, we can turn toward this uncomfortable and painful situation and, with curious ears and brave hearts, step

---

* In this book I use "Black" and "African American" interchangeably, as is standard in US literature. I humbly recognize that each country and cultural context might have different terms to describe racial groups and identities, and that all of these terms are imperfect ways to describe a wide and diverse range of peoples, cultures, languages, histories, and experiences.

forward into the unknown territory of our own group racial identity development.

## Mindfulness-Based Racial Affinity Groups

Over the years, I knew my path of Sangha building and embracing communal diversity was missing a key component. When a few years ago, I read Ruth King's book *Mindful of Race: Transforming Race from the Inside Out* for the first time, I was immediately captured by the power of her teaching. She had a clarity so many books on racism lack: a clear and concrete path of racial community healing through mindfulness-based racial affinity groups. King illustrates how the Buddha's teachings on mindfulness offer unique support for healing the roots of racism from the inside out. She writes, "How we think and respond is at the core of racial suffering and racial healing. If we cannot think clearly and respond wisely, we will continue to damage the world's heart." Mindfulness is exactly this training—to think clearly and respond wisely so that we avoid causing suffering. King was trained in clinical psychology, organizational development, and diversity consulting; however, these professional backgrounds alone did not heal her painful relationship to racial distress. Instead, she writes,

> *The best tool I know of to transform our relationship to racial suffering is mindfulness meditation. For more than twenty years, that practice has supported me in experiencing racial distress without warring against it.*[39]

Mindfulness helps develop stability, clarity, and compassion so we can sit with the pain of our racial distress, thereby transforming our relationship to it. At the same time, the most powerful way to practice is within a supportive community. Myriad other teachers and activists have voiced a similar insight of collective healing. Black feminist Audre Lorde boldly writes, "Without community, there is no liberation"[40] and bell hooks captures a similar sentiment: "Rarely, if ever, are any of us healed in isolation. Healing is an act of communion."[41] The findings of neuroscience and psychology offer the same truths: we need another brain, another nervous system to sync with, coregulate, heal, and transform—we cannot do this work alone.

It is the same with racial healing; we cannot just read books alone in our homes and expect more than surface level change. Real transformation must be relational, communal. King's approach to racial healing combines mindfulness with racism and diversity training within the holding container of beloved community. She is the founder of "Brave Space," a yearlong racial affinity leadership development program that "offers an intentional, structured, and graceful way over time to examine our racial conditioning within affinity community." Brave Space is structured by affinity groups with members of similar racial, ethnic, and gender identities, offering more focus and group safety.

In *Mindful of Race*, King also encourages people to form their own local racial affinity groups (RAG), offering a suggested schedule, format, and questions for groups to explore themselves. In both Brave Space and any RAG, the group size is fairly small—four to eight people—so the atmosphere is intimate, safe, vulnerable, and concentrated enough for the magic to take place. In each affinity group, White men are among other White men, Black women with other Black women, White genderqueer folk with themselves, and so on. This allows each affinity circle to share their own truths, confusion, pain, and insights without filtering their speech or inadvertently causing more pain to those of other identities. King writes, "To separate into same-race groups, in this sense, is not intended to divide us but rather to leverage the fact that within most contexts and often within our hearts, we are already racially divided." Such circles invite White men, for example, to assume care and ownership over their own gender and racial healing without depending on or burdening those of other races and genders to teach or do the work for them.

Forming a local RAG is not a replacement for participating in an expert-guided and facilitated course such as Brave Space. The subtle yet influential group racial dynamics need seasoned eyes and ears to discern and skillfully guide participants into greater awareness and individual accountability of internalized racism. At the same time, we must also engage and integrate this healing work in our home communities where transformation is desperately needed.

As Ruth King and other teachers make clear, a supportive anti-racist community—something the vast majority of White people lack—is vital, especially when mainstream forces are stacked in favor of White supremacy, unconscious bias, oppressive systems, and business as usual. *Witnessing Whiteness* author Shelly Tochluk, a White woman, states that White awareness circles have supported her, especially in the most difficult times, with a steady stream of "validation, inspiration, comfort, support, challenge, knowledge, skills, a space for reflection, and, above all, a sense of belonging. Knowing that I am not alone keeps me hopeful and motivated."[42] Further, Beverly Daniel Tatum, explains that communities—not only the individuals that comprise them—undergo a process of racial identity development.

> *Every person, whether they are conscious of it or not, has or is undergoing a process of racial identity development. Their notions, ideas, perceptions, whether known or unknown, reflect who they are in comparison to others. Communities also undergo and form a racial identity development.*[43]

According to Janet E. Helms, six distinct stages of racial identity development exist for White individuals and communities. The stages Helms identifies describe a steady progression from conforming to mainstream ideas and behaviors and then, through self-reflection and critical analysis of racial identity beliefs and racism, moving onward to developing positive racial group commitments and the capacity to relinquish racial privileges.[44]

Each individual moves through a process of awakening awareness, but for community racial healing, White people need each other to traverse this journey's various stages, just as birds need their flock to safely travel across great distances.

## Beginning a Group for White Men

When I moved to Charlotte to begin a new mindfulness center, my deep wish was to plant seeds for a multicultural community to take root and flourish, a home to many people of diverse racial and cultural backgrounds. Charlotte has a very racially and culturally diverse population, although the city is segregated in its neighborhoods, schools, and churches. As we began hosting days of mindfulness every Saturday, many White men showed up regularly and formed the majority presence at our gatherings. Most importantly, our center's founding team was three White guys: Roger, an older, White-presenting, Jewish man; Nick, fully White; and myself, a White-presenting Chinese American.* With White, male leadership at our foundation, I had serious doubts about whether our community would ever flourish with diverse leadership and become a home for practitioners of diverse identities. I believed that having exclusively White male leaders was a big deficit for us, and I felt ashamed of our lack of racial and gender diversity. But after reflecting on King's strong encouragements to form racial affinity groups, and discussing this with friends experienced in communal diversity, my perspective on these "limitations" changed significantly.

*This is my racial karma*, I thought. *It is both our limitation* and *our potential. As a White-presenting man, I have a unique ability to connect with other White men. We have the opportunity to embrace Whiteness and patriarchy within ourselves as a path of practice.* A dear Sangha friend, AJ Johnson, who teaches White Awareness workshops in Virginia, further encouraged me: "At the start of every workshop or retreat I lead, I look around and ask myself, *Where are all the men?* It's all women and non-binary friends, David. I don't see White men doing the work, unfortunately. I hope you can do this!" Friends like AJ encouraged me to believe in our potential to

---

* White-presenting means that someone has a mixed or non-White racial heritage, but they appear White and receive the privileges of Whiteness while they may or may not feel a sense of belonging or identity with White culture.

heal, lead, and not fall into the trap of believing that merely standing on the sidelines is our role in this game.

That summer, I began sharing my intention of starting a new mindfulness-based racial affinity group with male-identifying friends in Charlotte. Upon hearing about this group for White men only, many people's eyes opened wide with fear and confusion. "I initially felt kind of afraid when you told me about White men gathering together," one female friend confided. We were, in fact, in the American South, where gatherings for White men had historically been a terrorizing experience. Still, I persisted in my outreach efforts and initially received loads of positivity and encouragement from the White guys I spoke enthusiastically to about the group.

> "Wow, that's amazing David, I would love to participate in such a group—keep me posted!"

> "I'm really dedicated to this work. Let me know when it starts."

> "I used to be part of such a group but it died off, and I've been looking for another!"

> "Oh yes, I love Ruth King. Definitely interested! Let's talk."

For weeks, I heard such responses. And yet, words and actions can be so different. Mostly, I never heard from these folks again. When I followed up, I heard different responses, as if I were talking to completely different people.

> "This work is very important to me. But I just heard this Dharma talk about not taking on too much at once. So now is not really a good time."

> "Well, I would like to, I really would. But I'm struggling and need more support from a normal men's group right now."

> "Well, my kids are in lots of extracurricular activities, and I just don't have the time. They need me more right now."

"I'm just starting my career as a therapist, and I really need to focus on that right now. Maybe later, though!"

The reasons went on and on. I stayed optimistic and hopeful through the first dozen or so rejections. *It's okay, they'll come around soon enough*, I thought. Finally, one beloved Sangha brother said he was in, and another brother said he was interested as well. The support from these committed friends, like drops of rain in the desert, kept my hope alive.

As the months passed, though, and the rejections piled up, the group was going nowhere. I started drowning in disappointment and frustration, feeling heartbroken by people's indifference, and afraid this group would never get off the ground. *Doesn't anyone care?! If not us, then who? Isn't this important for our children and their children?* I silently raged. My initial hopes turned to resentment and despair about the depth of privilege and indifference to racial violence in our society. Inside, I started despising and hating White men, even strangers I never talked to. I silently judged, especially when I attended other meditation groups, thinking to myself, *Most White people are racially oblivious, scared of themselves, and selfish, refusing to look at our wounds and wicked past.* I was clearly suffering.

I soon realized, I was hating myself and my own roots of deeply internalized racism. It wasn't others I hated so much as I hated being White, myself. I hated sharing ancestry and identity with a culture that has been so unimaginably cruel and domineering. I hated the indifference and fear I'd experienced growing up as a White person. I hated sharing an identity with White men, those at the helm of our political and economic systems who were steering our world off the cliffs of civilization. I hated feeling so powerless toward my own racial family. I hated feeling so alone in this struggle. So, I took on being the righteous one, the good White guy, not like the bad Whites, and distanced myself as much as possible from affiliation with my White tribe. So much hating, so much grief, so alone, I wanted to cry. And I did.

Without the group forming, I had time to sit, breathe, and grieve. This period of self-compassion was the perfect preparation and practice for me. I considered that people may truly be scared and drowning in their own deep habits (and the luxury) of turning away from the inescapable pain within, occupying themselves with busyness, worry, pleasure-seeking, or personal survival instead. We were in the South, where the land itself embodies memories so brutal and terrifying that they are consistently ignored as if they never happened. Regional slave plantations are flipped into nature preserves or wedding venues that still carry the master's family names without any memorial or mention of those enslaved and tortured over the centuries. Many US states, including North Carolina, ban schools from discussing historical or contemporary effects of racism to protect White people from ever feeling uncomfortable or guilty.

One day, a longtime African American friend and mentor visited us at Greatwoods Zen to explore the possibility of his offering retreats there. Together we sauntered through the quiet forest. I confided in him, sharing my challenges and people's responses to the group. Without hesitation, he said, both matter of factly and with care, "That's what privilege looks like, David. Now you know how I feel in my life's work." I was grateful for his compassionate reflection. Even if my difficulties were infinitely small compared to what he experienced throughout his life, it was comforting to feel understood, to not feel alone. I felt reassured; if a wise, experienced teacher knew this feeling, there was still hope for me.

The anger and despair I experienced opened my eyes. I leveled with myself, seeing that my current tactics were too weak. I, too, I saw, was avoiding confronting my actual feelings and relationships, just like others. I told myself, *The group must happen, even if it's just a few of us. I need to be stronger, more direct.* I sent out an email with a start date and began approaching people more fearlessly, yet compassionately. I said to them, "This training is going to be the core of our Sangha, both now and for years to come. If you are ever interested in leadership, this is where it starts." With others I shared, "I know you're very busy; I also know how important this is for you. This will be the learning of a lifetime, and if you don't join, I'm afraid you're going to miss out and regret it later on." To the dads, I said, "I think of the legacy for your children as we do this work ourselves. You will be a model for them, giving them real hope and healing for their future." To my closest friends, I said, "This is what I want the most for our center. I humbly ask for your wholehearted support, please." I told everyone how special the group would be, how special they were to our Sangha, and that I hoped to build deeper friendships through learning and bonding together. I used whatever power I had, compassionately, to encourage people to commit.

The one-on-one and heart-to-heart conversations worked. Soon enough, nine men agreed to join a trial gathering. I knew that if we just gathered once, people would immediately see how precious and powerful it was. I attempted to spoil them, buying each an audiobook of *Mindful of Race* so we could discuss the first chapter together during our gathering. I cooked a pot of heartwarming autumn soup, kabocha squash and apples, and brought fresh baguettes and hummus to prepare for an evening of meditation, discussion, and dinner with the bros.

I will never forget that first gathering: nine men arrived with wholehearted smiles and hugs, and it seemed we were happy enough just to be men together. It felt so rare, yet so familiar; so simple, yet so right. We began by meditating in silence for thirty minutes. Then I invited each of us to share our intentions for joining the group and anything about our racial upbringing that we wished. One by one, each man poured an overflowing well of suppressed stories, tucked away aspirations, homeless grief, and hidden fears into the circle of support. Tears rolled down my cheeks like a quiet, meandering stream at almost every sharing. The overwhelming need for these men to speak to racism, both in their own hearts and in the world, had finally found a home, and relief. The group's safety and compassion bloomed beyond the chosen topic. One brother cried openly as he shared about a recent divorce. It was as if he laid out his defenseless body in the middle of our circle, trusting his brothers' arms to hold him in gentle strength. It felt empowering just to be men together, supporting, embracing, and celebrating one another.

Our sharing lasted about an hour and a half, and then we headed upstairs for a hearty meal. We let go of seriousness and laughed, joked, and lightheartedly enjoyed our brotherhood for the rest of the evening. Without hesitation, the group committed to monthly gatherings. It was the beginning of a dream finally coming true, a shared path of communal healing with my fellow men.

## Mindfulness and Racial Healing

The following sections offer both examples and ideas of how both individuals and communities can concretely practice mindfulness of race together. My teachers and friends have shown me over the years how to practice mindfulness in ways that recognize flickers of racial bias, White superiority, or racial distress in my daily life. The first step is to notice thoughts or reactions that have hints or edges of racial bias or discrimination. Then I pause to breathe with the associated feelings, opening into them with tenderness, curiosity, and compassion. In this way, insights into my own views, suppressed feelings, or ancestral responses that cause me and others to suffer may slowly surface, and I can consciously choose different ways to respond in various situations. The more insights emerge, the more liberation can occur.

Here is an example of how the practice of mindfulness and deep looking can translate into practical daily life interactions: Last week, I found an abandoned purse outside my train just before departure. Thinking it belonged to someone on the train, I opened it to find some identification and find the person on board. Just as I opened the purse, a young Black woman came running toward me from the train, visibly upset and yelling, "You leave my stuff alone! Give me back my money!" She grabbed her purse and quickly departed, unable to hear me blurting out a flustered explanation. We both boarded the departing train and for the next ten minutes, I sat alone, mindfully breathing with my frustrated and shaken nervous system.

I could have yelled back, considered myself a victim, or fed an ancestral belief about Blacks and Whites never trusting each other. I kept breathing, and recalled how rattled and frustrated I was when my computer was stolen a few years ago. I thought about how much has been stolen from African Americans for so many centuries by White people—practically everything. This interaction could have happened between anyone; but I was also aware of the racial tension in our situation. After some time reflecting alone, I looked around and found the woman in the car below and gently asked from a short distance if I could explain. She was willing, and having calmed down herself, she was very understanding of my intentions. We spent the rest of the train ride sharing past experiences of being stolen from, empathizing with one another, and laughing off distressing yet funny stories. She was a very nice and sincere young woman; it would have been such a shame if we had both walked away from our encounter without repairing the misunderstanding between us. With the practice, I was able to transform this stressful encounter into a meaningful connection and new friendship.

## Transforming Our Childhood

Many people have asked me what these mindfulness-based racial affinity groups actually do together, and how it works. Most importantly, I respond, facilitators lead from their own humble experience and then let people experiment together. One of the first White affinity groups I participated in was led by my dear friend Melina, a former Buddhist nun in Plum Village. After facilitating a meditation exercise, she shared personal stories of her own past ways of racist thinking and behavior, thereby offering us the courage and vulnerability to similarly look within ourselves. She invited us to journal individually about this topic for fifteen minutes before opening the space for sharing with the group if we wanted. I distinctly remember thinking to myself, *I'm pretty sure I won't be able to think of anything. I just haven't been a very racist person.* That day not much came up, but I kept on journaling in the weeks that followed. Soon enough, I was shocked by what was unearthed—racially charged, painful, and completely forgotten memories from my childhood, teenage years, and adulthood. I'll share the following story to encourage my White friends to similarly investigate their hidden past, with a content warning, especially for friends of color; it is not violent, but it may be upsetting.

In one of these memories, I was in sixth grade in my school in Southern California. As usual during lunch, my classmates and I were playing a heated game of basketball out on the blacktop. The bell rang, and I walked back to our classroom, stopping at the water fountain on the way. As I jogged toward my classmates lining up outside, I noticed one of my friends, eyes narrowed and brow furrowed, glaring across the courtyard. Some Latino boys in the other sixth grade class glared back. I looked to my friends and saw their chins lifted, eyes scowling, and chests puffed. Suddenly, with no other knowledge, I felt myself a part of the clash and joined ranks with my tribe, glaring across the courtyard in prideful defense. We arrived in front of our respective classrooms, our backs up against the beige, stucco building and a small field of grass between us. A few more friends joined our opponents, now looking larger and tougher than our gang. A few of their boys across the yard threw their arms out wide, taunting us: "Come on then!" *Were they joking and playing around with us, or did they really want to fight?* I hadn't yet been in any real fights at school; I imagined that they had. We were admittedly smaller in size. My friends and I were in the GATE program—"gifted and talented education"—and we were mostly White kids, with some Asian-American students. Their class, however, was mostly Latinx, with a few Black and White kids. I guessed that the boys across the courtyard were from Casablanca, a barrio with poorer neighborhoods and reportedly more crime.

I started feeling afraid that if it came to a real fight, we would be easily dominated. *What would we do?* Feeling scared and at a loss, I immediately changed tactics. Without thinking, I joked out loud to our side, "Whatever! At least we're not going to be picking oranges for the rest of our lives!" We cackled at the joke out loud for several moments. Soon after, their teacher came outside and ushered the boys into their classroom. I don't think they were able to hear my ridicule from across the yard, but I'll never know.

What was that conflict all about? And why did I utter those racist comments? Lacking the physical prowess to back up my pride or defend myself physically, I pulled out the hidden weapon, always tucked away unconsciously inside, ready to use if needed—the dagger of White, middle-class, educated supremacy. As a twelve-year-old boy, I already intuitively knew how to wield this dagger over the working-class, immigrant, Mexican American boys in my school. Feeling powerless and afraid, I resorted to the social and racial power at my disposal to put them down, shield my weaknesses, and come out on top. After all, as a growing, White, straight male in America, that is where I believed I belonged.

Neither of my parents openly espoused those beliefs, and we had good family friends who were Mexican American. Yet I still inherited society's ugly knuckles of White supremacy. When push came to shove, those racist attitudes came out in punches. Sadly, I and other boys of my generation didn't receive any education about the incredibly brave yet punishing plight of the agricultural workers in my own community, who helped feed and nourish so many. In California, the agricultural industry had exploited Mexican Americans' backbreaking labor for decades, squashing access to living wages and citizenship rights, ignoring healthcare needs, and exposing them to toxic pesticides, but it wouldn't be until 2014 that Barack Obama would create a national holiday to honor Cesar Chavez and his fellow farmworkers' accomplishments, thus bringing their dignity and struggles to the national consciousness.

While journaling about these stories, I felt shocked, heartbroken, and ashamed to recognize how clueless and indifferent I had been to other racial groups' pains and struggles. Even well after the White Awareness Retreat with Sandra, I carried a deep-seated belief that racism was outside of me. *Yes, racism is a real problem in the world, and I'm against it. But me racist? Of course not!* Living in a society whose history and institutions have been built upon foundations of White supremacy, we are like fish who can't see the water we are living and breathing in.

At the same time, uncovering these buried stories also brought an undeniable sense of relief—I could finally touch an old pain that had been lost deep inside of me. Whereas the retreat with Sandra had cracked open the doors of investigating White supremacy, it was back home in my community of friends and teachers like Melina that I could walk the long road back home to myself and the roots of racism deep within. Sincerely investigating these memories and my discriminatory habits fueled an even stronger sense of hope: I no longer felt powerless to transform racism in the world. It was already happening, right here, within me and my community.

## White Centering versus White Healing

This group- and mindfulness-based investigative work is crucial for White people anywhere, but especially those practicing in multicultural communities. "Why?" you may ask. "Why focus so much on White people's feelings? Isn't this just White centering? Shouldn't we be focusing on combatting racism and supporting people of color instead?"

Several years ago, a local Sangha I had been attending and facilitating for a few years had a significant conflict between two members who were previously friends. A middle-aged Black woman had voiced grievances related to the blatant, hurtful remarks and microaggressions of an older White woman. At the request of both, several group leaders, including myself, held a listening circle for each of them to share their experiences, feel understood by others, and hold the possibility for reconciliation. After each of them had spoken, we took a short break to decompress. I was outside, offering emotional support to the White woman. She shared with me, "Gosh, I didn't think it was going to be like this. Does everyone in there think I'm some bad person now?" It was clear she didn't fully understand how or why her remarks and behaviors had been derogatory and offensive to her friend. As part of the reconciliation, the Black woman requested that the White woman participate in a White awareness group to better understand unconscious racial bias and receive support. In response, the White woman asked, "One thing I would like to know is, will you be able to forgive me?" In a way, she was acknowledging her unskillfulness and humility, yet I still cringed. She was asking for the Black woman to wipe away her faults without committing to the inner work herself. The other woman contemplated the request for a few moments before replying, "I'll think about it."

By partaking in White affinity group work and cleaning up our own racial baggage, we avoid laying unresolved emotional burdens (guilt and shame, for example) upon the shoulders of our BIPOC friends. People of color have enough to do without carrying the extra emotional weight of other racial groups. Forgiveness and salvation are another inside job. We can offer them to ourselves or seek support from other White allies.

## Being with White Guilt

In any multiracial community that includes White folks, White guilt is as common as passing gas—it's there, disturbing the air, making things unpleasant, but rarely acknowledged. If I fail to recognize how these hidden feelings of guilt are impacting my behaviors and relationships, then the cycle just continues.

Mindfulness helps me to embrace with less judgment what is happening in my own mind, the thoughts and feelings operating subtly just underneath the surface of normal awareness. For example, I sometimes notice myself paying extra attention and giving extra care to my clients of color with the underground intention of feeling better about myself as a good White person. Deep down, I notice myself trying to relieve an unspoken feeling of guilt. The guilt starts driving the show, overriding my natural inclination to be genuinely present with this person's needs. If I become aware of the guilt, though, I have a better chance of shifting my ways of thinking and acting with greater integrity. Shelly Tochluk articulates it this way:

> When we move into community work without working through issues of guilt, we can often act out of a savior complex. There is nothing wrong with wanting to make a difference in a person's life. However, quite often, we go about this work in order to fill a hole within ourselves.[45]

When I first began to write about White awareness and healing racism in community for this book, I wrote a whole chapter filled with stories and examples of things I was proud of: profound friendships, meaningful collaborations, and engaged activism with BIPOC friends and communities over the years. I soon realized I was showing off what author Resmaa Menakem calls my "racial résumé." Thankfully, I was able to see this and delete that chapter. Reflecting on positive experiences of allyship and the fruits of racial healing work may be helpful at times—but not when it's covering up the deeper malaise of my own racial identity. The most important work is tending the soil of our own racial, cultural, and ethnic identity development. If the roots of our identity are withered or sick, cross-pollinating with other communities will be fruitless.

Given the extremely traumatic and violent history of colonial countries like the United States, experiencing shame and guilt as a White person is natural. These are healthy emotional responses of a psyche desperately seeking relief from the screaming wounds of witnessing or inflicting violent oppression, whether past or present. There's no need to feel ashamed about our shame. In fact, shame and guilt can be powerful teachers if we are willing to sit and listen deeply and respectfully to them. Whereas many psychotherapists I know regard shame as completely negative and toxic, Buddhist psychology regards regret and shame as indeterminate mental formations. That is, they are neither inherently skillful nor unskillful, positive nor negative; it depends on how we tend to them. Racial affinity groups offer the space to safely bring these wounds and afflictions to the surface, where they can be heard by others, lovingly accepted, and consciously worked with and transformed.

## White Awareness Community

White people have a lot of work to do on themselves, by themselves. When members of different racial groups come together to discuss race, especially when some groups have not done their own healing work, things typically get messy very fast. As White people, how can we possibly try to mend racial divisions across groups when we have not attended to the racial identity wounds in ourselves first? People of color similarly need space to heal collectively, within the safety and support of their own community, without focusing on the needs and ancestral wounds of White folks.

There is a tendency for White people as the dominant racial group in the United States and globally to try to solve problems or focus on others instead of being curious about their own racial group identity, suffering, and habits of harm. As opposed to people of color, White folks by and large don't begin questioning their own racial, ethnic, and cultural identity until much later in life, if at all.

I aspire to not leave this world with the stains of racism and White supremacy on my soul or its footprints on the soil of humanity bearing my name. White supremacy and racism deeply hurt us as White people. It fuels our loneliness, superiority complexes, greed, and alienation from others. It is an isolating and fearful way to be and live. The path of racial affinity groups naturally strengthens our capacity for allyship and living in collaborative and caring community, supporting the happiness of White folks as well as others. Even after participating in racial identity work for years, we will still undoubtedly make many, many mistakes. But with a supportive White awareness community, we have friends to help pick ourselves back up after each fall while we find our footing and learn to act more wisely moving forward. Where there are mistakes, there are great learnings.

Building communities with BIPOC affinity groups or White Awareness is not done in isolation from engaging in our larger community. White people come together as White allies and can then better engage in multiracial spaces. This movement is like the rhythm of our breathing: coming in, then moving out, energizing ourselves within, then flowing out to the world. We move together, then apart, learning and sharing, offering and receiving, healing and supporting.

## Starting a Racial Affinity Group

Joining a preexisting racial affinity group may be ideal, but many people do not have that option. If you already practice in a spiritual community, you can start building a racial affinity group right where you are. It can even be quite enjoyable and fun to gather weekly or monthly with like-minded friends. See how the following steps can help:

1. **Start small**: Talk with a few friends you already know who might want to join a conversation about race. Or connect with other like-minded people you can partner with. Tochluk says an easy way to start building a BIPOC affinity group or a White awareness community is to reach out to a friend, sibling, cousin, or colleague and "Let them know you have been working through some ideas and you could really use some support. In this way, the invitation is about becoming more connected to you and joining your process rather than suggesting the individual needs some work."[46] I love how this approach invites mutual growth and collaboration; we all need support. Even if you feel intimidated, you may be surprised by the positive responses you get.

2. **Community Support:** Brainstorm together how to create a group that will support each of your goals for racial healing and inclusive community building.

3. **Study and Dialogue:** Read, dialogue with, and practice exercises from books or online guides that inspire you. Appendix C offers a list of resources.

4. **Create Shared Agreements:** How can we support each other? What are our individual and collective needs and goals for the group? How can we be accountable to each other and our goals?

5. **Engaged Learning:** Talk about your experiences of working, visiting, or living in diverse spaces, your awareness of how White privilege and racism operates there, and your practice of

engaged relationships. When people are in very White spaces, look for White supremacy, no matter who is in the space. Share about what you notice and how you respond.

6. **Show up for and support events that others organize:** Look for events being organized in your community and offer your support. Specific holidays or events can be especially powerful: Juneteenth, BLM events, and racial justice collaborations, for example.

7. **Dream Big Together:** Share each of your visions for a more racially just community and world and consider creating a group vision together.

8. **Honoring Ancestor Allies:** Study and learn from pioneering allies who have walked the path before you. Becoming close with these inspiring figures and their legacy can support and sustain your efforts throughout your life.

9. **Broadening the Circle of Learning:** Once you have been meeting for a while, try organizing a workshop, day of mindfulness, or an online study group for others to join this work with you.

It may seem daunting to put some or any one of these ideas into action. If you are White, you may be thinking, *I don't know enough to start a White awareness group. I'm not sure that I'm ready yet.* It's so easy to believe that we ourselves don't know enough, aren't experienced enough, or are too insignificant to do anything within the overwhelming current of racism. Even Ruth King shared these doubts: "I have questioned myself: *Do I understand enough or know enough?* At some point I realized the answer was *No. I didn't understand enough or know enough. But I would have to go ahead and write the book anyway.* None of us knows enough, but we can't let that stop us."[47] Just so, we don't have to be an expert on race to take the next step forward in our community's practice of White awareness and racial healing. We just have to take it. In order for our descendants to inherit a more harmonious

multicultural community, a less racist society, and a legacy of hope, we
must step humbly and wholeheartedly into the unknown.

## An Inclusive Welcome

After deepening our understanding of our own racial and cultural
identities, including habits of racial harm, we have built the foundation for more genuinely extending safety, belonging, and inclusivity to
others. I would like to close these chapters on racial healing by offering a profound inclusive welcoming practice that you can explore with
your own community.

During our first Educators Retreat at Morning Sun Community,
we were blessed to have Valerie Brown, a Buddhist-Quaker Dharma
Teacher in the Plum Village tradition and author of *Healing our Way
Home: Black Buddhist Teachings on Ancestors, Joy, and Liberation*, join us
from Pennsylvania. During the orientation, Valerie offered an "Inclusive Welcome," setting a powerful tone of unconditional acceptance,
respect, and belonging that touched the heart of every person in the
room. Valerie did not merely read this practice out loud—she spoke
from the depths of her own personal experience and reflection. She
also invited three others to lead different parts of this practice with her,
including myself. A few hours before orientation, she offered some
brief guidance: "You can say what is already written in your section,
or you can change the words or add on according to your own inspiration. Enjoy reflecting on it. Just don't read straight from the page." I
was so moved by this practice and its effect upon everyone in the room
that I began sharing similar versions at every retreat I helped organize
or teach thereafter. Every time, people expressed deep gratitude for
being welcomed so genuinely and safely into the new retreat space.
Following Valerie's ways, I also invited others to present alongside
me, so that diverse voices and identities could welcome others into
the space and people loved cocreating this welcoming atmosphere at
the start of the retreat. Vishwa, a Sangha member at Greatwoods Zen,
wrote to me after our retreat, "This practice made my entire human

being come alive and all versions of me felt welcomed in that space. It made me feel safe and holistically supported in all that I am. That I didn't to be a certain version of me to be there at the retreat."

I finally told Valerie how much this practice impacted me and so many others during dozens of retreats over the years, and I asked her about its origins. Valerie personally developed the Inclusive Welcome from her years of spiritual practice with the Religious Society of Friends (Quakers) and the Plum Village Community. Over time, thousands of people have asked her how to offer such a practice, so Valerie developed a guide called, "How to Create the Inclusive Welcome." Following the ancient proverb "give someone a fish and you feed them for a day; teach someone to fish and you feed them for a lifetime," Valerie designed this step-by-step process to help people create their own uniquely tailored and lovely Inclusive Welcome for their home community.

## CREATING AN INCLUSIVE WELCOME

1. Enjoy quiet time to reflect on the people you wish to welcome. Who are they? What do you know about them?
2. Picture them in your mind and heart in the fullness of their lives, the challenges and the joys.
3. Reflect on the many elements that create their internal and external identity and reality.
4. Where are they from geographically?
5. What languages do they speak?
6. What faith or wisdom traditions?
7. What is their chronological age?
8. How might they be feeling at the moment you extend welcome?
9. What emotions do you think might be present for them?
10. Who supports them in their daily life?

Continue in this way, reflecting on these internal and external elements of people's identities. Extend welcome to these various elements that support these people and their lives. After you have reflected in this way, write your Inclusive Welcome, extending warmth and acceptance to the various aspects of them and their lives. Notice what happens as you offer this to others. How do you feel? How has the space changed? What is your own sense of belonging and community?

# CHAPTER 14

# SHARING BOUNDARIES, ADDRESSING POWER

*The most common way people give up their power is by thinking they don't have any.*
—ALICE WALKER

*The power of sexuality is enormous—it produces all of humanity; it is the creative force that dances through all of life. Yet its exclusion from much of spiritual life has been disastrous.*
—JACK KORNFIELD

*I am not interested in power for power's sake, but I'm interested in power that is moral, that is right, and that is good.*
—MARTIN LUTHER KING JR.

In building our community house, healthy boundaries are the roof that provides us with solid protection and safety against the elements, which can otherwise destroy our beloved home in the blink of an eye. I know the reality of this danger firsthand. I first started studying power, vulnerability, and healthy boundaries because I was feeling confused and heartbroken in my own community. No one around me, including myself, really understood how to clearly and skillfully navigate between the lines of friendship, intimacy, romantic relationships, and leadership in community. Everyone, including the community residents and teachers, seemed to have different ideas about what behavior and attitudes were okay and not okay. One summer, I developed an emotionally close and flirtatious relationship with a volunteer I was supervising at a meditation center. I asked my teacher and a colleague for guidance and support in dealing with this unsettling relationship. Although well-intentioned, their advice was inexperienced, unclear, and unhelpful to both me and our community. My lack of appropriate boundaries ultimately caused the volunteer a lot of confusion and suffering in her relationship to our community. I felt devastated, ashamed, and afraid; I did not know how to responsibly manage my own attractions and offer a safer presence in our community.

Over the next few years, I was determined to dig up these roots of misconduct in myself and learn what real safety and boundaries look like in a faith-based community. I repeatedly asked, *How can I protect myself and others in our Sangha who find themselves in similar situations? How can we prevent this together?* I took a course on healthy boundaries for Buddhist teachers and started voraciously reading material about power and vulnerability dynamics, sexual misconduct, and healthy boundaries in spiritual communities. I wrote a healthy boundary document for myself and my Sangha, and I started listening more to the stories of sexual trauma and healing shared with me by my female-identifying and non-binary friends. I have learned a tremendous amount about this topic, and I am grateful to know that my whole Sangha is safer because of it.

I wish I could say that this issue is easy to navigate now and I have no more questions. But living in and stewarding a spiritual community is complex and presents many nuanced situations. I still have questions at times about implementing boundaries, managing attractions when they arise, and consistently standing clear and strong in my yeses and nos. I am still humbly learning how my nuanced behaviors as a male-identifying community leader create feelings of safety or vulnerability in our community. At times, I need to check in with trustworthy friends and teachers and ask for guidance or reflection to support my utmost accountability.

Even though I have spent years engaging with this topic, it is still on the edge of my comfort zone to write these chapters. I humbly ask you, dear readers, for your understanding and patience for the short-comings and mistakes I will undoubtedly convey while addressing this difficult topic. These chapters, like each chapter in this book, reflect an ever-evolving distillation of my own learning, insights, ignorance, and limitations.

As a cisgender man, I hope these chapters serve as a humble yet rousing wake-up call for other men. The overwhelming majority of sexual misconduct in both spiritual communities and in society at large comes through men's ways of thinking, ignorance of power dynamics, and habits of harm. It is our time now as men to unmask and untangle the cycles of unevaluated gender power, its linchpins of ignorance and secrecy, our sexual enculturation as boys, and the resulting harm that reaches back centuries. As men, it can feel scary to turn toward this problem and deeply acknowledge the ignorance and violence that our individual minds and collective male psyche con-tinue to contribute. Simply facing it with a humble mind and open heart already begins the healing. We can do it.

Studying this topic is crucial not only for men, but for every person and community. Safety in the Sangha is not an individual matter. The greatest power we have as community members, both male and non-male, is to lean into this difficult topic together. Through collectively addressing and learning from stories of misused or abused power, mis-guided and ignorant leadership, and unhealthy boundaries, together we will steadily arrive at the shore of greater communal safety, dis-cerning leadership, collectively created ethical guidelines, and shared community power.

The following two chapters offer guidance for all community members, especially those in leadership roles, to 1) be familiar with the history of misconduct and risks in each of our communities, 2) better understand and skillfully relate to power differentials in com-munity life, 3) more skillfully navigate romantic and sexual attractions or dual relationships in general, and 4) write a healthy boundaries document with the intention of supporting greater safety for every-one. For our community's well-being, we must explore this challeng-ing terrain no matter how uncomfortable it feels.

## Relational Trauma in Religious Communities

Friendship, intimacy, and romance in spiritual community is com-plicated. On the one hand, falling in love with someone who shares your spiritual path can be a wonderful thing. Many close friends have developed flourishing romantic partnerships after being friends in their spiritual community. United in their aspirations, they offer expo-nentially greater presence, support, and leadership to their commu-nity than each could offer alone. Attractions between members is a natural part of community life, including in healthy and flourishing spiritual communities.

On the other hand, when romantic relationships between members break apart, the whole community feels it. Even more importantly, when teachers, pastors, or other leaders in a spiritual community become romantically or sexually involved with commu-nity members, the power differential creates enormous vulnerability and suffering for everyone involved. It is the way that people become aware of attractions, respond mindfully, and express appropriate boundaries that determines how safe or harmful these relationships become.

Our society has a longstanding historical precedent of male-perpetrated misconduct in religious communities that have left deep teeth marks of mistrust in our collective psyche. Spiritual communities should be the healing balm to these historical wounds of sexual trauma in our society. However, the opposite happens—these entrusted with spiritual authority inflict further even harm and betrayal. I have witnessed firsthand local groups, meditation centers, and entire traditions devastated by harmful sexual relationships and lack of boundaries between teachers and members. These community-wide traumas can take years or even generations to fully heal.

In the 1980s, Buddhist teacher Jack Kornfield published a survey of fifty-four teachers from different meditation traditions.

The survey posed two questions to forty-eight men and six women:

1. Are you celibate?

2. Have you had a sexual relationship with at least one of your students?

The results were hair-raising. 87 percent of the non-celibate teachers (thirty-four out of thirty-nine) admitted to having had at least one such relationship. Among all the teachers surveyed, both celibate and non-celibate, 63 percent of them had been sexual with one or more of their students. Kornfield's study is now decades old, did not include teachers in the Abrahamic traditions, and had a low sample size. It is still striking and extremely concerning, nonetheless. Even if these statistics might now be lower, spiritual teachers have earned the reputation of being the most sexually exploitative among helping professionals.

If renowned teachers and senior practitioners have made such fateful mistakes, what is stopping this from happening in our own community? It may be easy to shake our heads about others' mis-doings, but have we studied power and vulnerability dynamics, dis-cussed boundaries in community, and collaboratively created healthy boundary guidelines? Our society does not educate people to identify and skillfully respond to power differentials, and it is likely that you and your community are not prepared; spiritual groups, local Sang-has, and faith-based congregations must study and learn from these painful lessons to prevent such traumas from occurring close to home.

## Gender Power and Sexual Misconduct

The backbone of sexual misconduct in religious communities throughout the centuries has been patriarchal power. The intersection of gender power with positional power and religious authority has given men in spiritual leadership the freedom to commit misconduct without accountability. Most of the world's major religions are deeply rooted in patriarchal systems to varying degrees, and Buddhism is no different. Whether in the East Asian countries where Buddhism has originated and flourished or the European-dominated cultures where it has spread, society provides cisgender men an enormous power differential over women, trans, genderqueer, and non-binary persons. Multiple studies have revealed that 96 percent of helping professionals who had sex with their clients, patients, or students identified as men. Other studies have revealed that roughly 10–20 percent of males who serve in helping professions (doctors, professors, psychologists, therapists, for example) have been sexually active with their patients, students, or clients. Meanwhile, 30 percent of male clergy had sexual relationships with their congregants.[48] These numbers are simply staggering.

One thing we know helps to reverse this ancient trend of violence is to talk openly and acknowledge the harm of power without accountability. This is where our strength lies. Our communities can be a force of positive change by breaking old habits of complacency, silence, and exploitative power structures. To think that our community is immune to these problems is naive, given the consistent pervasiveness of misconduct. Male-identifying teachers and Sangha leaders need to be more than just aware of these problems. We can use the power that society or our community has bestowed upon us to be active learners and change agents who address these longstanding wounds by studying the roots of power in our community, implementing healthy boundaries, and establishing greater safety for everyone.

Individuals and communities cannot protect themselves until they can identify, understand, and talk openly about power dynamics. Power is usually most harmful when it operates invisibly, silently, and without accountability, quietly serving the one wielding it whether they are conscious of the harm being caused or not. Taboos and discomfort around discussing power undermine a community's ability to guide healthy power dynamics and provide accountability.

The key to dismantling unchecked power's potential recklessness is community awareness, speaking openly about power differentials, and clarifying boundaries that reflect community members' real needs. This collective awareness supports leaders and everyone else in making safe and informed decisions and fosters healthy relationships for everyone. This chapter aims to teach you how to identify and concretely break down power dynamics in your life so that you can have these constructive discussions in your home community.

## Sources of Power

The simplest definition of power is "the capacity to influence." It stems from the Latin word *posse*, meaning, "to be able," that is, to be able to influence others. Power in and of itself is not good or bad, positive or negative. It is like a raw resource, inherently neutral, and can be used to help or hurt, depending on the one's intent, skillfulness, and circumstances. Whether we recognize it or not, each person has various sources of power that are always influencing relationships. Whether power is beneficial or harmful depends on how well we understand and relate to it. In her foreword to *The Power Book,* Roxanne Gay encourages young people, "If more people understand power, they will be better able to handle the responsibility … and know what you can do with your power to create change for yourself and the people you care about."[49]

In *The Emotionally Healthy Leader,* Peter Scazzero clearly defines and describes six main categories of power. Adapting these categories for spiritual communities, we will take some time exploring these power sources, which are so foundational to community dynamics.

For each category of power described below, please reflect upon and write down examples in your own life and community, both in domains where you have more power and where others have more power. Remember that having power is neither good nor bad; rather, the key is to first recognize clearly and non-judgmentally where power exists in order to better understand relationship roles, vulnerability, and needs in any given situation.

1. The first source of power is *positional power,* which comes from particular roles in the community: facilitator, Dharma teacher, staff member, meditation instructor, or ordained clergy, for example. Whether these positions were authorized, encouraged by others, or taken up by individuals themselves, they all embody positional power.

2. *Projectional power* occurs when an individual or group projects their ideas, infatuation, esteem, or criticisms onto another person. For example, community leaders may have projectional power given their spiritual training, personal charisma, lectures, public recognition, or other reasons. In one instance I am personally familiar with, Thich Nhat Hanh had tremendous projectional power as an internationally renowned Zen master and author. After teaching events for two, five, and ten thousand people, he often shared with us monastic students, "It is easy to get caught and think people are here to see Thay as an individual. But Thay knows it is not me they are here for—they come for the Three Jewels (the teachings of the Buddha, the Dharm, and the Sangha)." Thay taught us how to cut through projections and aggrandizement and instead cultivate humility. Whether others' projections are positive, negative, or neutral, they are based upon limited perceptions.

3. *Relational or social power* is based upon relational proximity to others with power. Those with close relationships to an executive director or senior Dharma teacher—a teacher's attendant, the treasurer's wife, or someone with consistent contact with the board chair, for example—have greater relational power. How community leaders communicate and relate to their peers affects how expansive or concentrated relational power becomes. Communities which foster a dynamically connected

relational web with many strong relationships are more resilient and less vulnerable than ones with solo teachers at the
center of an isolated relational wheel.

4. *Power of resources* means owning, managing, contributing,
   using, or even possibly transferring wealth, land, materials,
   and other resources in the community. For example, donors,
   financial stakeholders, a treasurer, landowner, director, or
   others who manage community resources have this power of
   resources. Our society places tremendous esteem, adoration,
   and respect to those with resource power. This may not be easy
   to address, but it is very important in community life. It is not
   difficult to see how those with significant resource power can
   have an outsized influence on a community's direction or decisions. Transparency in resource management and decision-
   making is key.

5. *Personal power* includes attributes, talents, or skills that are
   transmitted to us biologically, socially, or by circumstances
   of opportunity, such as being charismatic, good-looking or
   having "pretty privilege," formally educated, athletic, able-bod-
   ied, skilled in the arts, or a gifted orator. Each of us has myriad
   sources of personal power, both active and latent, that may
   develop and change over time.

6. *Power of privilege* is an advantage due solely to socially attributed
   identities. For example, identities of gender, race, class, health,
   mental health, sexual orientation, nationality, or citizenship
   have associated privileges depending on the societal context.
   For example, since I present as a White straight man, which is
   the dominant race, gender, and sexual orientation in the United
   States, I have untold advantages in social, professional, legal,
   educational, and other domains that I have done nothing in my
   lifetime to earn. The more I open my eyes to the vast horizon of
   privilege, the more this mountain range is revealed.

It is never just one particular domain of power, but rather the con-
fluence of multiple sources of power that leads to exponentially stronger
power and vulnerability dynamics. When multiple sources of power
overlap and compound, this creates interdependent systems of advantage and disadvantage. For example, widespread sexual misconduct
in religious communities is rooted in the weighty combination of historical male gender privilege, exclusive male spiritual leadership, and
controlling resources in religious communities. The complex nature of
power is why identifying its various sources is such a crucial first step
toward understanding and then fostering healthy power dynamics.

How we relate to and express these sources of power also influences whether they are used beneficially or not; learning about classic
power dynamics as expressed in the "four expressions of power"[50] can
further strengthen the community's safety and healthy relationship to
power.

1.  The most familiar of the four expressions, "power over," is built
    on control, force, coercion, or domination. In this expression,
    power is a limited resource that some people have and others
    do not. It can still be used beneficially or harmfully toward
    others, but it is limited to being expressed by the dominant
    actor.

2.  The second expression, "power to," is someone's unique poten-
    tial to shape their own life.

3.  When combined with mutual support, "power to" opens pos-
    sibilities of collaborative power, or "power with." This expres-
    sion of power multiplies individual strengths, knowledge, and
    resources by finding common ground and developing solidar-
    ity and support; for example, when marginalized communities
    combine their power to generate large, collaborative social
    movements.

4.  Finally, "power within" reflects one's sense of self-worth and
    their capacity for self-actualization. "Power within" can manifest

as a capacity to cultivate hope, dignity, and fulfillment, even in difficult situations.

Thich Nhat Hanh often taught about spiritual power—the ability to cut through afflictions—which is partly "power within" and partly "power with." Sitting in a meditation hall together with other practitioners has the power to help each person cultivate peace and joy within; it is the power with others that encourages and supports our power within, and these powers interact in mutually reinforcing ways.

Leaders themselves benefit enormously from a stronger collective awareness that guides them to exercise their power more carefully and skillfully. Not only leaders, but also every community member has power that is continually growing and changing. Power affects all dynamics of community life; none are excluded.

## Examining Power in Community

Reflecting on and discussing sources of power and expressions of power as a community is a courageous and compassionate step to interrupt potentially harmful power dynamics and ensure healthier and more resilient relationships in our spiritual communities. Deepening awareness of one another's vulnerability within structural power dynamics also has great potential to deepen bonds of communal empathy and solidarity. When a community cracks open the taboo of power dynamics, open discussions greatly reduce the likelihood leadership power will be misused, intentionally or unintentionally.

For example, Mia Mingus, a writer and community organizer who focuses on issues of disability justice, coined the phrase, "access intimacy," which she describes as that "elusive, hard to describe feeling when someone else 'gets' your access needs." How is access intimacy expressed or built in community relationships? Mingus writes,

> It has looked like relationships where I always feel like I can say what my access needs are, no matter what. Or I can say that I don't know them, and that's ok too. . . . It has looked like able-bodied

*people listening to me and believing me. It has looked like people*
*investing in remembering my access needs and checking in with me*
*if there are going to be situations that might be inaccessible or hard*
*disability-body-wise.*[51]

Access intimacy acknowledges where structural power differentials
cause vulnerability for people and points to an ability to show up for
each other as an interdependent web of communal support.

I will be honest, though: while such group discussions can be
extremely helpful, they can also be uncomfortable, particularly for
those who need it the most. The first time I led a workshop on power
and vulnerability dynamics for a few dozen Sangha leaders, including some Dharma teachers, I asked participants to identify sources
of power in their community and personal lives according to the
six categories I previously described. A small handful of long-term
practitioners, including Dharma teachers, expressed that they felt
too uncomfortable or frustrated to even participate in the exercise!
At first, I was shocked by their reluctance to engage in such a simple
reflection. I did not understand until later that the topic touched old
wounds within them—people often associate power with manipulation or self-serving interests, and these individuals did not want to see
themselves as having power in their spiritual community of friends.
This state of collective denial, miseducation, and trauma around
power dynamics leads to blind spots in communal awareness and ultimately makes us susceptible to misconduct. These conversations need
patience, sensitivity, and follow-through.

Avoiding such discussions of power is where the most danger lies.
My experience is that the greatest harm occurs when people feel emotionally powerless inside yet simultaneously have significant power
over others. This can lead individuals to think and act in controlling
ways that overcompensate for their inner deprivation, often to the
harm of others—knowingly or unknowingly. Even in subtle ways,
many if not most of us think and behave like this at times. This is why
collectively learning about, identifying, and discussing our individual

sources of power as well as our inner emotional landscape is so crucial for mature leadership. Author and teacher of nonviolence and peace strategies Kazu Haga writes, "Real safety doesn't guarantee that we will not be uncomfortable. Real safety means that we create spaces that are safe enough to have brave and oftentimes difficult conversations, knowing that our relationship will only be strengthened by them."[52]

## PRACTICE: A COMMUNITY EXERCISE ON POWER

You do not have to be an expert on the subject in order to facilitate a discussion about it. Here's a blueprint for opening dialogue around power in your community.

First, make sure everyone involved understands that to create more safety in a community, it is essential for its leaders and members to identify and discuss sources of power.

Then present the six different categories of power, described above (power over, power to, power with, and power within).

Next, invite everyone to silently reflect upon and journal about each category, identifying relationships where they have more power as well as ones where others have power.

Alternatively, you can invite people to reflect upon just one relationship where they have several sources of power (such as with their children or a client) and another relationship where someone else may have several sources of power over them (such as with their teacher or mentor).

Lastly, invite people to share about their reflections with the group, identifying the sources of power, how they expressed such power, their emotional responses during the reflection, and any other insights that emerged.

## Caring for the Power of Attraction

With the help of the following example, I invite us to study more closely what happens to relationships in spiritual community when unexamined power dynamics and a lack of healthy boundaries are present. This is a story I encountered about ten years ago in a local Sangha. (Names and identifying information have been changed.)

Latisha, a Black woman in her late twenties, started attending a mindfulness group for young adults every Sunday evening, enjoying the support for her meditation practice and the company of a new group of kind friends. She increasingly felt a part of the community and developed a warm friendship with Jacob, a White man in his early thirties who had started the group at his house several months prior. Jacob loved bringing people together and was a natural at facilitating groups and explaining mindfulness.

Jacob was exploring dating, and his mentor Rebecca, an experienced facilitator, encouraged him to think about dating Latisha, given her wonderful qualities and their similar ideals. While Jacob questioned their long-term compatibility, he was open to exploring, so he asked Latisha to spend time together outside of Sangha. Latisha felt nervous about dating Jacob given their relationship in the community, but she was excited about having a more exclusive connection with Jacob. They started dating but never talked about what would happen if they broke up. After about six months, Jacob decided to pursue another relationship with someone outside their community, so he ended his romantic connection with Latisha, to her disappointment. While Jacob tried continuing a friendship, Latisha felt confused and heartbroken by the loss. She later learned that Jacob started dating a White woman, and this touched wounds of racial discrimination in Latisha that Jacob did not understand.

It became too uncomfortable for them to attend the group's mindfulness gatherings together, so they tried rotating weeks. But the group mostly met at Jacob's house, and Jacob had a central leadership role; Latisha began to feel excluded and hopeless. The group no longer felt emotionally safe for her, and she left entirely. She felt angry at Jacob and heartbroken about the loss of her community. On the one hand, Jacob felt terrible that Latisha no longer attended and that their friendship was ruined. On the other hand, he believed that breakups are a natural part of relationships and that they were both responsible for their own feelings.

What do the teachings on power have to say about this story? Jacob was unknowingly engaged in a *dual relationship* with Latisha. A dual or multiple relationship is when anyone in leadership has an additional role with someone within the group they're leading, for example, as both a teacher and friend, or as both a counselor and next-door neighbor. Dual relationships are common, cannot always be avoided, and are not inherently harmful. But when the power differential is significant, vulnerability is created for the client, student, or community. Dual relationships involving spiritual mentorship and romantic or sexual connection are extremely vulnerable, and are almost always considered sexual misconduct. Those in positions of spiritual leadership are 100 percent responsible for maintaining appropriate behavior and preventing harm within dual relationships. Even if a member projects feelings of attraction or makes sexual advances, it remains the responsibility of those in leadership to exercise safe boundaries in the relationship, given the original purpose and aim of their position. These suggestions are no different from the ethical codes of conduct for ministers, rabbi, counselors, physicians, or anyone else in positions of authority or power relative to participants, whether the position of power is voluntary or compensated.

Jacob's belief that he and Latisha were equally responsible adults on a fair playing field was misguided and ultimately harmful—the faulty foundation of beliefs gave rise to harmful conduct. It's not just Jacob—many people in Sanghas, especially young adult communities, also believe everyone is just friends and members of a couple are equally responsible. But this understanding is predicated on the assumption that everyone has equal standing and power in the community; this view, based on misunderstandings about power, is inherently wrong. In Wake Up communities, where young adults practice mindfulness in the Plum Village tradition, people almost never use the word "leader," preferring the words "facilitator" or "ambassador" instead. This language is intentional and meant to convey that many people can lead the Sangha—no one person assumes single ownership or control. Having no "president," "king," "queen," or "boss" in charge creates opportunity for horizontal leadership and shared power among members. However, not identifying people as "leaders" when they are in fact assuming roles of spiritual leadership (positional power) can be misleading. Whether people are conscious of it or not, the responsibilities that accompany positions of spiritual leadership are not the same as those of casual friends.

People often come to Sanghas or other spiritual communities in order to learn, grow, and heal, emotionally and psychologically. Thus, they are intentionally and vulnerably opening themselves to the support and trust of teachers, facilitators, and community. Given the emotional intimacy of this process, it is natural for feelings of infatuation and attraction to occur (i.e., projectional power). This makes their safety with Sangha leaders so much more crucial.

In my own experience as a mindfulness teacher and therapist, I am continually learning to pay vigilant attention to the seeds of attraction and infatuation that may be touched in me while serving others. People's praise and positive regard helps me feel more confident, safe, appreciated, and worthy—all really pleasant feelings! This may lead me to consciously or unconsciously speak, look, or behave in ways that elicit further projections or attraction. Noticing rather than ignoring my attachment to these pleasant feelings is my best protection. Recognizing and embracing my own needs for self-worth and acceptance helps me not depend on my clients or students to have these personal needs met. It can be humbling to talk about such attractions or attachments to praise, yet the more that I speak openly with mentors, friends, and therapists, the easier they are to work with. Caring for one's inner landscape of attractions is a precious offering of leadership to one's community.

While leaders are responsible for their roles and behavior, what is the responsibility of the rest of the community, given that power exists multi-dimensionally? As Scott Edelstein writes in *Sex and the Spiritual Teacher*, we all have some power and responsibility to keep each other and our community safe and accountable. Each of us has a responsibility to the whole, and the whole community is responsible to each member. How can we put this into action? This is the aim of our next chapter.

# CHAPTER 15

# COCREATING HEALTHY BOUNDARIES

*Boundaries are the distance at which I can love you and me simultaneously*

—PRENTIS HEMPHILL

*As philosophers have long recognized, true community depends on a shared commitment to virtue.*

—BHIKKHU BODHI

*What do I value the most about living in a mindfulness community? The opportunity to face my fears. Especially fears around setting boundaries and trusting others. It's a chance to explore what my needs really are.*

—CECILIA REED, WAKE UP LONDON

With a fierce tone and plea of compassion in his eyes, Michael addressed the hall of Buddhist teachers from over thirty traditions. "We never think it's going to happen to us. These scandals are something that only happens in other communities, right? No, that's wrong. Because it's happened to us, and it will happen to your community, too, at some point." He paused, letting his words sink in. "We have to prevent this from happening now and in the future, and we know how to do this," he continued resolutely. "Please don't wait. Discuss this with your community and write a code of conduct together now."

In 2019, I was attending the European Buddhist Union's annual conference in Barcelona, where I had been invited to give a keynote lecture about Sangha-building practices. Michael was a Dutch man from an international Sangha still reeling from grave misconduct. Their founding teacher, Sogyal Rinpoche, had been recently exposed for secret sexual relationships with dozens of young female students, all in the name of transmitting sacred teachings. Their entire tradition, including Michael's local chapter, experienced a painfully sobering disillusionment and community-wide trauma. Not only Michael, but two additional teachers from other traditions on the panel shared how sexual misconduct had ravaged their international communities.

As Michael shared, the creation of ethical codes of conduct and healthy boundaries is the safe path out of this mess. Such documents are not mere pieces of paper; they are living and breathing agreements of wise guidance and accountability, created by and embodied within community. Given the complexity and crucial importance of community safety, this chapter offers thorough guidance across diverse domains of leadership, friendships, and community life, including: step-by-step guidance to create community-led ethical guidelines; questions and prompts to guide challenging yet fruitful discussions; stories from other communities' challenges and successes; culturally respectful considerations in establishing appropriate boundaries; clear guidance for community leaders to avoid mistakes and misfortune; and ways to safely navigate romantic interests between Sangha members.

## Creating Healthy Boundaries in Your Community

Experts suggest that setting boundaries is the root of both self-care and care for the community. In her book, *Set Boundaries, Find Peace*, Nedra Glover Tawwab defines boundaries as "Expectations and needs that help you feel safe and comfortable in your relationships." She goes on to clarify, "The root of self-care is setting boundaries."[53] In faith-based communities, boundaries help lay a foundation so further healing can occur in safe parameters. The following quote is widely attributed to Prentis Hemphill, an African American teacher and writer:

> *Boundaries give us the space to do the work of loving ourselves. They might be, actually, the first and fundamental expression of self-love. They also give us the space to love and witness others as they are, even those that have hurt us.*

Healthy boundaries help people to both feel safe and express themselves vulnerably in community—benefiting themselves and the community—because they offer a trustworthy foundation of protection from physical or emotional harm. Based on the combination of my own experience and researching other communities, here are the key steps in creating healthy boundaries for your community, further expounded below:

1. **Take inventory of your own power in community and dual relationships**. Invite your community to engage in reflection exercises about sources of power and privilege, and their influence on relationships.

2. **Learn about and discuss** topics of safety, power-vulnerability dynamics, dual relationships, and healthy boundaries in your community.

3. **Write a healthy boundaries document with your Sangha.** Actively involve everyone's ideas and contributions so that it is a truly cocreated and living document. Everyone's needs for safety are important, and care is needed to center the needs, well-being, and safety of those most vulnerable in the community.

4. **Understand and discuss the cultural context** of your community when drafting and implementing healthy boundaries.

6. **Create a Harmony Council.** Composed of at least two people, preferably different genders, Sangha members can go to them with questions or concerns about Sangha safety.

## Steps One and Two: Taking Inventory and Shattering Taboos

The first step in creating community safety is to take an inventory of power in your community, especially among community leaders, as explored in the last chapter. The second step is to hold community discussions about power-vulnerability dynamics and healthy boundaries. Ethical guidelines should never be followed blindly. Rather, you can start with communal conversations about these taboo subjects, seek counsel from others, and come to collective agreements.

Due to widespread pain or trauma around issues of misconduct, your group may first want to discuss *how* to create a brave space for such discussions. Is there someone everyone trusts to facilitate such delicate and meaningful conversations? Based on their own gender expression, racial identity, or other identities, can they relate safely and empathetically to the needs of other members? Otherwise, you can invite external facilitators more experienced in this field to educate and safely initiate such discussions.

Along the same lines, it is important for men always to remember that the vast majority of sexual misconduct in spiritual communities (and everywhere else) is perpetrated by men. These conversations can be triggering for people, and cisgender men in the room must try to listen as deeply and receptively as possible. At the same time, men must be willing to show up and contribute as much as needed for discussions and implementation. Receptive willingness on the part of men, even when they are uncomfortable, is an expression of compassion and radical friendship toward women, genderqueer, and BIPOC members. This paradox between receptive humility and willingness may be confusing at times for men, but it is a paradox we, as men, must embrace in order to both help others and heal ourselves. My friend Sophie Sarkar, BIPOC activist and author of the children's book *Mixed Rice*, offers these words: "I find myself relieved when cis men are proactive in upholding their own and each other's healthy boundaries so that the labor does not fall on those who are most often recipients of sexual abuse and misconduct, such as women, queer, trans, and non-binary folks. I also believe that this work can be transformative for cis men, who have often been socialized from an early age to dominate and exploit the bodies of other genders. It is an invitation for them to heal the deep wounds of this superiority complex and recover their humanity and capacity to love."

Another friend and Sangha leader, Laurie Rabut, shared with me that when she facilitates discussions related to community safety, restorative justice, or healthy boundaries, she asks the community, "What are people's needs on this important issue?" In response to safety and healthy boundaries, people may say, "Helping people, especially women and non-binary friends, to feel safe and empowered," or "providing guidance and education to Sangha leaders," or "having accountability in place for appropriate behaviors." Laurie writes these answers down on a board where everyone can see them. This deep listening approach invites the whole community to understand one another's needs and priorities more easily before discussing or arguing about specific strategies.

Once the group has sufficiently shared their needs related to safety, trust, and respect, Laurie invites the group to brainstorm together: "What ideas and strategies do people have to meet these various needs?" The participants discuss different ideas and then decide which ones to focus on. For example, someone may suggest that several members attend a healthy boundaries training and then educate the community. Someone else may recommend that different meditation facilitators be trained so that the community leadership does not rest with just one person. Another person may propose that the Sangha write a code of conduct to be shared on the website.

Please remember that no matter how much a community studies these topics, people are bound to make mistakes related to their roles, power, unclear boundaries, insensitivity to trauma, and cultural ignorance. While mistakes can be difficult for all parties involved, they can also, when tended to with great care, be prime opportunities for learning and growing together. Inevitably, your community will continue to make mistakes; now, they may happen with greater care and there-fore greater learning and hopefully less painful consequences.

## Step Three: Ethical Codes of Conduct— An Ancient Practice

The greatest prevention to misconduct of all kinds is through collec-tively creating or adopting an ethical code of conduct agreed upon by all members—the third step of creating communal safety. A code of conduct is like the rib cage of the Sangha, protecting its vital organs and preventing injury from misused power.

I once had the opportunity to eat lunch with a small group of close students of Thanissaro Bhikkhu, a senior American monk in the Thai Forest tradition, along with the teacher himself. After the meal, I asked him, "What do you consider most important in building a harmoni-ous and thriving Sangha?" He answered simply, "Having a practice that you all follow and having precepts that you all share." Just to be sure, I asked, "That's it?" He nodded, "Yes, that's it." It was cut and dry, emphasizing the no-nonsense wisdom of shared ethical agreements.

Pioneering American teacher in the Vipassana tradition Jack Kornfield similarly writes, "The most obvious principle in the main-tenance of a wise spiritual community is the establishment of clear ethical guidelines that are followed by all." The advice is so simple, yet practicing it is another story. To emphasize this point, Kornfield recounts, "One Zen master told me that the moral precepts were very important for students to follow, but, of course, Zen masters didn't need to bother with them since they were 'free.' You can imagine what troubles later visited that community."[54] This chapter is offered to sup-port our communities and prevent at least some of such troubles!

Broad ethical guidelines such as the Five Precepts (or Five Mind-fulness Trainings in the Plum Village tradition) address sexual mis-conduct in the form of adultery, child abuse, or generally "misusing" sexuality, but they don't concretely address the vast spectrum of inap-propriate sexualized behaviors related to power and vulnerability dynamics that is especially needed for teachers or community leaders.

Over the course of centuries, the Buddhist monastic Sangha developed both precepts and fine manners to protect the monastic Sangha's practice and the connected lay community. The dramatic rise of lay Dharma communities in non-Asian countries is still evolving and generally, although not exclusively, lacks these strong ethical foundations to concretely support lay teachers and leaders to use their power appropriately. For those of us in these lay communities, creating such ethical codes is our work.

## Cocreating Ethical Guidelines

The most empowering and sustainable path of safety for a community is to cocreate its own ethical guidelines. This should especially relate to appropriate sexual conduct, given the severity of the harm that can be caused. But ethical guidelines can also more broadly address how members should speak, touch, and relate to one another. Creating such guidelines should involve as many core community members as possible, not just the few "in charge." A document that is collaboratively discussed and created will be more deeply embodied in the community consciousness and therefore more effective in manifesting experiences of safety. Community safety never comes to fruition by one person alone. Rather, safety is both alive and relationally dynamic—therefore, it is optimally supported, protected, and enhanced by collective awareness and relational strength. This is extremely important—real safety, both the guidelines and expression of it, must come from the community body itself.

In my Sangha, Greatwoods Zen, we are currently expanding upon our healthy boundaries guidelines to address a broader range of needs for safety, trust, and friendship in our Sangha. While we already had firm guidelines for right sexual conduct, a few of our female members courageously and skillfully shared their lack of emotional safety and discomfort in different situations. We humbly invited those members, if they wished, to help lead a discussion or offer suggestions for new community guidelines about how members relate safely to each other, for example, relating to how people touch or speak about others' appearances. For example, during retreats we now maintain and remind the Sangha that people should always ask for consent before any kind of physical touch toward any Sangha member, including hugs, and that consent is alive, subject to change at any time. This raises people's awareness about how touch affects people differently, including their sense of safety, and reminds them to exercise sensitivity and care. I am extremely grateful that our Sangha is becoming safer and stronger with the leadership and insights of our members. By collaborating together, we are cocreating a deeply desired environment of trust and security that our society is not yet able to consistently provide for women and other groups who consistently experience a lack of physical and emotional safety.

## Healthy Boundaries for Sexual Conduct

No matter how wise and stable people appear, no spiritual teacher or leader is perfect; they too need the community's awareness and accountability to help guide their actions, both subtle and obvious, for the well-being of all.

In general, there are three forms of sexual misconduct which necessitate clear, healthy boundaries:

1. A sexual relationship is never appropriate between a teacher, mentor, or supervisor with someone they are mentoring, teaching, supervising, or to whom they are providing spiritual guidance. Any suggestions of a romantic or sexual relationship between a teacher and student are also inappropriate.

2. It is inappropriate for those in positions of leadership to begin a romantic or sexual relationship with those they're leading.

3. It is always sexual misconduct for an adult within the Sangha to engage sexually with any minors in the Sangha. Full responsibility for avoiding such relationships lies with the adult.

Power differentials (projectional and relational) still continue after mentoring relationships are formally over. Therefore, it is questionable whether romantic or sexual relationships are ever acceptable for former teachers or mentors and students, given the great potential for harm, and considering the level of vulnerability in the relationship. "Romantic" here is defined as "relating to love or sexual relationships." At the very minimum, those in leadership involved should wait until the teaching relationship has been over for some time before exploring a romantic relationship. Additionally, both parties should always consult with experienced community leaders or outside professionals before beginning a relationship.

Lama Rod Owens illuminates the crucial need for boundaries by acknowledging the human reality of his own sexual needs, the vulnerability of his students, and that a sexual relationship within his community is never truly consensual due to his power as a teacher. In an interview about sexuality, he says,

> As a spiritual teacher my practice is first and foremost accepting and acknowledging that I do have physical, sexual attractions to many people.... As a teacher, I cannot engage in any kind of sexual relationship with a student or mentee because there is a power differential in my relationship with students, which makes authentic consent very difficult if not impossible. So, when I seek sexual relationships, it's always outside of my spiritual communities.[55]

Ultimately, every community must develop specific guidelines according to their particular cultural, organizational, and individual needs. For example, Spirit Rock, the meditation center in Northern California cofounded by Jack Kornfield, openly explains in their code of conduct that several teachers in their community developed partnerships and marriages with former students. They assert that such healthy relationships are possible, but that great care and sensitivity are needed. Their guidelines maintain that the student-teacher relationship must be over for at least three months and that both individuals must consult with a senior teacher before developing a romantic relationship together. This allows some flexibility combined with standards of safety. In contrast, at Great Vow Monastery, a Zen center in Oregon, the teacher-student relationship is at the core of their spiritual practice and thus embodies a deep vulnerability for the student. Thus, their code of conduct requires higher degrees of safety, stating, "We vow to refrain permanently from engaging in romantic or sexual relationships with current and previous students." If any romantic or sexual attractions develop, the teacher must consult with a senior teacher and determine whether the teaching relationship should end.

When friends and I started Greatwoods Zen in 2023, one of the first policies we created was to set healthy boundaries for leadership. We drafted several iterations over time before finally adopting a policy similar to Spirit Rock's ethical code in three categories:

1. Teachers, mentors, and supervisors are never allowed to become romantically involved with students or staff.

2. Those in any leadership position, even minor roles, are not allowed to start a romantic or sexual relationship with people currently involved in the community.

3. Current members must wait at least three months before approaching a new member with any romantic interest.

4. Those in leadership roles may develop a romantic interest with those who have formerly been attendees or members of the community, waiting at least three months before approaching them. They should also consult with at least one senior Dharma teacher who is knowledgeable about healthy boundaries before pursuing or developing a romantic relationship with the former member.

The document discusses and explains each guideline in greater detail; it can be read at *Greatwoodszen.org*. Our policy is not perfect, yet it has provided us with a foundation of safety and ethical conduct that we can continue to grow with over time.

Whenever I begin formally mentoring someone, I say, "Since you have asked me to mentor you, I am committed to always supporting your safety, well-being, and spiritual growth. As such, I will never express romantic or sexual interest in our relationship."

The first time I said this to a young woman who asked for mentorship, I felt quite uncomfortable and embarrassed. The words would barely come out of my mouth. Yet I also felt relieved and strong in myself, and I experienced that a close trust between us arose immediately after. Identifying as a straight man myself, I initially only said this to female mentees. But now I see that everyone I mentor, regardless of their gender and orientation, deserves such clarity, trust, and respect.

## Nuances

Leadership conduct also applies to more nuanced behaviors; there are countless aspects of healthy boundaries your Sangha may consider developing. Aside from entering into an explicit relationship, spiritual teachers and leaders should maintain awareness about how their speech and behavior may contain flirtatious or sexualizing messages that threaten the actual or perceived sense of safety in the relationship. This includes refraining from expressing sexual gestures, verbal innuendo, invasive personal questioning, scheduling of dates, inappropriate touching, intimate self-disclosures, romantic gifts or expressions, and other forms of flirtation. Moreover, the practice of consent is of utmost importance, even if the intentions are not romantic. Care must be taken not to put someone in an uncomfortable situation where they may not feel safe to refuse an interaction, such as personal gifts, hugs, or spending time alone.

Certain boundaries are clear, black and white distinctions. But more often, gray areas need discernment and discussion. Your Sangha may like to discuss questions such as: Can experienced members date new members; if so, what conditions must be met before someone approaches a newer member with romantic interest? If someone formerly attended the community, can a Sangha leader become romantically involved? What extent of closeness and friendship can Sangha leaders have with other members? Such discussions illuminate the Sangha's awareness of power-vulnerability dynamics, shine the light on potential risks, enhance every member's understanding of safety, and pave the way toward greater relational harmony.

## Avoiding Misconduct

Preventing misconduct begins with community standards created by individual initiatives for safety. At a young adult Sangha that I co-led many years ago, I started noticing romantic attractions occurring among others in the group as well as myself. Our facilitator team decided to address the issue at the beginning or end of each gathering by saying:

> We are all young adults here and attractions between people are normal. But we are here first and foremost as friends—to support each other in embracing our suffering and finding joy within. The Sangha is not a dating site—it's a friendship site! We want everyone to feel safe, be themselves, and trust each other. If we notice attractions coming up, that's okay; they come and go, and we can breathe with them compassionately while respecting each other's space here.

It was a little awkward addressing this at first, but people understood and respected it. The reminders helped to ground and refresh the group vibe, encouraging people to let go of their constant thinking about, pursuing, and defending against romantic attractions. People need to feel safe in their environment in order to relax into meditation, genuinely open up to each other, and bond joyfully as a community.

## Supporting Leaders

What kind of practice will support leaders to consistently think and act wisely? Understanding misconduct is easy when reading a book or talking about another community's problems. But having clarity during personally evocative circumstances is another story. Just think about all the renowned male teachers across spiritual traditions whose sexual misconduct brought down their entire community: How and why did those teachers act so foolishly when their life intentions and actions were previously so compassionate and wise? Bruce Lee supposedly said, "Under duress, we do not rise to our expectations, but fall to our level of training."

Here are several strategies to support leaders in their training to consistently strengthen healthy boundaries now in order to minimize or avoid great harm tomorrow:

1.  Newer Sangha leaders should sign their agreement to previously developed guidelines.

2.  Those in leadership, especially men, should reflect upon possible scenarios and provoking questions. "What will I do if I feel attraction to a student, or if a member approaches me with romantic interest? If I feel confused, what is a safe response, and who can I talk to for wise counsel?" Reflect alone, but also share your thoughts with other community leaders. In the book *Teachings on Love*, Thich Nhat Hanh writes that when a spiritual teacher considers having a sexual relationship with a student, he should meditate on the tremendous suffering that would be caused by such an act, even for generations to come. Meditating on this future suffering will naturally foster compassion in his heart and lead him to avoid such behavior.

3.  Sangha leaders should have a network of friends, mentors, and teachers for support and consultation. Loneliness is one of the biggest underlying causes for spiritual leaders to become sexually involved with their students or congregants. Having close friends who are in similar leadership positions or who are outside the community nurtures one's social and emotional well-being so that one does not depend on students to meet such needs. When attractions manifest, it is best to talk to multiple confidants, especially those who are knowledgeable in healthy boundaries. One confidant is not enough, as most people, including those in leadership, are clueless about power and vulnerability dynamics; as such, their judgment may not be soundly relied upon.

## Step Four: Cultural Needs and Appropriateness

Aside from the main pillars of ethical sexual conduct, each Sangha will express safety and boundaries differently depending on its cultural values and group norms. Understanding and discussing cultural context is the fourth step of creating community safety.

Before the COVID-19 pandemic, several friends from Mexico told me that during their Sangha gatherings, everyone hugs each other, puts their hands on one another's shoulders, and generally exudes warmth and physical connection. One friend who recently moved to the United States from Mexico shared, "It's not like here in the States where people are so distant that it feels cold. Us Mexicans, we like being physically close and affectionate with each other." She shared this with warm eyes and a big smile, her face quite close to mine. I admired her freedom and closeness; admittedly, I also felt curious whether other members felt less comfortable in such physically affectionate environments.

Other Sanghas from Vietnam and Europe that I've visited have been almost the opposite. When I visited a young adult Sangha in Vietnam, people looked very happy to see each other, but instead of hugs, they offered big cheerful smiles, exuberant eyes, and a bow before exchanging greetings. In some all-ages Sanghas I visited, like the Heart of London Sangha, the practice begins and ends in silence. A gentle smile and half-bow before quietly taking one's seat is enough greeting. People feel free to come and go with ease and concentration, free from distraction. After meditation is over, those who wish to hang out may gather in the lobby or at a nearby cafe. In many other young adult groups across North America and Europe that I've visited, social and physical affection can be pretty loose. During Wake Up retreats or after weekly gatherings, I've witnessed or experienced young people relaxing on sofas or lying on the floor in friendly "cuddle-puddles" while enjoying post-meditation vibes together. The language of physical touch nurtures bonds of connection, joy, and care for each other. The risk, however, is that boundaries between members, especially those in leadership, can become murky.

How can communities balance intimacy and safety given multi-faceted cultural expressions of touch and intimacy? One approach is for leaders to ask the community for people's preferences, needs, and guidance. This is not only a safe move, but also generates empowering discussion and insights. Facilitators may ask, "What are people's thoughts about an optional hugging meditation practice after we close?" Or "How do people prefer to be greeted or say goodbye at the beginning and end of a gathering?" Such questions give people space to directly speak their needs, and help inform community members how to support one another and make each other feel safe. For some people and cultures, touching and hugging without asking is an everyday occurrence. In other contexts, touching someone without their consent can feel unsafe and disrespectful. Many people, especially women, queer folks, and BIPOC carry the mark of centuries of oppression and violations to their bodies. As such, a community may wish to develop guidelines to invite more sensitivity and respect: "We agree that during gatherings, we will ask permission and receive consent before touching anyone's body, hair, or belongings, including hugging."

Boundaries are not only important, they are something to appreciate and celebrate! Communicating boundaries gives others implicit encouragement to name their own. When someone expresses a boundary such as not wanting a hug, they are trusting you enough to say how they really feel. Once, a close Sangha female friend told me that my hugs were "lingering" and asked me to be briefer. At first, I felt surprised and ashamed that my hugs had unknowingly caused her discomfort. But after reflection, I felt extremely appreciative for her honesty, which allowed me to better understand and respond to her lived experience. As a White-presenting cis man who grew up feeling generally safe in my body in the United States, I must continually strive to better listen, learn, and engage others' needs and expressions for safety and trust in community.

If someone oversteps your boundary, it is not your fault and it does not reflect how you care for yourself. If you previously liked hugs but hugging without consent no longer feels good to you, it is okay to communicate that. Chances are, you are not the only one who feels this way. It can be as easy as saying, "Well, I prefer you ask me before giving me a hug in the future—thank you."

### Step Five: Creating a Safety Council

In order to develop and oversee an ethical code of conduct and appropriately receive grievances, every spiritual community should have some kind of "safety council." Whatever name you give it, this is a group that practices what we call "Sangha eyes," looking after the well-being of the community. As a group, they can see and hear more clearly than any one person alone. The council can listen deeply to the Sangha's needs for safety as well as facilitate discussions within the whole community, thereby contributing diverse insights into a healthy boundaries document. Members can approach the council members with questions or concerns about their own or others' safety and well-being. The council should have at least two people who are known in the Sangha as trustworthy, approachable, and knowledge-able about power-vulnerability dynamics and healthy boundaries. The group should strive for diversity among gender, racial, and cultural backgrounds as well as other identities so that all community members feel supported. People in significant leadership positions, such as founding teachers, should remove themselves from chairing the council if possible. There are many wonderful resources available to help educate and guide Sanghas in grievance procedures, codes of conduct, and responding to allegations of misconduct. (Please see the Appendix for more resources.)

## Supporting Sangha Friendships

A friend of mine, a Dharma teacher on the West Coast, shared that her Sangha's healthy boundaries needed to go beyond sexual relationships to include platonic relationships: male Sangha members sometimes offered friendly invitations to both single and married women, where the women did not know the intention and felt uncomfortable or unable to refuse. The men, who composed the majority of the Sangha, were unconscious about this effect on the women. Drafting guidelines for platonic relationships meant openly addressing these uncomfortable issues, but it helped produce a shift toward greater gender awareness, feelings of safety and support, and more ease in community friendships.

My experience is that men, including myself, are typically quite unaware about how their behaviors impact the feeling of safety in women or genderqueer friends. These examples beg the questions, "Why are men typically not aware of such dynamics? In what kinds of contexts are men more supportive? How can we raise awareness among men?" While I believe men should take responsibility for educating other men in these matters, it is also important for community leaders to address these matters openly in the community, and for women to feel supported and empowered to refuse whatever feels uncomfortable to them.

Maintaining a safe communal atmosphere takes consistent discernment. Many years ago, I founded a young adult Sangha in California that enjoyed regular hangouts, potlucks, and games after our Friday night meditations. One evening, the young woman leading our meditation invited everyone to hang out in the sauna after our potluck, clothing optional. She had just returned from Burning Man and was inspired to connect the group in this free-spirited, clothes-less way. I felt caught off guard by the invitation, so I didn't say anything at first. While I appreciated her enthusiasm for this experience together and felt tempted to partake myself, it also felt unsafe to me. I waited for the right moment before sharing with her and the group, "Thank you so much for this idea, it sounds really fun. But I think it is better to do it outside of a Sangha gathering if people want to." Everyone was cool with this casual sounding yet clear boundary I set. I knew that being naked together could complicate our relationships as Sangha members, jeopardize others' trust in me as a leader, and raise serious eyebrows from others outside our group.

## Dating between Sangha Members

Feelings of emotional and sexual attraction are a natural part of a healthy community. Acknowledging and honoring our sexuality is part of creating an environment where conscious relationships, whether platonic or romantic, can be safely cultivated. I have often heard those in young adult Sanghas ask, "Is it okay for us to date?

Sharing a spiritual path while developing a loving partnership can bring tremendous joy to both the couple and their community. It is understandable for people to fall for someone in the Sangha, a place where so many compassionate, creative, and friendly people share deep values and a spiritual calling. I have often heard senior monastics encourage lay practitioners who are searching for romantic partnership to select someone who shares their spiritual path because of the harmony, support, and shared purpose they can generate together throughout their lives.

While I fully support people safely exploring romantic relationships rooted in spiritual community and practice, there are a few serious questions to consider before dating in one's Sangha. The first is whether significant power differences exist, as previously described. Second, one should be aware of how approaching another member with romantic interest may impact feelings of safety and ease in the other person and in your group as a whole. Consider: Will so-and-so feel safe if I approach them with romantic interest? In what context? How may this affect our friendship and our comfort in being a part of this community? This last concern touches on what may happen if you stop dating. While not a very romantic question, it is a crucial one, and it takes emotional maturity and communal wisdom to truly consider it. I have seen and heard countless stories of a hastily-considered romance turning south and the refuge of a spiritual community changing drastically as a result—not many people want to meditate every week with their ex. Inevitably, either one or both people no longer feel comfortable in the group, and losing one's Sangha is a high price to pay.

Before initiating romantic involvement, I wholeheartedly encourage people to share their attraction with friends and mentors. It takes time to truly know someone, whether partnership has a real chance, and if the risk is worth it; candid conversations can help bring clarity. Here are some questions to ask yourself or reflect upon with others: What is the true nature of my attraction to this person? Is the other person new to our community and do they already have a network of friendships? What if things don't work out—how will that impact my and our relationship to the Sangha? Talking with friends can deepen these reflections and help point out blind spots. When it feels safe and appropriate, discussing these questions with your heart crush can initiate a respectful and caring beginning to your relationship. Such courageous questions will deepen your trust and intimacy moving forward, support your decision making, and encourage your mutual happiness, whether shared or individual.

Some communities begin exploring healthy boundaries and writing a code of conduct after some calamitous event traumatizes their community. But hoping that misfortune will not cross your path when the preventative solution lies right here before us is foolish. We can even begin right now by asking our friends or community members what their actual needs are for emotional and physical safety and how we can directly support them. If we listen wholeheartedly, they will offer many truths, whether easy or difficult to hear. Such communication begins the process of cocreating a living culture of safety that protects and nurtures our community's well-being, now and into the future. By offering safety to ourselves and each other, we offer safety to the world.

# CHAPTER 16

# GOING FORTH AND THRIVING TOGETHER

> *If we are a drop of water and we try to get to the ocean as only an individual drop, we will surely evaporate along the way. To arrive at the ocean, you must go as a river. The Sangha is your river.*
>
> —THICH NHAT HANH

One of the most powerful teachings I ever received on starting a new intentional community was at Dharma Gaia meditation center on the subtropical North Island of New Zealand, land of the Indigenous Māori people. During our world tour, Vanessa and I traveled from the concrete streets of Athens, Greece, to this vegetal paradise of a retreat and residential mindfulness center that the Dharma Gaia community had steadily and simply built over fifteen years. After two weeks there, Vanessa and I had the opportunity to meet privately with the founding teacher, Sister Shalom, and her Sangha cofounder, Anton Bank. I asked Sister Shalom, "We would love to hear the story of how you built this gorgeous retreat center and community—would you share with us?" Cutting through the surface and getting to the heart of the matter, Sister Shalom said in her casual, yet fierce Zen way, "You want to know how we did it? We rolled up our sleeves and learned as we went. That's how we built it." It was simple, no-nonsense wisdom. Initially, I was disappointed by her brevity—I had been hoping for a long, dramatic portrayal of community spirit and challenges overcome (which she and Anton did eventually share with us later.) But when I began developing a new meditation center and Sangha years later, the simple wisdom of her first response came back to me during many trying moments.

Feelings of doubt plagued my momentum in the first several months I moved to Charlotte alone. *Who am I to start a mindfulness center anyways? Maybe I'm not a strong enough leader and teacher to succeed here. People will see that we're inexperienced impostors!* I began questioning my decisions and leadership capacity, feeling afraid of failure and intimidated by my own shortcomings. Then I remembered flashes of Sister Shalom's gestures as her hands had rolled up her imaginary sleeves. "This is how we built it!" I started telling myself the same: *Time to roll up our sleeves…. This is how we build it!* This mantra gave me an inner push of confidence to believe in each step of the work, regardless of future results, and trust in the great experiment of community-building, step by step, mistake by mistake, friend by friend, and moment by moment. Although I may be disappointed if we didn't succeed, I would never regret having offered my very best to this noble effort.

Building community is an act of trust that what we have to offer is already enough, that we are already enough. We trust that our intentions to serve, learn, and grow alongside others are enough. We trust that our ancestors are there within us, supporting, guiding, and encouraging our every move towards our lost heritage of loving community. With such trust, fear no longer holds such a heavy burden on us. We know that we will fall down and fail, hundreds, even thousands of times; yet we will grow even stronger, rebound even higher, and experience more collective joy than before as well. As a community, our greatest task is to simply show up, roll up our sleeves, and dig in together.

## Harmony is the Nature of the Sangha

After digging into community building, is there one thing that keeps a Sangha alive and flourishing above all else? Throughout every chapter, harmony has been the enduring theme that profoundly affects every other principle of community life, from visioning to friendships, silence to service, appreciation to joy, and racial healing to healthy boundaries. Harmony is the nature of the Sangha. It is the lifeblood and heartbeat of the community. If you take only one message and practice out of this book for your community, may it be the power of harmony.

When I started visioning our Sangha of volunteers in Greece, I had a chance to meet with Brother Phap Huu, the abbot of Plum Village Upper Hamlet. Brother Phap Huu was in his mid-thirties at the time, but he entered the monastery at just fourteen years old, so he was extremely experienced in Sangha life. He served as Thay's personal attendant for over a decade before becoming the abbot in his late twenties. Brother Phap Huu has the heart and smile of a playful child, but he leads the community like a wise sage.

I asked Phap Huu for his advice and for encouragement to help make this challenging project a success. Without hesitation, he looked me in the eyes and said with a knowing smile, "It's all about harmony—that's the key. This is my experience. If your community is harmonious and joyful, you can do so much together, you can help so many people, you can do whatever you want. But without harmony, you got *nothin'*!"

I nodded, and thought to myself, *Yeah, we can organize morning meetings and everyone can discuss things together.* As if reading my mind, Brother Phap Huu added, "But you don't have to be super formal and strict about it—that can kill the joy."

I heard about Brother Phap Huu's harmony skills from many of the monks, young and old. My friend Chad, who entered monastic life for several years in Plum Village, explained, "Phap Huu has this amazing ability to help everyone in the Sangha feel deeply heard and included. Sometimes you're in a meeting and someone says something that everyone else just groans at—maybe it seems ridiculous or it's just difficult to hear. Phap Huu will listen and pick out the one hidden gem of that brother's sharing and reflect it back for the rest of the community to hear and appreciate. It brings the whole community together." Harmony is not merely a state of mind; it is a practice to cultivate and offer to each other.

I've tried to emulate Brother Phap Huu's practice in community living, and I've found it quite challenging at times, actually. It can be very easy to get caught in my beliefs about what is right or what is best, which leads to small standoffs with others, even about minor decisions. This frame of mind doesn't allow me to listen in ways that understand, validate and support the diverse ideas, opinions, and needs that others bring to the table. I need to be reminded about what is most important to our community's well-being—harmony. Does the Sangha's happiness depend more on whether my views are implemented or whether others feel heard and encouraged? This is the ancient dance of being right versus being happy.

Just this morning, Roger, one of our Sangha founding members, demanded that we keep a small couch in the mediation hall for him to sit on whenever he came. When I heard his staunch opinion, I was ready to go toe to toe with him to make sure we maintained the correct and best environment in our meditation hall, which in my opinion didn't include couches. As the programming director and experienced practitioner, I was ready to use my expertise and leadership role to combat and override his views. But using force and personal power to achieve desired outcomes that fit my personal views is dangerous, I've learned—whether or not we get our way, this approach erodes the sacred fabric of inclusive collaboration and harmony of views. When I recognized this habit arising, I went for a slow walk outside and followed my breathing while listening to spring frogs croaking freely and the babbling brook running through the red bud trees. The harmony between the forest creatures sounded so effortless. I remembered Brother Phap Huu's beaming smile and gentle words, "The most important thing is harmony." My face relaxed, my righteousness softened, and my attitude downshifted. By the end of my walk, I knew I would initiate a conversation in which both his needs and my perspectives could be fully heard and included.

When harmony becomes the ultimate aim, everything else orients around it. No matter where our solar system travels in the Milky Way, the planets always circle around the Sun.

## Learning as We Go

Even after Sangha building for over twenty years (and writing this book for what seems to be many of those!), I still have so many questions. Many limitations, mistakes, and challenging situations continue to arise in stewarding my own community. Bringing curiosity and kind attention to these questions unleashes a gentle and sustained power. Acknowledging uncertainties and shortcomings naturally unlocks two doorways to a thriving community: humility and receptivity. The resident venerable at Deer Park Monastery, Thay Phuoc Tinh, an older Vietnamese Zen monk, was one of the most brilliant teachers I ever studied with. He once shared during a public talk, on the verge of laughing, "When the monks start getting arrogant, you can sit back and watch all the laypeople running away in the other direction!" In his typical light and humorous fashion, Thay Phuoc Tinh taught us the dangers of hubris and overconfidence while highlighting the virtues of humility.

In community life, can we respond humbly when difficult situations arise and we don't know how to help? In the past, whenever I worked with clients or faced community dilemmas that exceeded my experience and insights, I tried to hide the nervousness and shame I felt about my own limitations. As a cover, I pridefully projected confidence and pretended to know the answers. That almost never worked out very well, as you can imagine. Over the years, I've grown by allowing myself more space to not know, to not be wise, to feel vulnerable, even to be a fool. During difficult situations, I try my best to pause and breath slowly with the feelings of discomfort, curiosity, and wonder of not knowing. Then I tell myself, "It's okay not to know, David. Let the Sangha be your teacher. Let this difficulty be your teacher. What do they have to teach me in this moment?" The Dhammapada reminds us, "A fool who knows his foolishness is wise at least to that extent."

Instead of trying to be a teacher, I simply show up and try my best to learn, love, and heal, just like everyone else. The key is always to listen deeply and trust that the wisdom needed is already right there, inherent within each person, community, or difficult situation that arises. Listening in this way, with humility and receptivity, magic naturally unfolds and the way forward emerges more clearly.

When I first started writing this book nearly seven years ago, I felt a calling to transmit the depth and power of the joy I had experienced participating in building mindfulness communities over the years. What I didn't anticipate was how much each of these chapters would further build upon and strengthen my own house of community. Even though I had over twenty years of Sangha-building experience before starting Greatwoods Zen, I still found myself feeling completely stuck at times, doubtful about my capacity, and unsure about what steps to take next. In the beginning especially, I felt very alone. I had just separated from my partner, best friend, and fellow Sangha-builder, and I was learning to facilitate and organize everything by myself.

For the first six months, we had low turnouts at our weekly days of mindfulness. I started rereading these chapters on Sangha-building as if I were a brand new practitioner and community builder, as if someone else had written them for me. Each chapter boldly invited me into new, inspiring reflections, providing me a clear direction and practice to follow for that week alone. Small step after small step, the Sangha grew. When I felt alone and friendless, I was reminded of how to cultivate my own inner kalyana mitra, and I wholeheartedly planted seeds of spiritual friendship into new community soil. Later, when our founding visions strayed into dangerously divergent directions, I knew what to do right away. Our small founding team dedicated a whole morning to just meditate and drink tea together by the pond, relishing the vibrant autumn leaves falling around us. Then we spent an hour rewriting out our visions to clarify our core purpose as an intimately committed team.

Living in a deeply racially segregated city, our leadership team dedicated itself to White awareness work during our first year. The chapters on racial healing provided me with clear reminders, encouragements, and faith to keep on walking that path, no matter the obstacles. The garden of our Sangha's cultural humility and diversity continues to grow slowly with new blooms, deeper roots, and richer soil every month. When my Sangha partner, Nick, and I started having more frequent disagreements in the midst of developing our mindfulness center, the chapters on reconciliation encouraged us to re-initiate regular Beginning Anew sessions, something I had lost track of. The hills we climb and peaks we ascend in our reconciliation, brotherhood, and gratitude for one another seem to reach no limits.

When I fell in love with someone who attended a nearby sister Sangha, we convened our five-member Harmony and Safety Council and reviewed and renewed our healthy boundaries policy for those in leadership positions. We also sought counsel from elder practitioners in the region, bringing further safety, transparency, and ethical integrity to our young Sangha, myself, and everyone involved.

The process of writing this book has offered me a ceaseless fountain of inspirational suggestions, compassionate reminders, and concrete guidance on how to build my own beloved community from the inside out. No matter how long we have been practicing mindfulness, we all need supportive encouragement and reminders at times, especially during trying moments. While the wisdom of community exists in the depths of our heart, bones, and chromosomes, in every generation we are still young students of this ancient art, with so much to learn and grow. With the nine principles offered in this book as a guiding light, I feel a bright torch illuminating my path, bringing clarity and fearlessness to the obstacles and darkness we will surely encounter ahead.

In true community, we don't have to face the difficulties of our world alone. As my teacher, Thay, frequently and enthusiastically encouraged, "Let us climb the hill of the next century, not as separate individuals, but as a Sangha." Because I have a strong, loving community both at my back and in my heart, I feel ready and excited for whatever challenges and happinesses lie ahead. What we cannot do alone, we can do as a Sangha. What we can embrace and heal together is far greater than what we could ever achieve individually. This is true not only for practicing mindfulness successfully, but especially for our capacity for building greater friendship, racial healing, shared joy, meaningful service, communal safety, and more. There are no limits to what we can grow together, as everything becomes more powerful in community: love, learning, hope, and our aspirations for the peaceful, harmonious world in which all of us can be ourselves fully and realize our potential.

# NOTES

1. Kaiser Family Foundation Aug 31, "KFF/Economist Survey: One in Five Americans Report Always or Often Feeling Lonely or Socially Isolated, Frequently with Physical, Mental, and Financial Consequences," KFF, August 31, 2018.

2. Survey Center on American Life June 29, "Men's Social Circles are Shrinking," June 29, 2021; *www.americansurveycenter.org*.

3. Miller McPherson, Lynn Smith-Lovin, and Matthew E. Brashears, "Social Isolation in America: Changes in Core Discussion Networks over Two Decades," *American Sociological Review* 71, no. 3 (2006): 353–75.

4. Cigna (2018) US Loneliness Index, (Cigna Philadelphia, 2018), revealed that at least a quarter of the US population feels they don't have anyone in their lives who understands them.

5. Kim Parker et al. "How Urban, Suburban, and Rural Residents Interact with their Neighbors," Pew Research Center, May 22, 2018.

6. Joe Cortright, "Less in Common," *City Observatory*, September 6, 2015.

7. An eighty-year study by Harvard University quoted in Robert Waldinger, "The Good Life," TEDxBeaconStreet, November 30, 2015.

8. Poor relationships have a greater influence on health than even physical inactivity and obesity. Holt-Lunstad, Julianne Smith, Timothy Baker, Mark Harris, Tyler Stephenson, David. (2015). "Loneliness and Social Isolation as Risk Factors for Mortality: A Meta-Analytic Review." *Perspectives on Psychological Science*, 10. 227–237.

9. Vivek Murphy, "Work and the Loneliness Epidemic," *Harvard Business Review*, September 28, 2018.

10. bell hooks, *All About Love: New Visions* (William Morrow, 2018) 11.

11. Mia Birdsong, *How We Show Up: Reclaiming Family, Friendship, and Community* (Hachette, 2020), 14.

12. Diane Leafe Christian, *Creating a Life Together: Practical Tools for Nurturing Community* 2nd ed. (New Society Publishers, 2003), and Chris Coates in

Sally Howard, "Is the boom in communal living really the good life?" *The Guardian*, January 17, 2021.

13. Karen Liftin, *Ecovillages: Lessons for Sustainable Community* (Polity Press, 2014), 16.

14. Bhikkhu Bodhi, *The Buddha's Teachings on Social and Communal Harmony: An Anthology of Discourses from the Pali Canon* (Wisdom Publications, 2016) 38.

15. Liftin, *Ecovillages*, 32.

16. Christian, *Creating a Life Together*, 5.

17. Larry Yang, *Awakening Together: The Spiritual Practice of Inclusivity and Community* (Shambhala Publications, 2017), 170.

18. Yang, 171.

19. Bhikkhu Bodhi, *The Buddha's Teachings on Social and Communal Harmony*, 86.

20. Thich Nhat Hanh, *Chanting From the Heart, Vol. 1: Buddhist Sutras and Chants for Recitation* (Parallax Press, 2023), 14.

21. From the poet Joseph Rubano's blog: *https://josephrubano.com/friend-by-friend/*.

22. Kate Johnson, *Radical Friendship: Seven Ways to Love Yourself and Find Your People in an Unjust World* (Shambhala, 2021), 169.

23. United Nations High Commission for Refugees, "Syria Situation," Global Focus, March 13, 2024 data, accessed October 31, 2024.

24. M. Scott Peck, *The Road Less Traveled: A New Psychology of Love, Traditional Values and Spiritual Growth.*(Simon & Schuster, 1997), 86.

25. Lawrence Robinson, Melinda Smith, Jeanne Segal, and Jennifer Shubin, "The Benefits of Play for Adults" (HelpGuide.org, 2024).

26. Monica S. Hammer, Tracy K. Swinburn, and Richard L. Neitzel (2014), "Environmental Noise Pollution in the United States: Developing an Effective Public Health Response" in *Environmental Health Perspectives* Vol. 122, issue 2, 115–118.

27. Deepak Chopra, *The Seven Spiritual Laws of Success: A Practical Guide to the Fulfillment of Your Dreams* (Amber-Allen Publishing and New World Library, 1994) 23.

28. Bhikkhu Bodhi, 54.

29. Kahlil Gibran, *The Prophet* (Alfred A. Knopf, 1965), 68.

30. Robert A. Emmons, *Gratitude Works: A 21-Day Program for Creating Emotional Prosperity* (Jossey-Bass, 2013); Wood et al., "Gratitude influences sleep through the mechanism of pre-sleep cognitions," 43–48; Jackowska et al., "The impact of a brief gratitude intervention on subjective well-being, biology and sleep," 2207–2217.

31. Jackowska et al., "The impact of a brief gratitude intervention on subjective well-being, biology and sleep," 2207–2217.

32. Gordon et al., "Have you thanked your spouse today?: Felt and expressed gratitude among married couples," 339–343; 257–274.

33. Lambert et al., "Benefits of Expressing Gratitude," 574–580.

34. hooks, *All About Love*, 121.

35. Sister Chan Khong, *Learning True Love: Practicing Buddhism in a Time of War* (Parallax Press, 2009).

36. Martin Luther King Jr., *A Gift of Love: Sermons from "Strength to Love" and Other Preachings* (Beacon Press, 2012), 45.

37. bell hooks, *The Will to Change: Men, Masculinity, and Love* (Washington Square Press, 2004), 29.

38. Rick Hanson, *Buddha's Brain: The Practical Neuroscience of Happiness, Love, and Wisdom* (New Harbinger, 2009), 68.

39. Ruth King, *Mindful of Race: Transforming Racism from the Inside Out* (Sounds True, 2018).

40. Audre Lorde, "The Master's Tools Will Never Dismantle the Master's House" in *Sister Outsider: Essays and Speeches* (Crossing Press, 2007), 112.

41. hooks, *All About Love*, 215.

42. Shelly Tochluk, *Witnessing Whiteness: The Need to Talk About Race and How to Do It* (R&L Education, 2010), 234.

43. Beverly Daniel Tatum, *Why Are All the Black Kids Sitting Together in the Cafeteria? And Other Conversations About Race* (Basic Books, 2017).

44. Janet E. Helms, *Black and White Racial Identity: Theory, Research, and Practice* (Praeger, 1993).

45. Tochluk. *Witnessing Whiteness,* 236.

46. Shelly Tochluk, *Witnessing Whiteness: The Need to Talk About Race and How to Do It* (R&L Education, 2010), 239, Kindle Edition.

47. King, *Mindful of Race*, 12.

48. Scott Edelstein, *Sex and the Spiritual Teacher: Why It Happens, When It's a Problem, and What We All Can Do* (Wisdom, 2011).

49. Roxane Gay, foreword to Claire Saunders, Georgia Buckthorn, Minna Salami, Mik Scarlet, Hazel Songhurst, *The Power Book: What is it, Who Has it, and Why?* (Ivy Kids, 2019).

50. Lisa VeneKlasen and Valerie Miller, *A New Weave of Power, People and Politics: The Action Guide for Advocacy and Citizen Participation* (Practical Action Publishing, 2007), 55.

51. "Access Intimacy: The Missing Link," *Leaving Evidence*, published May 5, 2011, https://leavingevidence.wordpress.com/2011/05/05/access-intimacy-the-missing-link/.

52. Kazu Haga, "Fierce Vulnerability Considerations" (Garrison Institute, 2020).

53. Nedra Glover Tawwab, *Set Boundaries, Find Peace: A Guide to Reclaiming Yourself* (Penguin Random House, 2021), 5, 6.

54. Jack Kornfield, *A Path with Heart: A Guide through the Perils and Promises of Spiritual Life* (Bantam Books, 1992), 266.

55. Leslee Goodman, "Conscious Sex: An Interview with Lama Rod Owens," *The MOON magazine*, March 29, 2020, *https://moonmagazine.org/conscious-sex-interview-lama-rod-owens-2017-12-30/*.

# SELECTED BIBLIOGRAPHY

Bhikkhu Bodhi. *The Buddha's Teachings on Social and Communal Harmony.* Wisdom Publications, 2016.

Birdsong, Mia. *How We Show Up: Reclaiming Family, Friendship, and Community.* Hachette, 2020.

Brown, Jr., H. Jackson. *Life's Little Instruction Book.* HarperCollins, 1991.

Chopra, Deepak. *The Seven Spiritual Laws of Success: A Pocketbook Guide to Fulfilling Your Dreams* (One Hour of Wisdom) Amber Allen, 2015.

Christian, Diane Leaf. *Creating a Life Together: Practical Tools for Nurturing Community.* Second Edition. New Society Publishers, 2003.

———. *Finding Community: How to Join an Ecovillage or Intentional Community.* New Society Publishers, 2007.

Haga, Kazu. *Healing Resistance: A Radical Response to Harm.* Parallax Press, 2020.

hooks, bell. *All About Love: New Visions.* William Morrow, 2018.

Johnson, Kate. *Radical Friendship: Seven Ways to Love Yourself and Find Your People in an Unjust World.* Shambhala, 2021.

Kagge, Erling. *Silence: In the Age of Noise.* Vintage, 2017.

Khong, Sister Chan. *Learning True Love: Practicing Buddhism in a Time of War.* Revised Edition. Parallax Press, 2007.

King, Ruth. *Mindful of Race: Transforming Racism from the Inside Out.* Sounds True, 2018.

Menakem, Resmaa. *My Grandmother's Hands: Racialized Trauma and the Pathway to Mending Our Hearts and Bodies.* Central Recovery Press, 2017.

Nhat Hanh, Thich. *Silence: The Power of Quiet in a World Full of Noise.* HarperCollins, 2015.

Scazzero, Peter. *The Emotionally Healthy Leader.* Zondervan, 2015.

# RESOURCES FOR HEALTHY BOUNDARIES

FaithTrust Institute—includes courses for spiritual teachers and facilitators on healthy boundaries. Visit *Faithtrustinstitute.org*.

## Books and articles

Edelstein, Scott. *Sex and the Spiritual Teacher: Why It Happens, When It's a Problem, and What We All Can Do*. Wisdom Publications, 2011.

Peterson, Marilyn R. *At Personal Risk: Boundary Violations in Professional-Client Relationships*. W. W. Norton, 1992.

Senauke, Alan, ed. *Safe Harbor: Guidelines, Process, and Resources for Ethics and Right Conduct in Buddhist Communities*. Buddhist Peace Fellowship, 2004.

Sawyer, Lauren D, PhD, Emily Cohen, MDiv, and Annie Mesaros, MDiv., eds. *Responding to Spiritual Leader Misconduct: A Handbook*. FaithTrust Institute, 2022.

Kornfield, Jack. *A Path with Heart: A Guide Through the Perils and Promises of Spiritual Life*. Bantam, 1993.

# ACKNOWLEDGMENTS

My goodness, it has taken quite a community to give birth to this book. I'm happy to say that this writing on community has been nothing less than the culmination of generosity, effort, and love of an incredible family of friends. To everyone who supported this work, enriched my learning, and contributed to our research tour in various ways, I bow deeply towards the earth, and with a joyous smile, open the wellsprings of gratitude within to you.

First and foremost, I give limitless thanks to my wonderful parents, who nurtured the writer in me from an early age, and in whom I still call upon for proper grammar, sentence flow, and grounded feedback. You have been and always will be my biggest supporters in writing and life! How incredibly lucky I am for this.

To the rest of my family, who all read, edited, and re-edited my first few chapters until they were polished like little gemstones. You have supported and celebrated my every step along the way, through more than six years of writing!

My unconditional gratitude goes to my root teacher, Thay Nhat Hanh. Since my first winter retreat with you in 2003, you offered bright, unwavering dedication and compassionate guidance on the art of Sangha building, a beautiful and noble path through this challenging world. I give thanks to the countless generations of ancestral teachers who carried this lineage of Sangha over the ages to its current expressions today. Each writing session, I invited your hands to hold the pen and let your wisdom flow through the ink and onto these pages.

To Fern Dorresteyn, for your wholehearted mentorship and spiritual friendship with me over the years as I wrote this book, always inviting me to move at a pace that brought peace and happiness to myself first. And to the whole Morning Sun family, who taught me so much about living in a loving and harmonious lay practice community.

To Melina Bondy, who read my first drafts of the chapters on White awareness and racial healing—the most challenging yet rewarding chapters to write. Your patience, humble tolerance, and gentle, wise guidance helped me take those first leaps of faith forward.

To Sophie Sakar, who provided crucial feedback and guidance on the chapters on healthy boundaries and power, the second most challenging to write. Your friendship and willingness to share knowledge, insights, and compassionate reflections have spurred both me and my writing to greater maturity.

To the amazing team at Parallax! This book has grown and bloomed thanks to your collective passion, discerning eyes, and caring hands. Matt, you have been an outstanding editor and even more than that, a good friend who has stuck by my side throughout this process. I'm happy to say that we've had fun together doing this!

To Jessie Raye, for helping me create the title and subtitle for this book, for your overflowing love of the Sangha, for your partnership in community building, and for teaching me how to embody self-love and true freedom through your own writing.

To Verena Böttcher, for your precious friendship over the years, for facilitating our research tour in the Netherlands, and always encouraging the teacher and writer in me to come out and play, especially during difficult moments.

To Emily Buckley, who read all of my earliest drafts, always encouraged and celebrated my efforts, and truly believed in my potential.

To Karl and Helga, my favorite "Dharma Dinosaurs," thank you for your unbelievable generosity and support for our community research tour in Germany and Italy. You are true trailblazers on this path.

To Noah Walton and Joe Holtaway who wholeheartedly welcomed me to dive into and partner with the London Sanghas and stay at their Wake Up houses, which were always filled with so much love and laughter.

To Omar, Sylvester, Mohammad, Kadar, and so many other friends from migrant backgrounds with whom we spent time in Greece. Thank you for offering your trust and friendship, imparting your stories of survival and resilience, openly receiving our community, and making us a part of yours.

To Anton and Sister Shalom at Dharma Gaia, for generously sharing your beautiful community and inspiring stories, and for embodying the life of true community and service so profoundly.

To Stefano and the community at Avalokita, for generously hosting us at your gorgeous community and treating us like your Italian family.

To all the communities, both large and small, that we visited, and to the many hundreds of people we met, befriended, and who shared their heartfelt stories and wisdom with us. It is you who have made this book come to life. Thank you.

# ABOUT THE AUTHOR

Between 2003 and 2007, David Viafora studied closely with Zen Master Thich Nhat Hanh as an aspirant and novice monk in Plum Village, France, and Deer Park Monastery in California, before finding his niche in community lay life. In the past two decades, since his early twenties, he has founded over half a dozen local Sanghas or intentional communities, several of which are still thriving today. Over the last ten years, David has dedicated his life to building Sanghas, visioning and organizing mindfulness retreats, and mentoring young adult facilitators. David's deepest belief is that compassionately engaged communities are the key to the healing and transformation people deeply long for, on an individual and global scale. Pushing the envelope of compassionate communities, he is changing the world one breath, one community, and one smile at a time. He lives in Charlotte, North Carolina.

Monastics and visitors practice the art of mindful living in the tradition of Thich Nhat Hanh at our mindfulness practice centers around the world. To reach any of these communities, or for information about how individuals, couples, and families can join in a retreat, please contact:

PLUM VILLAGE
*24240 Thénac, France*
plumvillage.org

LA MAISON DE L'INSPIR
*77510 Villeneuve-sur-Bellot,
France*
maisondelinspir.org

HEALING SPRING
MONASTERY
*77510 Verdelot, France*
healingspringmonastery.org

MAGNOLIA GROVE
MONASTERY
*Batesville, MS 38606, USA*
magnoliagrovemonastery.org

BLUE CLIFF MONASTERY
*Pine Bush, NY 12566, USA*
bluecliffmonastery.org

DEER PARK MONASTERY
*Escondido, CA 92026, USA*
deerparkmonastery.org

EUROPEAN INSTITUTE OF
APPLIED BUDDHISM
*D-51545 Waldbröl, Germany*
eiab.eu

THAILAND PLUM VILLAGE
*Nakhon Ratchasima
30130 Thailand*
thaiplumvillage.org

ASIAN INSTITUTE OF
APPLIED BUDDHISM
*Lantau Island, Hong Kong*
pvfhk.org

STREAM ENTERING
MONASTERY
*Porcupine Ridge, Victoria 3461
Australia*
nhapluu.org

MOUNTAIN SPRING
MONASTERY
*Bilpin, NSW 2758, Australia*
mountainspringmonastery.org

For more information visit: *plumvillage.org*
To find an online sangha visit: *plumline.org*
For more resources, try the Plum Village app: *plumvillage.app*
Social media: *@thichnhathanh @plumvillagefrance*
To donate, visit *thichnhathanhfoundation.org*

PARALLAX PRESS, a nonprofit publisher founded by Zen Master Thich Nhat Hanh, publishes books and media on the art of mindful living and Engaged Buddhism. We are committed to offering teachings that help transform suffering and injustice. Our aspiration is to contribute to collective insight and awakening, bringing about a more joyful, healthy, and compassionate society.

View our entire library at parallax.org.

THE MINDFULNESS BELL is a journal of the art of mindful living in the Plum Village tradition of Thich Nhat Hanh. To subscribe or to see the worldwide directory of Sanghas (local mindfulness groups), visit mindfulnessbell.org.